barcode on next page

Out of the Blue

Out of the Blue

A Pilot with the Chindits

TERENCE O'BRIEN

COLLINS
8 Grafton Street, London W1
1984

William Collins Sons & Co. Ltd
London · Glasgow · Sydney · Auckland
Toronto · Johannesburg

British Library Cataloguing in Publication Data

O'Brien, Terence
  Out of the blue: a pilot with the Chindits.
  1. Great Britain *Royal Air Force*—History
  2. World War, 1939–1945—Aerial operations,
  British—Personal narratives
  3. World War, 1939–1945—Campaigns—Burma
  I. Title
  940.54'25'0924   D767.6

        ISBN 0 00 217198 8

First published 1984

© Terence O'Brien, 1984

Photoset in Linotron Plantin by
Rowland Phototypesetting Ltd
Bury St Edmunds, Suffolk
Made and printed in Great Britain by
William Collins Sons & Co. Ltd, Glasgow

To Flight Lieutenant Stanley Douglas Mayhew, RAFVR and Lieutenant Peter Birley Wilmot, 4/9 Gurkha Rifles, two friends who were killed out there

FOREWORD

From the time I left Australia in December 1939 until a little beyond the end of my war I kept a series of notebooks, not in diary discipline but written up from time to time when the urge became compelling. These were private records of scenes and events and feelings never intended for publication, just for imprint on memory and occasional nostalgic review. The habit persisted throughout my time with the Chindit Force, but in addition I also kept a brief diary going for the three months actually spent behind the enemy lines. Whilst convalescing afterwards I combined the records of the note-book and diary and immediate memory into a unified account of the whole Chindit experience. Two years later, when working at Air Ministry back in England, I wrote up the whole of my war experiences and at that time I added to the already completed Chindit section a few items of later information; the pencilled sheets and exercise books were then put away, unread, for nearly forty years.

It was my son who finally prodded me into taking out the old faded sheets and typing up the full war story so that it would be easier for him to read at once, and then more convenient subsequently as a family record – for it dealt also with his mother, and with friends we have kept ever since those wartime years. When it came to the Chindit section, I showed the opening chapters to a friend who encouraged me to edit this section (cutting out the private notes) for general publication: the same encouragement came from the publishers, and this book is the result. It is taken entirely from

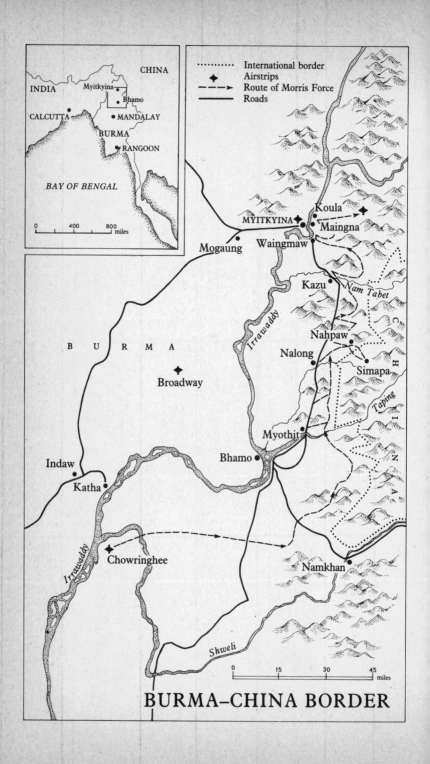

BURMA–CHINA BORDER

International border
Airstrips
Route of Morris Force
Roads

CHINA

INDIA

Myitkyina
Bhamo
CALCUTTA
MANDALAY
BURMA
RANGOON

BAY OF BENGAL

0   400   800
miles

Koula
MYITKYINA
Maingna
Waingmaw
Mogaung

Kazu
Nam Tabet

B   U   R   M   A
Nahpaw
Nalong
Simapa

Broadway

Tapeng

Myothit
Bhamo
Indaw
Katha

Chowringhee
Namkhan

Irrawaddy

Shweli

0   15   30   45
miles

the record in the old pencilled sheets but I have added one or two items of military background – such as the Wingate signal quoted at the end of Chapter 6 – which have since been released from the archives.

It should be clear therefore that this is not, and was never intended to be, a purely historical study of our particular operation, nor of the Chindit expedition itself and the Generals involved in it. Those who want such a balanced account, of Wingate and Stilwell and of the whole campaign, should look to the works of the military historians – by far the best on our campaign is Shelford Bidwell's *The Chindit War*. Mine is a personal memoir, not a military study. It is what I as a young man saw, and did, and knew, and felt, back in 1944 whilst serving with the 4/9th Gurkhas in that remote mountainous region between northern Burma and Yunnan.

I

The Army was a foreign land; they had a different language, different institutions and customs and gods. They talked of things like 'acquittance rolls', had Battalion Lines, assembled for orders, and their god was not the Air Ministry but the War Office. The RAF signal calling for volunteers had referred to the group as Special Force and I found them in the centre of India camped near a station called Ghateera. The train arrived one early afternoon in May 1943 and once out of it I was standing there, dazed in the ringing heat, when a soldier approached and said something either in Gaelic or such a broad Scots accent it was equally unintelligible, picked up my canvas grip and strode off towards a truck shimmering in the haze beyond the hissing engine. I followed with the sleeping roll. Having been in India over a year I knew enough to test the front seat first with my hand, then withdrew it sharply and instead went around to the back and slung up my gear. Clambering up after it I just had time to grab a strut before the truck started off and went juddering over the corrugations, churning up so much dust you could see nothing but a straw-coloured cloud, and when you licked your dry lips they grated like coarse cloth against your tongue.

The camp was pitched about a river that at the height of the dry season then was only a series of disconnected waterholes, a big one the colour of milk-chocolate being close at hand; walking away from the truck I saw a buffalo deeply immersed in it, just the top of his head showing so that he looked like a horned crocodile, and on the bank nearby a snow-white egret was stepping with dainty precision across the mosaic of dried mud. There were then just two battalions in Special Force, the First Cameronians and the 4/9th Gurkhas; this I learned when I walked into the basha shelter indicated by the truck-driver with an arm and a comment – only the first of which was meaningful – and found a man sitting alone in khaki shorts and without a shirt at a bare table, drinking tea from an enamelled mug. He was rangy in build, skin dryly tanned.

'I'm Lentaigne,' he said. 'The Brigadier.'

He called out in Gurkhali to an orderly who brought another mug of tea and as I began to sip – and exude it at once in perspiration – he told me his force would be starting operations behind the enemy lines in October; another Brigadier called Wingate was just coming back from such an operation. Lentaigne's two battalions would be split into four columns, and each would have its RAF officer. He suggested I join the Cameronians and thereby avoid the language problem, not realizing I was an ignorant Australian untuned to northern accents.

The air was crammed with arid heat in those pre-monsoon weeks. The moment you sat down the seat of your shorts and the back of your shirt became clammy with sweat, then when you stood up they dried stiff in an instant, the sweat evaporating in the scorching dryness. Your lips cracked and the harsh dryness inside your nostrils made them feel as if stuffed with brown paper. A yellow haze enveloped the countryside, avidly searching every trace of moisture. There was only one real tree anywhere near my tent – a blackwood with creamy white flowers now almost finished – and all the rest of the land about the camp area had been grazed down to roots so that the only cover left on the dusty surface was leafless scrub, and mostly thorny at that. All movement was an effort. I used to marvel at the persistent energy of a small pied kingfisher that had a regular pitch just behind my tent; he would hover still as a dragon-fly over the brown flat water, suddenly plunge like a dart and rise with a tiny fish or tadpole in his beak, then once back on his perch would go on beating his catch with demonic fury again and again until you wanted to cry out: Enough, enough!

I thought at that time that the whole area about the camp was just truck-high scrub, parched and tough as the mulga in Australia, but then the rains came, the whole countryside turned from a dry-straw colour to a glistening butterscotch brown, the heat haze and the dust clouds were washed away and you saw tall green trees in the near distance and discovered the direction in which the river ran. It rained for days on end. There was no escape from the damp, the atmosphere was so heavy with moisture it penetrated everywhere; one rare fine morning a foot-high carpet of cloud covered the tent floor and the mud outside, and so solid was it that I could clear a temporary path with my hands then watch it roll back honey-slow to fill the gap again. Small bottle-green frogs crawled into your boots, mould grew on your watch-strap and rotted it through, the staples of the note book rusted over, and the spines of your books became tacky as the damp revived the old glue and set it oozing through the cloth binding.

With the rains too came Stanley Mayhew, wearing a great pot of a topee, peering at me warily by the rail track as I approached in jungle-green outfit and drooping bush-hat, till recognition suddenly penetrated the disguise and he grabbed my hand and began to beat me joyfully on the back.

'Pat! I knew you'd work it somehow. I knew.'

I had been, simultaneously, the Commanding Officer of the RAF Stations at Juhu and at Santa Cruz, of a Navigation School near the beach, and of the RAF-Naval Liaison Office in the town, a disgruntled Pooh-bah of the Bombay area, and had arranged that Stanley whom I had known from squadron days in England should come to run our flight of aircraft at Juhu. Shortly after his arrival, however, a signal came to all units in India calling for volunteers for 'a dangerous mission'; I grabbed at this chance to get back to operations and although the Air Commodore blocked me at first on the grounds that the call had specified Flight Lieutenants, the rank below mine, I was able to work a stunt that bypassed his opposition, dropped down a rank, and so got into Special Force. That left Stanley stranded in Bombay, not happy with the New CO, and barred from joining me by the obstructive group commander. He could not use the same stunt I had devised – Stanley was a most incompetent liar, particularly to senior officers – so I wrote an official letter to Air Headquarters saying the Brigadier had asked for him specifically, having worked with him on Army Liaison in Singapore. All lies, of course, but there was no realistic chance anyone in Delhi would ever check and sure enough the letter did the trick. Stanley was posted to the last vacancy and so landed up at Ghateera station that day in July.

I tried to get him into the Cameronians but could not persuade the other RAF officer to move. Fortunately the fourth volunteer had not yet actually arrived so I got in first and wangled a quick switch over to the Gurkhas – I went to 49 Column, Stanley to 94, and both of us to a friendly welcome.

With the Gurkhas the language problem could not be lazily solved by a gradual osmotic process, as was happening with the Scots, it had to be learned by deliberate study. Stanley chose to learn Hindustani – the battalion provided teachers for both languages – because he thought it would be useful afterwards in India, but I did not bother about afterwards and stuck to Gurkhali, being helped by my orderly Lilbahadur who, like so many Gurkhas, could not speak Hindustani anyway. He, like all the others in the 9th Gurkhas, was a high caste – they were all Thakkurs and Chettris, slimmer and taller than the other groups but just as friendly whether sober and slogging along the track on the march, or drunk on rum and singing around the fireside on a

14

festive evening. They laughed a lot, the Gurkhas – unlike the local Indians who looked at you in solemn silence when you passed along the road. Lilbahadur was too helpful in language practice for he learned quickly to grasp my pidgin Gurkhali and accepted it, never correcting nor explaining, so my standard remained shamefully low throughout the whole time with the battalion.

The area where we were then training, about three hundred miles south of Delhi, is covered in thin jungle through which in parts you can walk for a day without sight of a village. It is geologically young country, seamed with low rocky hills and strewn with a fine webbing of tracks made by men and game so that someone out with a rifle on shikar would have a pleasantly easy passage. For us however, it was not so pleasantly easy. We were not sauntering along with just a light sporting rifle, a retinue of servants in attendance nearby, we had monstrous packs on our backs and were engaged on a relentless test of endurance.

My pack, an average load, was made up of spare clothing, canvas shoes, water-bottle, ammunition, grenades, rations, mess tin, compass, binoculars, ground-sheet, lightweight blanket, toilet articles and a book or two (I had Palgrave and a tree book at the least). When carrying five days' rations at the start of a march this weighed eighty pounds. *In dry conditions.* When it was raining then your green cotton trousers and flannel shirt became sodden-heavy, as did webbing and pack and practically everything in it, and it was then no longer just an oppressive weight but a belted restraint against movement – as though the straps over your shoulders were fastened down to powerful springs in the ground and you had to heave up and forward against their pull at every step.

On training we marched for exactly fifty minutes with this load on our backs – not a second more: then we stopped for ten minutes – not a second less. Along roads we expected to complete just under four miles in every fifty-minute slog, a marching speed of 4 mph that yielded about thirty miles in a full day. In Burma however, even in the fine early days when we were in good condition and on the flat, we could only average about 2 mph because hold-ups were inevitable; later on in the mountains and thick jungle we were sometimes down to five miles of anguish achieved in a whole day.

The first month or so our progress through the jungle had been loudly proclaimed by the braying of the mules but then the veterinary surgeons operated on the animals' vocal chords so the braying stopped. But not completely. A ghost remained. Though the mules no longer had chords to vibrate they could still force air through the vocal chamber, so you kept hearing a noise like the gasping of a water-starved tap, going on and on with decreasing pressure until ending at last with a prolonged rasping sigh. Later, as the chords regenerated, their voices began to grow back again, but the change was fitful and uncontrolled, like the period when a boy's voice is breaking, so you would get a piercing wheeze or a loud piece of bray in the middle of the gasps.

We had a mule officer whose job it was not merely to look after their health but to check their loads constantly. All loads had to be balanced, and though some were carried in leather yakdhans many such as mortars and radios had their own special crates and their own special mules – the largest mules were needed for the big RAF radio, and particularly for its petrol-engine charger which was the heaviest load carried. The business of loading up and unloading the mules cut severely into the free time of the Gurkha muleteers; they would be already saddling-up in the early misty mornings when we were still having a last sip of hot tea, and in the evenings, when we others had loosened the laces of our boots and were lying back on the ground, watching the arrows of geese passing overhead or flicking biscuit crumbs to a hoppity mynah, the muleteers would be feeding or rubbing down their charges. On the march too they were rarely at rhythmic peace like the rest of us, they had to guide the mules through obstacles, readjust loads when they slipped, and somehow persuade the animals to get moving again when for no obvious reason they stopped and then leaned back on their haunches against the fierce pull of their drivers. They hated noisy loads and would stop, embedded still, or bolt – anything to force the muleteers to silence the rattle or the squeak that was so offensive.

I thought them marvellous animals, independent, stout-hearted, astute, altogether admirable. Nothing like the horses. We had several horses, pampered creatures that carried only trivial weight in their little saddle bags; they were meant for reconnaissance work and inter-column liaison, but particularly for carrying the sick and wounded – however, never as tough as mules, they succumbed easily on operations to all sorts of diseases and not one survived the campaign. On our training tortures in India I used to resent the horses with their empty saddles, strolling along contentedly with plenty of energy left for a little fastidious grazing at the halt or a discriminating sip of appraisal when crossing a stream, immune from the punishment we and the mules were suffering as comrades in distress.

When in camp we lived well, but mostly we were out on exercise and then we lived on the rations we carried. These were miserably inadequate. Designated 'Indian Light Scale', they comprised biscuits, dates, cheese, tea and powdered milk, and a separate small tin of bully beef. You had to tap the biscuits first so as to shake out the weevils; in the dates there was a shiny brown insect with a forked tail that could not be shaken out so if you were still determined to eat them you had first to ease them apart and flick out these burrowers – or shut your eyes and eat the writing fruit whole. You also had a packet of Indian V cigarettes and in dry weather these had to be opened carefully and horizontally otherwise all the tobacco poured out quick as sand; in the wet weather they were almost unsmokeable because the ration package was not waterproof, on the contrary it was avidly absorbent, so the cigarettes became a soggy part of the biscuits-cheesemilkpowder clod which was usually blue-furred with mould. Trying to subsist on such rations while marching thirty miles a day and carrying an eighty pound penalty on our backs had a steady debilitating effect on even the toughest Gurkha. The line on the sickness graph moved inexorably towards the top right-hand corner of the chart.

During one of these exercises there occurred the first of two similar incidents for which I never did hear a satisfactory explanation. We were on a night exercise in an area assumed to be enemy-infested. It was a moonless night but there was sufficient starlight to see the shapes around us when we stopped about midnight, weary and hungry, and prepared to sort ourselves out into circular defensive grouping. There was a delay for some reason or other, a common occurrence, so we stood there stilly. We had to speak in whispers, our position was supposed to be dangerous, most of the men believed this and were tense – unbelievers like me were drowsy beyond care and wanted only to sleep. There was a smell of sweat and manure trapped under the trees about us on the road, mules snuffled, and the harness clinked and clattered softly in the warm still night. I was about to sit down on the road to relieve the weight of the pack when I was halted by a sound, something like that of an autumn wind sending the dead leaves scurrying. It came from the blackness towards the head of the column. Just as I looked in that direction, stilled for an instant by the strange noise, it swept down over us in a swift and devastating crescendo – a sound composed of bounding mules, flailing men, panic cries and gasps and groans. Lilbahadur swiped me across the chest as he hurled himself somewhere beyond, another Gurkha crashed into me and somehow ripped my trousers wide open along the seam before sending me down to thump on the unyielding pack with a spine-thudding jolt that forced out a yelp of pain. By the time I recovered the panic wave had passed. Mumbling figures began to scuffle about searching for their places again, mules were being retrieved, equipment being collected. No one seemed to know what started the wave of violent energy that had swept so rapidly along the complete length of the column, and it took us almost an hour to get the whole unit sorted out again. The second time this happened we were behind the lines in Burma, I remembered the sound at once and flung myself sideways in time to escape without damage.

The RAF section comprised an officer and two radio-sergeants per column. We were responsible for arranging supply drops, constructing emergency airstrips to get out our wounded, and directing all types of air support for the column's actions. These comparitively straightforward duties were not enough for an elderly Wing Commander who now arrived at brigade headquarters to be nominally in charge of us; he had been in Balloon Command and felt he had to prove himself as fit as any of us, so he exercised his position at once by ordering all RAF officers to parade with full pack and do standard drill under his command. This was not for me. Stanley did turn up the first day but I went sick, saying I had a twisted knee, and that evening went to the brigade major, Jack Masters, asking that he quell the old man's enthusiasm and so keep us in Special Force – none of us had, or would, volunteer for work that entailed being given pointless drill sessions by an ancient from Balloon Command. Happily Masters was sympathetic and managed to stifle the old man temporarily before he was removed anyway, as the training proved too arduous for him. An air gunner took his place and sensibly left us each alone to get on with our jobs in the columns.

However, we then learned in August that the entry into Burma was postponed until November and instead of being given a refreshing leave we were kept in camp, forced into mere repetitious exercises that no longer had anything to teach us. There was no explanation why the leave was not granted – pure inertia on the part of headquarters staff, probably. So I went to the Colonel and told him, with suitable gravity, we felt it essential to fly on a few supply drops the better to appreciate the pilots' problems; he was duly impressed by this conscientious sense of duty, backed up by a letter I prepared for Air Headquarters and they promptly detached us to a Dakota squadron in Assam. We did a couple of trips, then I told the squadron commander we had been urgently recalled, so managing finally to get us a few days illicit leave in Calcutta. We flew down to Dum-dum airfield late one afternoon under a lowering sky, vultures sliding past on rigid wings, the palm-strewn land below showing a black grid of paddy bunds on the flooded fields, and in the city itself the myriad water tanks like fragments of a mirror that had shattered against the clutter of roads and bridges and buildings.

We paused for three days, and Stanley found cause to rebuke me for misconduct – it was not the first time. There was a delightful Anglo-Indian girl whom I had met there after our escape from Java the previous year; Stanley joined us at dinner one night, then the next morning reproached me with some embarrassment but refusing to be diverted. She was serious, I was not – so she should be told that. I laughed but this was never a successful defence against Stanley's disapproval; he had a way of looking at you with wide brown eyes, gravely and without saying a word, that penetrated any cover you had arranged over conscience. It was a discomforting habit, just looking at you steadily as you tried to make him laugh – or were fabricating a story to disarm him. He adhered to a strict moral code that could rarely be shaken and was often mortifying. Out on a party he acted as a back-up to conscience; when your moral values softened and became malleable under the flow of alcohol his always remained rock-solid. One night in Delhi we took a bicycle from outside a restaurant and went racing off for a couple of miles on a most unsteady ride, him on the handlebars and me pedalling. I would have left it where we finished our perilous journey but Stanley would not allow this so we had to go all the way back to Connaught Circus to replace the thing. From a book-seller there on the pavement that night he found a book called 'Common Trees and Plants of Northern Burma,' with coloured pictures in most atrocious tones, which he later gave to me because I borrowed it so often.

The monsoon had been curtailed, the rains stopped, when we arrived back at camp. There we heard the brigade was not going to operate independently but would now become part of a larger group under Wingate. There had been an explosion of publicity about Wingate's expedition, poor Lentaigne with his similar group was wiped out in the blast, all was now Wingate's to command. Our theatre of war had been starved for good news, and the fact that this first expedition had cost hundreds of lives for no direct military benefit was irrelevant against the powerful psychological boost it had given our forces; all the talk about the Japanese mastery of jungle warfare, it was suggested, had now been proved unfounded by the march of Wingate's brigade right through the enemy lines into Burma and then out again. In effect, its major achievement was to spotlight Wingate. He was carried on the crest of the publicity wave not only to London but thence onwards to the Quebec conference so impressing both Churchill and Roosevelt with his personality and ideas that he was given practically all that he wanted – at the moment. His wants became wildly excessive, delirious perhaps, later on; but although his imperious manner and gradiose plans antagonised many of the staff at Delhi we in the columns certainly benefitted materially when he rocketed to stardom. Special equipment and rations began to pour in for us. The title of Special Force began to have practical benefits as well as those for morale.

I only met Wingate about half a dozen times, apart from the public meetings when he addressed crowds of us. During the flying breaks that I arranged for Stanley and myself at an aerodrome near Force Headquarters I took Lentaigne up on several flights and met Wingate on two or three such occasions; later he stopped to watch one day in Assam when we were preparing a landing strip, and again there we met him by a Dakota one afternoon. The last time I saw him was when he arrived on the airstrip in Burma a few days after we had landed. Most of the officers spoke of him in the tone reserved for a deity, but the brief contacts I had with him would never have tempted me to pray to him for aid; in the first place he would be unlikely even to hear the prayer, being so engrossed in his own thoughts, but if he did happen to listen then any solution he offered would probably have been far more dangerous than the original problem.

When comparing him to other commanders – to Lentaigne particularly – I don't think of his original mind, compelling oratory, fanatical dedication, the aura of his personality and other such characteristics which he undoubtedly possessed, but to his lack of common humanity. It is difficult to imagine Wingate shedding a tear over a dead comrade. All generals will kill you, of course, that is part of their job and should be irrelevant to any consideration of their character; for that reason I can never see the point of Sassoon's bitter lines about the passing General in the first World War:

> 'He's a cheery old card,' grunted Harry to Jack,
> As they slogged up to Arras with rifle and pack . . .
> But he did for them both with his plan of attack.

So what? What's so damnable about a General whose battle plan produces casualties? As well criticise a butcher for a bloody apron, or a gardener for muddy hands – these are concomitants of the job. And if a general will probably kill you anyway in the end, then surely it is preferable he be a warm and friendly character in those last few days rather than, like Wingate, an aloof and self-absorbed genius? Military commentators say fellow-feeling is misplaced in a Commander, he must be cold and hard, but the fact is that friendliness inspires sympathy and sympathy might well have practical benefits in a desperate situation. In the early days after first joining Lentaigne's group I often shared a drink with him in the evening, sitting under the hissing pressure lamp, drinking rum and listening to him and Masters telling stories about India and the Army, and I would have done a lot for him. He met me in Calcutta one day months after we got back, called me by name and approached with a smile and outstretched hand. Wingate however looked at you like the ancient mariner, 'long grey beard and glittering eye', sensing you if at all not as a fellow human-being with a life and mind of your own but as a tool for him to wield in some God-given mission. Why risk your life for such an egocentric visionary? Or even do him a favour?

There was no doubting the passionate enthusiasm he roused in most of the officers. They spoke of him with a sort of religious fervour. After that famous meeting at the cinema in Jhansi when he addressed us in his flat harsh voice, most of the officers came out with shining eyes, transformed into excited crusaders. They were so inspired by his personality that his actual words escaped scrutiny; one or two however (Masters, I remember) were not completely bewitched, were uneasy about some of his military ideas and said so. These were matters beyond my competence, the most junior subaltern knew far more about ground fighting than I did, but I did know something about air warfare and I thought he was talking fanciful nonsense on the subject of air support. He said we had no need of artillery, that the US Force of fighters and bombers commanded by Cochrane would act for us far more effectively than any field guns, and far more massively. Certainly Cochrane himself, speaking with enthusiasm, offered a willingness to try anything we might devise – 'Just dream it up for us,' – but he made no such extravagant guarantees about air support as Wingate did. Wingate was dogmatic:

'The planes are our artillery. They will bomb and destroy the targets you produce.'

Not a doubt in sight. The believers, and these were the

vast majority of the audience, were thrilled, but anyone who had ever flown in an aeroplane in action could have told him and them that this was nonsense. A Major-General in his position should have known that – and if not, should have been aware of his ignorance – because to think otherwise could at best lead to disappointment and at worst to a bloody shambles. To many Wingate was omniscient but in one detail, the matter of air warfare, I did know more than he did. I had practical experience in three theatres of war, in bombing and ground support, had actually been lecturing on these matters just prior to joining Special Force, and I knew he was wrong. The pilot drops his bomb on a target, misses, and is finished; but guns *open* fire, the gunners then adjust on the fall and can start hitting. To a pilot a miss is an end result, to a gunner it is the preamble to the bombardment proper.

When I tried to argue about this with the Gurkha officers just after that conference they thought this was a typical example of internecine jealousy, the American pilots were going to do what the RAF could not or would not do. However Cochrane had not guaranteed results, what he actually said was that he would *try* anything for us; his enthusiasm perhaps was such that few people examined the actual words, and anyway with Wingate being so dogmatic about the subject any such scrutiny would have been sacrilegious, so it was not until we had had the test of actual experience in Burma that they were forced to recognize the severe limitations of aircraft when used as a substitute for artillery.

One day in Assam there was a close contact with him that brought to mind another general I had met, and again the comparison was invidious. It was an Australian, General Sir John Laverack; in the closing days of the Far East debacle he turned up in Sumatra to assess the possibility of another Australian division, one from the Middle East, being brought into late action there. I took him on a reconnaissance, a three hour trip about the coast and nearby islands, examining some of the beaches in low-flying detail, and on the return he began to ask questions – he knew I had led a raid on a Japanese task force up the Malay peninsular a week earlier when half our bomber force left in the Far East were shot down. We now had less than twenty bombers left – Singapore had fallen, even the aerodrome in Sumatra to which we were returning was to last only a few more days – and he asked what we survivors could do about further Japanese landings in Sumatra or Java.

'If they come with the same naval and fighter escort as at Endau,' I said, 'we certainly couldn't stop them. And they'll finish us off when we try.' (As they did.)

His questions about our personal experiences, our background and opinions, continued right until landing, where he finally thanked us all for 'an illuminating discussion', wished us good-luck, and went on his way (that extra Australian division was never committed, incidentally.) The point of the story is that he was prepared to hear from anyone who might have something to contribute, even from us lowly officers in the RAF – as was also a General in AA Command in 1941, asking for a comparison between the defences of Plymouth and those of Brest, and a Vice-Admiral that same summer seeking information about our methods of bombing ships.

It was different however that day with Wingate by the aircraft. Stanley and I were by the door of the DC3, checking a ramp, when he approached with two staff officers trailing behind. He was wearing his coal-scuttle topee, carrying a staff, bearded once again, heavy brows, aggressive in approach. Without any preamble he asked if we had been practising the use of the radio to give homing signals for supply aircraft. We had not. Stanley and I had long agreed on the wasteful futility of this scheme and I welcomed the opportunity of telling Wingate why, foolishly assuming he would listen – just in case we had a contribution to make.

'No, sir,' I said. 'The reason is –'

'You will practise it.'

I tried to go on, to point out the serious waste of battery power it entailed, but it was impossible to contact the man. He was leaning forward, resting on his prophet's staff – he always seemed to have a slight stoop – and peering into the dark interior of the aircraft. I must have said only a word or two before he cut in, impervious to reason and still not noticing us with his attention.

'You will practise it. At every opportunity.' It was not even a firmly insistent order, just a confident assertion. Then he left us.

And to hell with you too, I thought. There had been no contact between us. He might have been dictating an order, so flat and impersonal was his tone. I don't think he heard words from me, just a noise to be stopped.

Stanley was distressed he had not given me support but he could have done nothing anyway. Wingate was deaf to us. Stanley suggested we wrote an official report setting out our arguments and asking that the homing-signal orders be cancelled. I dissuaded him. His column commander, Peter Cane, gave him a free hand anyway, and I could usually befuddle the Colonel, so there was no point in seeking an official review; it might only provoke a more definite instruction.

'We'll just ignore the bloody order,' I told him. 'Say the radio wasn't working if anyone asks questions.'

It took very special treatment to incite someone as honest as Stanley into a conspiracy of deceit. Wingate managed it, in that one brief contact.

2

We were a restless force. We would clear an area, set up tents and establish a habitat, then one day suddenly pack everything on to mules and our own backs and set off on a hundred mile march to a new befouling area. There was no obvious purpose in these moves. The one in September was for about eighty miles, just after there had been a brief resurgence of the monsoon – three days of massive rainfall now ended – and for the first two sweltering days we heaved ourselves through thick mud higher than boot-level across flat country where maize and cereal crops were just starting to shoot; so sticky was the mud you had to lean sideways to get leverage for each uplifted boot, which would be released finally with a sharp 'hluk'. We must have looked like weird mechanical toys crossing the flat landscape, vaguely human-shaped but green and with monstrous humps, rocking our way through the mud to the sound of 'hluk . . . hluk . . . hluk.'

All this time we were becoming steadily weaker under the accumulated effect of poor diet and over-strenuous exercises in appalling conditions. Nor did things improve at the new camp by Dukwan Dam. Here, the mosquitoes were present in such force as to make them sound at night not individual whines but a continuous high pitched note reminiscent of cicadas, and among the hordes were anopheles searching for the blood-meal essential to their breeding cycle. So presently we were decimated by malaria.

The depleted force continued training however, shattering the jungle tranquillity with explosives. People were firing rifles and machine guns, throwing grenades and setting off explosive charges, and the inevitable accidents included three deaths. It was a strange and disturbing experience for us pilots to discover the brutal immediacy of army warfare. We had been accustomed to bombing and machine-gunning 'targets' – ships, docks, airfields – inanimate objects outside our own cockpit world; but the army stabbed and shot 'the enemy', fellow human beings on the ground right in front of them. I will never forget the chilling shock given by an instructor one day when taking us for a lesson on ambushes. We had gone to a road bend which, he said, was a perfect site – not just for the dense cover to hide the ambush party but particularly for the open space on the far side.

'That's the killing ground,' he said. 'It's the only place they can go, and you can kill them there without any problem. Always try to ensure you have a good clear killing ground.'

Our rifle company commander, David Anderson, glanced at me with a conspiratorial wince of distaste at such cold-blooded clarity but other officers discussed the matter studiously and I saw Peter Wilmot, his second-in-command, make a careful sketch map with the capitals KG marked on the open space. David, who was about my age, had just come down from Cambridge when war started, from the same college where I had done my RAF cadet course, and had at once joined the army; Peter Wilmot was younger than us, had come straight from wartime Cambridge into the Army and was much more of a soldier than David or myself. Peter was the studious type to be selected for staff college, would end up as a general if he chose an army career; he was serious about his work, highly intelligent, dedicated. But David was just dabbling in the army, he was gentle and unassuming, shied away from disagreement, the most unlikely person in the world to shoot bullets at anyone. I spent a lot of time with him on the campaign, never had a cross word from him, and the worst I ever heard him give a Gurkha was a mild remonstrance; we used to have long sessions with Peter trying to rouse us to discuss such important matters as the ideal structure of a Chindit Force, or the role of Gurkhas in the British Army, but we would keep drifting away towards more languid topics like sunbathing on a houseboat deck in Kashmir, dining at the Taj by the window looking out at the moonlit harbour entrance, or drinking a glass-frosted Tom Collins on the veranda of the club at Naini Tal as we watched the boats on the lake.

The camp site was close to the dam itself, a grey granite wall about twenty feet high, now filled with water up and over the flaps – these were a line of rust-red metal plates which could be hinged up to add six feet to the containing height of the dam wall. We did all sorts of water exercises about the dam, but particularly we tried to train the mules to cross rivers. They were not co-operative. It was easy to get them into the water, provided it was shallow, but they were reluctant to go to swimming depth and always tried to keep close to the launching bank; right to the end of the campaign, let alone the training period, the problem of getting mules across water and still keeping one's temper, was never solved.

We actually lost a few through drowning. It happened with me one day when trying to get an unusually stubborn radio-mule across by close-tethering him to a boat. It is astonishing how quickly they can drown. I was holding the lead, the animal was barely out of its depth and its head was within inches of the gunwale, then a slight bow-wave came up to nose level and in that very instant it ceased to move. No struggle, no sound, just collapse of body when the water gushed into the lungs. We dragged it immediately to the bank, only about ten yards away, hauled it on to dry land but it remained motionless. I tried artificial respiration, bumping down on to its rib cage with a thump about fifty times, but to no avail except bruise my behind. Just that one short inhalation had proved fatal.

By this time, the Force was vastly greater than the four columns of the original Lentaigne group, for we now had more than forty columns scattered over thousands of square miles in the Central Provinces. There was little contact between the various brigades; we, for example, in 49 column, stayed close to 94 which was the other half of our battalion, but had only vague contact with the other six columns of our brigade, and of the others in the Force we knew little more than their titles on the distribution list of orders. We would meet troops in the jungle of the area and not know if they belonged to us or not, for our uniforms had varying touches according to the battalions of origin – only when the yellow Chindit flashes were issued much later did we have a discernable common identity. Skin colour was no guide; we ranged from the glistening purple-black of West Africans through the range of Gurkha browns and suntanned Europeans (and an Australian) to the pallid white of a Cameronian's buttocks, seen exposed one day in the muddy waters of the Nerbudda River – he looked as if he were towing a large mushroom that kept bobbing up and down behind him as he jerked in breast-stroke across the flat brown water.

One group, the so-called Merril's Marauders, had the whole colour range within itself, negroes and Spanish-Americans and American-Japanese and Caucasians. This group was part of our force only for a short period before they had the misfortune to come under the direct command of Stilwell, but they continued training with us until the new year. I visited their camp twice, and also was with a small group in an aircraft which crash-landed on one occasion.

They probably had the worst combat time of all because as Americans directly under Stilwell they had no saviour like Slim or Mountbatten to whom they could appeal in extremity. And there was a lot of extremity under Stilwell and his henchmen. The Marauders were all volunteers, had expected to rush off at once in a do-or-die mission, and were boisterously impatient of mere training. Going through their camp was like going through a set of a Wild West film, a man would suddenly pull out a revolver and start firing not directly at you fortunately but at a nearby tree or tin or simply a passing cloud. Their final opinion of Stilwell was perhaps summed up by one of the survivors, coming out on a plane near the end of the campaign:

'That bastard ain't no American. He was born in his God-damn Myitkyena, and I hope he dies there.'

Stilwell was a menace. Wingate might have had no consideration for human beings in pursuit of his dreams and this could result in incidental casualties but Stilwell seemed to have a positive hatred of his fellow creatures, to lash them towards destruction. The treatment by him and his assistant Boatner of fellow Americans in the Marauders was disgraceful by even the harshest war standards; their conduct was such that many of his junior staff went out of their way – and probably took great risks – to show kindness to their fellow sufferers. Stilwell was said to hate the British but this is to particularize irrelevantly, he killed off American troops just as wantonly, his Chinese too for that matter; he was an unprejudiced misanthrope.

By early October the effects of our training regime were being clearly reflected in the sickness returns and the C-in-C sent inspectors from Delhi to discover why we were in such wretched physical condition. They were appalled by our training schedule and our rations, and at once ordered a period of pampered convalescence. Medical specialists came to examine us, special food was brought in, we were forced to take a disgusting drink of shark-liver oil every day, and all started on a course of Mepacrine. This was administered with strict discipline, and men were not given food until they had been seen to swallow their pill; in case anyone, including officers, felt tempted to cheat, it was announced that anyone who contracted malaria would be put on a charge for failing to take Mepacrine. The presumption was not accurate, later

31

we discovered that people could and did go down with malaria despite punctilious adherence to the Mepacrine drill, but at the beginning it was so effective that a case of malaria presently became a rarity – instead we looked as if we had all caught jaundice and bathed our eyes in a weak solution of curry powder.

Wingate himself at this time went down with typhoid and because of this and the appalling condition of the men, our entry into Burma was postponed again, this time to January 1944. I arranged for Stanley and me to go off on another flying jaunt in this interim period – merely telling Air Headquarters that the Brigadier had suggested this. No one bothered to check and shortly afterwards a signal came back detaching us to a Blenheim flight at Bhopal.

It was marvellous to be back with the Blenhein. At first we stuck to the brief and did local flying, taking Lentaigne on a few trips but then the temptations of the Blenheim range were too much and I told the Wing Commander that our brigade had gone to Assam for jungle training and wanted us to do some air exercises with them. He raised no objection, so presently we were going off when and where we liked. Stanley was uneasy at first, worried we might be discovered but as carefree time passed he too began to relax and enjoy the wide freedom we were given.

We saw the sights in privacy from our Blenheim cockpit, taking turns to fly. We circled the Taj Mahal one crisp winter morning when the grass was still glistening with dew, the marble dome dazzling as a snow-slope, shadows of the curved arches black and sharp as cut-outs of a collage. We flew beside the level of the Jaipur walls on the hillcrests surrounding the rose-pink city, swept down the valley over the Amber palace where two children waved and danced in bright excitement as we banked overhead, and one evening in the still hour of sunset we saw the Golden Temple of Amritsar as sharp and clear in the lake reflection as its reality above. In Nepal we flew along a valley between mountainsides where terraced rice fields wavered down the slopes like map-contour lines drawn on the very landscape, and we climbed up to snow level by the Himalayas with white peaks still jutting higher like sharply chiselled cumulus against the Tibetan sky. We stayed overnight at airfields north in the Punjab, west in the dry sands of Baluchistan and down south on the palm-fringed coast of Coromandel, and no one ever seriously queried our purpose. Occasionally an officious adjutant questioned our landing, whence we came and on what authority, and we would reply with impressive modesty:

'We are with Special Force.'

We were rarely bothered further after that demure announcement. No one knew the unit and the title was too awesome to risk a challenge – curiosity perhaps, but that could be discouraged by apologetic hints about security. And we did appear special anyway, dropping in like that, completely out of the blue not only metaphorically but also literally, for we wore not the blue caps and rank stripes of RAF officers but Gurkha hats and the black pips of army captains – although we signed in as Flight Lieutenants – were dressed in weird jungle-green outfits not khaki, and were not accompanied by the usual bearer with inscribed tin trunk but had simply a pack which we carried on our own backs. We were creatures from an unknown world, at best treated with friendly curiosity, at worst with guarded wariness.

The final test of Special Force was in December, a major exercise code-named THURSDAY which involved every brigade. I have no idea of the purpose of the exercise, an ignorance that was shared by the vast majority of those taking part. This is the difference between the operations of the other services and those of the Army: the Navy can send a task force after an enemy battleship or the RAF put a hundred bombers on to a dockyard, and in each case the men involved can actually see how their contribution is part of the whole. Not so in the Army. A platoon sent to capture a bridge

33

cannot physically see how this affects an assault twenty miles away, nor can the soldier in a rifle section easily perceive the chain of logic that links possession of a wooded hill in front of him with the fortunes of an Army dispersed over a thousand square miles.

We marched over eighty miles to start with, that much was painfully clear. This lasted three days, along a metal road through a landscape bare except for an occasional isolated temple standing clear like one of those eroded pinnacles in the deserts of Arizona. Then we had a supply drop before continuing for another two days of bright harsh sunlight across paddy fields now already cracked dry again and dusty as in the scorching days of June. There were large herds of goats in the area, and these had contributed heavily to the loss of cover. I saw a man one day walking across the goat-stricken fields and each footfall sent up a puff of grey dust; he could have been splashing his way across a storage pool of talcum powder.

The air drop, which we had practised before, was this time a memorable one. It introduced us to K rations. What bliss it was to be alive that day! They came in neat packages marked 'Breakfast', 'Dinner', and 'Supper', each one about the size of a brick sliced in half, wrapped in waxed brown waterproof security that kept the bright contents in all their pristine splendour – shiny little tins of pressed meat, of chopped ham and egg, of processed cheese, varieties of biscuits, sealed packets of coffee, of milk, of sugar, lemon drink powder, cellophane-wrapped cigarettes of world famous brands, silver-wrapped candy bars and other delicious sweets, all sparkling new and crisp and fresh in their tightly sealed packets and sending us into excited cries of delight. We were like children opening our presents on Christmas Day as we showed one another our treasures, for there were minor differences in each of the packages that made opening a thrill of anticipation in novelties to come; this variation not only kept interest alive for many weeks but also introduced all the fun of the market place in the development of barter values for the different items.

I had a swop arrangement with our battalion commander, Colonel Morris, my processed cheese for two packets of his dextrose tablets – I had a passion for these things, they did not so much melt in your mouth as disperse in delicious coolness. The Colonel looked the type of elderly Indian Army officer you see in films about the North-West Frontier, peppery, authoritarian, obstinate, impetuous, and he could be all these things, but he had, too, his times of doubt and uncertainty. He usually treated me more gently than the army officers; I was outside his experience and when, as happened from time to time, I expressed disagreement about some order on RAF matters from brigade, he would often look bewildered, confused by this casual rejection of an order from above, and would let me have my way. At other times, unpredictably, he would just explode.

'I don't care what you think,' he shouted one day, suddenly going wild in the middle of a gentle discussion about the positioning of the radio on the drop site. 'We'll do it exactly as they tell us.'

When we were having our practice drop on exercise THURSDAY he was jerky with nerves, knowing we were under observation, and after having agreed on my arrangement of pick-up groups, he then changed his mind when the pilot on his first run dropped mostly in the overshoot area, one parachute finishing high in the crown of a mulberry tree. In a panic he ordered all our main party into that area and obstinately refused to admit his mistake when the pilot subsequently dropped on target, consequently our collection was seriously delayed. Two staff officer umpires were actually with us, this was the compelling reason for not admitting a mistake, and he questioned me at length afterwards about their comments. They had been innocuous, I assured him, they appeared not to have noticed the muddle, but he remained anxious. He had in excess that respect for senior staff always so obvious in regular officers awaiting promotion – he was well into his forties, so at a critical stage of his career.

Exercise THURSDAY finished with some result or other and then we had that once-and-for-all meeting of all the Chindit officers in the cinema at Jhansi. It seemed the uninformed among us might then discover what the purpose of the exercise had been, and the meeting did start with a staff officer giving some comments which provided an inkling. During this time however we were distracted by Wingate's performance; he was on the stage back-right, blur of new beard on his pale face, taking tea with another general. They were at a cloth-covered table, cups and saucers, teapot, tinkling spoons and sugar bowls, in a separate scene of their own, blithely unconcerned with the action on the front of the stage. All chance of understanding THURSDAY was ended when Wingate suddenly stood up, interrupting Lentaigne almost in mid-sentence, and took over the centre stage in an exposition of his theory of Long Range Penetration, the role we must play in Burma, discipline whilst behind the lines, the splendour of the equipment he had obtained for us, and much other irrelevant material. Midway through this harsh lecture he reverted abruptly to the business in hand, not to clarify however but to deliver a most embarrassing denunciation of one of the battalions that had taken part. He did not specify it at once, and there were probably a few others in the cinema apart from Colonel Morris who had to wait in agony whilst the tirade continued.

'Such people will be expelled from the force,' Wingate declared.

I don't know if this was a conditional 'will' or one of his future definites, but the Colonel must have felt he was doomed – my heart bled for him, glancing across at his rigidly-tense face. But then the offending battalion was finally identified and my relief almost matched his. Oh frabjous day, callooh, callay! We were in the clear. The umpires had not noticed our Supply Drop kerfuffle. Even better, Wingate actually mentioned our battalion amongst the star performers; then the Colonel seemed to overflow his seat and thereafter kept nodding his head and giving enthusiastic grunts at every pause in the lecture. I never discovered what happened to the wretched offending battalion but later on Wingate did seem to manifest a genuine concern for fellow humans when he spoke of the Burmese people.

'If I find any person has ill-treated them I shall deal with him ruthlessly,' he grated.

The final word was uttered slowly, after a slight pause, and stilled the hall with menace. Perhaps it was an oratorical device – he had, after all, recently been in close contact with a master orator at the Quebec conference – but he did seem genuinely determined the people of Burma should not suffer from our passage. It was surprising in him, this apparent concern, and you began to warm to him a little. Later however you wondered about this performance when you heard about him encouraging the hill tribes to rise against the Japanese, with fervent promises of support; they had suffered cruelly afterwards and some of his own senior officers from that first campaign were publicly bitter about this betrayal.

The best part of that Jhansi-conference day was not the meeting in the cinema but the long and pleasant afternoon that followed. In relaxed holiday mood David and Peter and I went over to the far side of the dam for a swim but once we had sat down on the grassy slope in the lazy warmth of the December afternoon David and I decided that was pleasure enough. Peter tried to rouse us, urging the benefits of exercise, but finally abandoned this unprofitable effort and went out alone, thrashing about in the cold water and shouting to us about its tingling delight, but we remained unmoved on the dry grass as we looked up at the pale blue sky and chatted idly about Cambridge on soft summer days, and punting on the river, and laughing girls in gay summer frocks. And Peter came back, blinking without his glasses, and towelled himself vigorously as he went on about the treat we had missed. Then while he was dressing, a spoonbill came circling low about the dam, making a wing-creaking squeak as if its hinges needed a drop of oil – there was a huge swampy area just a little to the north where vast flocks of migrant birds from Europe and Asia passed the winter, so many of them that when you flew over low in an aircraft it was like a flurry of snow down below as they rose in their thousands from the tree-striped swamp. And back at the camp afterwards I was sitting outside the tent, under the cloudless orange sky as the sun went down, writing a note about the day's incidents when Peter brought me a glass of rum and ginger ale and asked me about the memorable event in *his* day.

'What have you put down about the meeting?'

I read it to him – it was mostly about the Colonel's apprehension, with just a short note of Wingate's comments on air support and one or two other snippets.

'Is that all?' he cried. 'What about the theory of Long Range Penetration? About our purpose? About morale? About . . .' he went on and on, giving what was probably a complete precis of the Wingate lecture, outraged that I should have reduced it to what he called mere trivia.

It was astonishing what he had remembered, but for all the passionate enthusiasm of his comprehensive review there was still precious little of substance one could grasp from the Wingate lecture, you remembered the feeling of the audience not the facts from the speaker, and despite Peter's reminder I can still recollect nothing more of Wingate's actual message that day than the 'mere trivia' I had myself recorded in my original note. It is the afternoon I remember best, not the morning.

A week or two later, at the beginning of January 1944, we left for the war zone in Assam.

3

I went to school in northern New South Wales some two hundred miles away from home in Maitland, so remote from family as to make personal contact almost impossible until the holidays. Both of these, the June midwinter and the long Christmas summer, were a time of golden promise. From the day of return to school we would start marking months, then weeks and finally days until we would be going home again. At last, the long count ended, we would catch the Brisbane Express late in the evening and then spend most of the night as the train puffed and hissed its way southwards through flurries of rabbits, talking about the forthcoming delights we had been promising ourselves during the long months at school. And that's how it was when we set off for the eastern frontier in January 1944 – the long period of training was finished at last and now, after all the postponements, we were finally setting off for the great adventure that had always been the promise.

The image of India is of massed humanity, streets and bazaars and maidans and ghats smothered in white-clad figures, a countryside strewn with overpopulated villages. But when you travel across the subcontinent by train you pass through vast areas of emptiness, mile after mile of flat desolate landscape, the grey earth withered and dry like the skin of the aged, and even in the lush green lands of the East, with their paddy fields and palm-ringed villages, you still see far less people than on a journey through the centre of England. So long as you keep moving. The instant you stop however they burst into view. You drive along the Grand Trunk road with not a sign of life in the vast landscape, stop to look at a tree – or relieve yourself behind it – and at once people appear all about you. On that journey to Assam all the stations we passed were lifelessly still, but if we stopped then people instantly materialized and crowded about the train – the official stationmaster and attendants, camping families, coolies loping up with head-loads on bouncing poles, beggars scuttling across on deformed limbs like giant crabs, water-carriers with battered brass pots, food vendors guarding their trays against the swirling kite-hawks, a bustling noisy community galvanized into temporary life by the halting of a train.

Ours was a special, never stopping at the big towns and having to pause often during the seven-day journey, chuffing quietly in a siding to let the thunderous expresses go charging past; the ground would shake, whistle wail, steam-clouded monster rush past giving flame-red flash from open boiler door, flickers of light between the flutter of carriages, and then it was gone. Our engine would give a plaintive whistle, screech of wheel-spin, hissing and clanking and joggling of carriages, and we would be on our way again, back to compartment life.

In our compartment was Tiny Langford – as the nickname might suggest he was well over six feet high and weighed some fifteen stone. He looked like Bacchus in battledress. He had lived for several years in Burma, working with a teak company and had little respect for army rank. As Intelligence Officer he was, like me, a non-army oddity attached to headquarters; I lived with him most of the time we were behind the lines and thought him the most diverting person I had ever met in my life. His vocabulary was at its best at its most bitter, whether the target were ill-fitting boots, a cantankerous Colonel or an injustice to the Burmese, but he was really a gentle soul who looked incongruous with a pistol in his hand – which he was most unwilling to shoot.

'They make such a beastly row,' he said – his hearing was more attuned to bird song, in which he was far more helpful to me in Burma than any reference book could have been.

I remember seeing him approaching along a track one day, together with David Anderson and Peter Wilmott, thinking how marvellously appropriate was the manner in which each carried his equipment. Tiny himself, indifferent to regulations, lumbered along with bits and pieces dangling all about his huge figure in a personal un-army arrangement, David had pistol and pouches in the authorized location but with such carelessly adjusted straps that all was slightly askew as he strolled along with languid gait, and Peter looked like a moulded unit with pack and every item of equipment in correct place and firm against his body as he strode in marching order just fractionally ahead of the others.

Our leisurely train journey went on and on until one morning I looked out to see that the scatter of palm trees about the plains of Bengal had given way to great thickets of giant bamboo; and, instead of flat paddy fields, here were terraced steps up the hillsides; there were patches of dense jungle with glossy-green rubber trees predominant, two women went swaying along a track wearing not saris but sarongs, and there was a misty moistness in the air that reminded me vividly of the Burma we saw when flying through to the Singapore debacle two years earlier. The railway skirted a ridge smoothly covered with serried rows of bulging dark-green bushes, women in red blouses with baskets on their backs picking at the bush tops like nibbling animals, then a clearing with store sheds and open-sided driers with red-tiled roofs, a little beyond that a spotlessly white bungalow surrounded by emerald green grass set on top of a little knoll like the centrepiece of a cake decoration. Tea plantations . . . we had arrived at last in Assam.

We reached railhead the next day. Our mules were following in a later train, but we had the loads with us so it took time to clear the train. The scene by the railway track that afternoon was like a busy caravanserai, the jumble of equipment being laid out in loads, thronging people in search of their pile, shouted appeals for sightings, a bustle of collecting and hauling and packing; I was involved most of the time with the two RAF sergeants trying to find our equipment and to get it positioned together to await arrival of the mules. Then we all gathered into milling groups to collect our K rations, fifteen packets in all to last us through the five-day hill march to the concentration area.

All this time a large group of the ubiquitous crows of India were hopping about the periphery of the action, cawing and squabbling about the scraps of food being cleared out of the train. Suddenly there was a fluttering commotion as they gathered in a noisy active crowd on the far side of the line and, going over to investigate, I found a staged fight in progress. An extraordinary spectacle. There was a little cleared space about six feet across, the two fighters in the centre, and the other crows ringed closely about them, just like two members of a gang fighting out their differences to the cheers and jeers of their fellows. The onlookers were partisan, occasionally one would give a peck at a combatant when the fluttering fight came close to the edge of the ring and this interference would provoke a squawking stab from a nearby spectator. The fight broke up abruptly when a kite hawk came swooping down to snatch a scrap thrown from the train, instantly the whole mob including the fighters went chasing after the interloper in cawing fury. We humans presently marched on for a night halt only a few miles away.

The plan was to wait there till the mules arrived, then march off to the concentration area a hundred miles up into the hills near the border, but this had suddenly to be abandoned. A little background may help appreciate the problem that arose. Burma in this context can be imagined as a long thin shovel, open end facing the sea, ridges of mountains up each side and around the top. The north is a cul-de-sac. No wheeled vehicle had ever made a passage across the mountain barriers between India and Burma. We in the Chindit force therefore had to find our own way across that congested series of mountain ridges which were covered in malarial jungle and separated by turbulent rivers which on our line had never been bridged since time began.

What would have been an appalling trial however suddenly became a tactical impossibility. The Japanese arrived. When they had flooded into Burma the previous year their invasion had stopped well short of the northern borders but now in a sudden new surge their waves rose high against the mountains, reaching up into all the valleys. The mountain routes across our path became clogged with enemy troops preparing to launch a major assault towards India. There was no way through for us. Our sister column, 94, came back a day's march to join us by the river, other columns en route continued to the concentration area, and then we all waited while the staff gave thought to the problem.

The days passed, we began to settle in, the Gurkhas rigged up semi-permanent buildings – a mess for the officers made of bamboo with tarpaulin covers, individual group bamboo shelters for all ranks as protection not only from occasional smashes of rain but also the heavy dew, a makeshift shower, even beds of thin bamboo slats that provided a springy base. I was now sharing a shelter with Stanley, and in accordance with a training bulletin we began to go off together on recces for possible airstrips, drop sites and testing our radios. Much was waste of time but Stanley assumed all memoranda from HQ were important, he always worried about compliance, so I usually agreed to do the superfluous exercise.

One pleasant afternoon we watched an elephant at work – there were plenty of wild ones in the hills of Assam but we never encountered any. This day we had been out on the higher ground to the west of the river and were heading back down in packless ease towards camp. On a hillock overlooking the road we stopped for a rest and to enjoy the view. To our right in the east the indigo-blue mountain barrier to

43

Burma was topped by a long thin ripple of silver-white cloud, lying on the ridge like the decorated squiggle of icing on the rim of a cake, and westwards in the gem-clear air left by the showers, the sun was setting in a turquoise sky, dipping down to the shadowed range of the hills about Shillong. Immediately below us a blue-grey elephant was lolling along the road towards a small working party and we strolled down the slope to watch. Tiny Langford had often talked about the intelligence of these animals at work – he was a friend of 'Elephant Bill' Williams who had trained them for their Bombay-Burma Corporation – and this particular one seemed to have a sense of fun as well. He was piling logs on a grassy shelf at the side of the road; as we arrived he had just set one down, then stepped back as if to turn and go off for another one – but instead he stopped, without a word from his mounted mahout. Then I saw that the log had toppled back from the pile and begun to roll down the slope towards him. He made no move however until you felt certain it would crash into his legs and then, at the last moment, with perfect timing, he lifted a front foot lazily just high enough and at just the right angle to stop the log dead with the sole. He stood still for a moment, his trunk flopping relaxed – waiting for applause? – and then the mahout spoke to him in an impatient tone and he lifted the log again and this time put it securely behind the others on the shelf. It was a masterly display of timing. You wanted to pat his trunk and give him a bun or some other little gift of appreciation of the perform-ance. Sadly we had no packs, and so no biscuits to dispense.

In our camp by the river we actually sat down at a bamboo table to eat, and had cooked meals. We had to carry our plates over from the basha cookhouse to the leafy shelter where we sat at the slithery bamboo table, a perilous crossing during which the plate had to be held close to the body and protected by a covering hand. Never have I known such daring and skilful predators as the kite-hawks in that region of Assam. The first time I lost a meal it was unguarded for about two seconds only; I was walking across to the safety of the mess shelter and moved my guard hand behind to scratch my back. I had even taken the precaution of looking up at them circling above, but the thief swooped from the side and hit the plate so hard with his talons he knocked it from my hand. If you sat outside you risked the spoon being knocked from your hand as you raised it from your guarded plate to the mouth, and one of them took most of a ball of meal which was about to be fed to a sick mule – it contained a huge pill which was shed clear when the bird struck the mass. Their eyesight was as good as their flying expertise; I tried to trick them by putting a mixture of brown river mud and pebbles on a plate and carrying it provocatively unguarded across the danger area but not one of them even made a pass at it.

The kite-hawk is a dull brown bird at rest and many of them look scraggy and battered, with gaps in the trailing edges of their wings and even in their tails, but this seems to make no difference – they still fly like angels. They can swoop down fast as a swift, turn sharp as a humming bird and are accurate in strike as a pipistrelle. I used to stand on the river bank and throw scraps of food into the air to watch their brilliant turns at full speed as they aligned themselves to dive for the catch. Watch closely and you see they don't just flatten back their wings and plunge down under the force of gravity, they give actual impetus to the dive with a downward flick of wings as they do the half-roll turn. Often, when food was caught high, they would continue the dive down almost to water level, gathering speed for an upward swoop which would finish in a graceful and perfect stall-turn that brought them back directly into line for the next plunging catch.

Wingate suddenly came up with a new idea. All this time the basis of our training was Long Range Penetration (LRP), a type of warfare devised in the Western Desert and practised by the first Wingate expedition. The basic idea was simple: a force was implanted deep in enemy territory, it attacked roads and outposts, then it dispersed into the jungle leaving

45

no substantial target when the enemy arrived in strength. But now, at the last moment, Wingate changed all that. Instead of melting away into the jungle we would return to a stronghold.

'Turn ye to the stronghold, ye prisoners of hope' was the heading of his paper on the subject. I remember the day he first expounded the theory to us. Wearing his Wolsey helmet, he stood there in a little sandpit with a model of his plan, a long staff in his hand, and we all gathered about the bearded figure; you felt you were part of an illustration in 'Bible Stories for Children', of Moses addressing the Israelites somewhere in the desert during the march from Egypt. The Stronghold, he told us, was to be our refuge – its heart was the airstrip. I don't know if he actually conceived this plan as a consequence of our impasse at that stage, or whether it had been developing in his mind all the time, but it did solve the immediate problem of getting us into Burma. A small advance party would go in by glider to construct a strip and the main force would come in a day or so later. Over ten thousand men and nearly two thousand mules, together with all their equipment, would be landed quickly at improvised airstrips and be ready to fight the moment they landed.

We began training at once with Cochrane's Air Commandos, spending hours of practice getting ourselves and the mules, our packs and their loads, into some sort of order within the Dakota fuselage. There was a complicated structure of bamboo poles and ropes at the top of the fuselage which allowed three mules to be jammed tight in line abreast, unable to move or lash about with their heels; when you entered the Dakota you saw these three mule-behinds lined up at the cockpit door, as if jammed in a rush to get through to the pilot's compartment. The mules took to the air far more equably than they ever did to the water.

The question of where the Chindit forces would actually construct their stronghold-strips had then to be resolved. There were two sites on the near side of the Irrawaddy which were suitable, both in open areas of indaing, a jungle made up of mixed deciduous trees found on laterite soils of the Burmese plain – one site was where an aircraft had actually landed to bring out some wounded from the first expedition, the other was a natural clearing not far away from it. From these two Strongholds our forces could keep up constant attacks on the road-rail link to Myitkyena.

There was a problem however about the smaller force destined for the far side of the Irrawaddy to attack the Bhamo-Myitkyena road link. It was felt that this group, composed of only one battalion, was not large enough to establish a stronghold so it was decided they would abandon their landing area at once, move quickly into the mountains on the Chinese border, and thence operate against the road according to the attack-and-disperse principle of the original Chindit plan. This most remote group would be called Morris Force after its commander and was composed of just 49 and 94 columns. So, having been introduced so dramatically to the concept of Stronghold warfare we in the 4/9 Gurkhas now had to forget it immediately and go back to our original role.

Colonel Morris went out with Jack Masters to inspect a suggested site for our landing and came back to camp all chattery and buoyant with excitement. They had been in a B25, it was equipped with a 75 mm cannon and had carried bombs; both had been used against a remote little railway siding somewhere, the Staff having decided that there must be a bombing as a cover for the reconnaissance. The sortie gave the Colonel the thrill of a lifetime. He could not stop jabbering about it. Yes, yes, they had seen a good landing site, a natural clearing in the jungle, but had I ever seen bombs burst from an aircraft? They made a little sort of circle that shivered. The landing site – oh yes, quite big. Had I ever felt how the aircraft judders when they fire the guns?

Not unnaturally, neither Stanley nor I could rouse a great deal of interest in a perfunctory raid on an undefended target, and this obvious indifference was as usual marked down as another example of the critical attitude affected by the RAF officers towards some of the Air Commando operations and promises. There may have been something in that charge – people who had done more than fifty operational sorties in three theatres of war naturally had opinions about aerial warfare and were prepared to express them. But reasoned argument tended to be inflamed by the attitude of the Army officers in discussing the Commandos; they were always provocatively lavish in praise and given to invidious comparisons when talking to us RAF officers – just as on this occasion when the Colonel told about the pilot calling him into the cockpit, he added the gratuitous:

'Not like the RAF – he let me come right up beside him in the cockpit.'

He was not trying to bait us, the words came bubbling out of his excitement, and Stanley was driven to mumble some objection – he never liked to argue with the Colonel. But in practice, an outsider in the cockpit can sometimes be a downright nuisance, particularly if the aircraft is being thrown around for some reason or other. I had a general up beside me in England, he wanted advice about search-lights in Plymouth, and after a couple of sharp evasions from the beams he suddenly vomited into the shielded view-screen of the ASV – we had to strip it down completely on return. When I told this story that day however it only provided Peter Wilmott for a supporting criticism of the RAF.

'If he'd had more co-operation he'd have been accustomed to such flights and not been sick,' he said.

Peter, typically, had a considered opinion on this subject. He believed the army should have its own air service and was always tiresomely eager to engage in argument about it. He maintained that the RAF was used too disproportionately for strategic purposes, some of which sorties were of doubtful value anyway. The Americans on the other hand were much more disposed to give the sort of air support that ground forces had a right to expect, as shown by their commitment to the Chindits.

He was crying for the moon. I don't think he, or many of the others for that matter, understood quite how exceptional was the air support we were given by the US Air Command. The American ground Forces themselves would never expect such lavish air backing. It was on an unprecedented scale. The Chindits numbered only about two-thirds of a regular division, yet we had the following *exclusive* support from the Air Commandos:

> 100 L1 and L5 Light aircraft
> 35 Dakotas
> 50 Mustang Fighters
> 30 Mitchell Bombers
> 10 Helicopters (Sikorskis)
> 100 Gliders

On top of this largesse we had occasionally all the resources of the US and British Air Forces in India – there were, for example, two US Air Force aircraft and two RAF for every single Air Commando plane used in transporting us into Burma. To supply whole armies on such a munificent scale would have taxed even the immense resources of the United States. It was reasonable to be grateful for this extravagant back-up but downright stupid to carp at the RAF for not providing it normally to every unit in the British Army.

Not only were we lucky that Wingate had been given this very special service but we were also lucky in the man chosen to lead it. Cochrane was an enthusiastic supporter of the campaign from the start; he was in the fortunate position of having complete control of his Air Commando, answerable only to the Pentagon, so there was no superior officer nearby who could grab some of his planes or crews for other tasks, never any need for him to get higher authority's approval for a particular operation. He enjoyed the job he had been given, had all the aircraft he wished for, and all he asked of us was to nominate the tasks. All in all we had struck it fabulously rich. I agreed with everyone it was marvellous – until, as so often happened, someone would start making those invidious comparisons and then the discussion would turn sour again.

During the actual campaign however promises and theories were put to the test of action – things were different after that.

4

About mid-February we moved camp close to the airfield where the Air Commandos were actually stationed, and so were able to train on site with them. Though very few of the Gurkhas had actually flown in one, an aeroplane presented nothing novel; the gliders however were something else. Every day after we moved to the airfield officers would come in with stories about the men's reaction to our practice glider. When would the engines be fitted? Where did they go? Most of the men however believed it was just a mock-up designed for training. Proper ones would have engines.

I went with Peter Wilmott when he took his platoon down for their introduction. Conscientious as ever in preparation he had told them beforehand about the lack of engines, explaining the machine's capability by example of the circling kite-hawks, but he was not confident they accepted his story. He was right. When we were gathered about the thing on the strip the Havildar said casually (in Gurkhali, of course):

'It has one engine? Or two?' He obviously believed it a mock-up.

'No, no. I told you. They do not have engines.'

Again he explained that an aeroplane towed the gliders. I called the Havildar over, showed him the tow point under the fuselage, then with my limited vocabulary tried to explain the whole process – the aircraft pulling up glider . . . mid-air release . . . glider floating down to ground. Peter listened closely, re-phrasing where necessary, and gave a running commentary as I illustrated a glider's landing with a sweep of hand down towards the ground.

'You see. They do not need engines.' He explained patiently. 'Even aeroplanes do not use engines to *land*.'

This was a terrible mistake. We might have won through to them but for that last sentence. The glider was by a dust-flaked straggley pomegranate tree about fifty yards off the strip and just then an aircraft came in to land, making such a din that he actually had to shout above the engine roar to be heard. It was a DC3 rumbling in on half-throttle. The whole platoon did a marvellous mime, turning heads in unison like spectators at a tennis match, watched for a moment the noisy DC3 as it spluttered on down the strip with a loud popping of exhaust stubs, then they all turned back together to look at the man who had just told them that aircraft do not use engines to land – just looked at him silently. Awaiting explanation. At a loss, he turned to me, but I waved him off:

'Give a lecture in aerodynamics? In Gurkhali? You're crazy!'

'No, it's serious, Pat. Please. Why did that chap use engines to land?'

I told him I had no idea. Perhaps he was practising powered landings, or he liked rumbling in, or he was under-shooting, or speed had dropped too low, or . . . God knows. There were hundreds of reasons. I suggested he tell the men the extra power was unnecessary – riding a bicycle down a slope some people might use pedals and others not, a matter of personal preference irrelevant to actual progress. He tried very hard as always, peering at them through his big horn-rimmed glasses, but they listened in patent, though polite, disbelief.

He needed help. I tore off a sheet of my message pad and began to make one of those arrow-shaped planes most of us have launched about classrooms in the past. Peter, in de-lighted relief, exclaimed:

'Ah! Watch what the hawaijaha-sahib is doing.'

He started an eager explanation, telling how the paper plane would float down safely without any engine power, just like the glider. Watch closely now! I launched it across in front of them and in the dead still air, with no reason whatsoever for unruly behaviour, the thing perversely turned on its back and dived steeply into the ground with such force the nose crumpled back at right angles. They observed this experimental proof in complete silence, then turned back as a group and looked at him.

I burst out laughing. Peter was distressed however. He begged me to treat the matter seriously, I was the expert, they would believe me. I did try to retrieve the situation by taking the bedraggled paper-plane in hand and bringing it down manually to a soft landing, with Peter giving a commentary on the turn and glide approach, but the men were not impressed by this staged exhibition. It was obviously phoney. The actual aeroplane, and the experiment conducted by the hawaijaha-sahib had been striking proofs of their own convictions.

Late in February Wingate spent a morning with us, watching a practice loading and afterwards talking about our projected role. The Chindit main force was to go in first to the two planned Strongholds on the near side of the Irrawaddy – code-named BROADWAY and PICCADILLY – and about a week later we would be flown into our landing site on the far side. There was a rumour that a small group from our column would go in by glider to protect the US engineers preparing our temporary strip – it was named CHOWRINGEE – but the Colonel would not discuss this matter. He gave me a starchy rebuff when questioned. He had become very rank-conscious at this period, in close daily contact as he was with so many senior officers of Force HQ and visiting staff, and when you met him in their company his attitude was distinctly aloof.

Security was tightened. Even in training days we had

53

never been permitted to suggest the type of operation being planned but now all outgoing mail was completely blocked – it would be posted on after D-day. Incoming mail was to be dropped with our supplies once we were behind the lines, and there was a special arrangement about outgoing mail; a stereotype airgram would be sent to one only nominated relative or friend every month. My nominee was Timmie, my fiancée back in England, and here is a transcript of one she retained:

Dear Madam,

It is probable you will not receive any letter from your (fiancé) No. (88689) . . . Rank (F/lt) Name (T. P. O'Brien) for some time to come. This does not mean that he is unwell. For the present however the type of operation in which he is taking part makes it impossible for him to write to you, but he will do so as soon as he can. Please however go on writing to him as your letters will greatly cheer him, and please ask his friends and relatives to write also. If you use the normal address your letters will be delivered. Until he can write to you himself, letters similar to this will be sent to you once a month.

(Squiggle)

. . . .

We were also given a sentence we could include in a last letter to other relatives and friends with whom we wished to maintain contact, and this was the only reference that could be made to our operation. The permitted phrase was:

If at any time you do not hear from me as regularly as you have been accustomed, write to . . . (the airgram nominee) to whom I will always send news of my doings.

Who chose that ugly final word, I wonder? Certainly not the sort of biblical phrasing you associated with Wingate . . . 'News of my smitings' would be more his style.

On the first of March we heard a definite date for the first time. The Colonel announced we would fly in to CHOWRINGEE on March 10th, but a small glider party would go in with the American engineers the night before to protect them. On the 5th March however this was changed abruptly when it was discovered that the PICCADILLY clearing which the gliders planned to use that very night was covered in logs. In a wild endeavour to retrieve the situation they decided to divert some of the frustrated gliders to BROADWAY, which seemed to be clear of obstacles. Those that could be prepared in time took to the air in double-tows with the BROADWAY gliders, but these unpractised double-tows were a disaster and most had to be shed even before reaching Burma. Worse still, fatally, were the casualties caused at BROADWAY by stumps of trees and other obstructions that even a casual survey would have revealed.

So, late that night when the great expedition had finally started, the staff had suddenly to re-plan all the loading schedules which had been so laboriously finalized for the three sites. Now only two were available. Things get confused here and it might be useful to set down the summary noted later that week in my diary.

	THE PLAN	THE EVENT
March 5.	Glider parties 77/111 Brigades land BROADWAY and PICCADILLY.	Only 77 land at BROADWAY, as PICCADILLY is blocked and useless.
March 6.	Strips prepared at BROADWAY & PICCADILLY Rest of 77 and 111 start to fly in	Fly in to BROADWAY only. Morris Force rushed in to CHOWRINGEE 3 days early.
March 7.	Landings continue at BROADWAY (77) and PICCADILLY (111 Bde)	Strip at CHOWRINGEE not yet made, owing to to accident. Morris Force and 111 Bde still stuck in India.

March 8.	Landings completed BROADWAY & PICCADILLY Gliders towed back to base in India.	Landings at BROADWAY completed (incl. some of of III Bde.) Rest now to go to CHOWRINGEE.
March 9.	Morris Force glider party to land at CHOWRINGEE.	All landings now finished, but most of III Bde on wrong side of Irrawaddy.
March 10.	All Morris Force in. CHOWRINGEE to be abandoned.	It finished previous day.

The Wingate disciples – and they comprised the vast majority of Chindit officers – all managed to minimize or even ignore altogether the almost incredible obstinacy of Wingate that was manifest in the chaotic last-minute change that had to be made to his plan. For this is the extraordinary fact: there was no close survey made of any of the three sites where the gliders were to land. From Colonel Morris at the time, and others later, I heard that this was on Wingate's personal and precise instructions. When I spoke to the Colonel about it the following morning, asking why the build-up of logs had not been noticed on the photographs he said he was surprised that I of all his officers should ask such a question.

'You can't keep on taking photographs of the place where you're going to land,' he lectured. 'That would tell the Japs at once.'

He really believed that. Such ignorance about air reconnaissance was excusable in his case, his experience was limited to peace-time Indian Army and he had no real need to know about such matters. But Wingate had no such excuses. He was surrounded by more pilots willing to help than any army commander had ever had before. And his own staff were not idiots; they were highly skilled professionals, as their handling of the launching showed, they must have known something about aerial reconnaissance and could have advised him – had they been allowed, or dared. Apparently they were not, or did not. It seems that Wingate had the same naïve belief as our Colonel, that the passage of an aircraft over a country jeopardizes the security of one particular field in it. He had rigorously banned all reconnaissance in those final weeks, and his staff bowed to the edict. Hard to believe that some people could have been so meekly deferential, and one man so barbed against advice.

Wingate had decided that photographs were a risk and that was the end of the matter. He himself had seen BROADWAY on the ground the previous year, the Colonel had flown over CHOWRINGEE and someone else over PICCADILLY and there was precious little more contributed to planning than that. It was as though the decisions about allied landing beaches for D-Day in Europe were made on information supplied, for one of them, by a General who had passed it once on holiday, and for the others by a rear gunner who had flown over them one dawn coming back from a raid.

This was the worst blunder – simple negligence. But even apart from that, the basic plan itself would have been vastly improved had Wingate and his staff taken advantage of facilities available within the command. What about all the lessons learned by special duty squadrons operating behind well defended and vigilantly guarded coasts of Europe? Such experience, and advice, was actually available in India. There was an RAF unit operating from Bengal whose sole task was to parachute agents into occupied territory. I joined them subsequently and by the end of the war had actually landed behind the enemy lines in Burma, Siam, Laos, Indo-China, and in China itself, without ever jeopardizing a site or losing a single life. Wingate must have known about the existence of these illicit organizations – and if he didn't, then he should have – and surely must have at least guessed at their expertise.

All the well-oiled machinery was there for a most efficient

and successful landing of his forces, and Wingate rejected it. The obvious way to have done the job would have been to utilize the expertise of the RAF specialist unit and the illicit organizations with which it worked – SOE (Force 136), the ISLD, or the OSS, all experienced in this field. Parachutists from one of these groups could have been landed with radios weeks before, the fields prepared and marked on the night, water supplies and enemy locations pinpointed, and all would have entered safely. All Wingate had to do was to talk to any *experienced* pilot in his force, British or American (or the one from Australia, for that matter), ask for ideas about either photographic security or illicit landings and he would have discovered his ignorance. But he did not ask for help and he was not prepared to listen to gratuitous advice. He knew.

I personally had reason to be grateful to Wingate because he gave me the opportunity to escape dull ease down in Bombay and become involved in an exciting adventure. The whole of the Chindit force had reason to be grateful to him for the successful way he sold the idea to Churchill and Roosevelt and other mighty figures, and so was able to obtain for us such splendid equipment, rations, and the marvellous resources of a private air force equipped on a lavish scale and manned by enthusiastic and skilful pilots. He had many unusual qualities – he must have had, for many of those who respected and admired him were not fools. For all that I have no doubt whatsoever that in blocking scrutiny of the landing sites he acted with almost criminal stupidity. There was no need for so many people to die that first night.

It always surprised me that no one on his staff secretly disobeyed this foolish injunction right from the start. It would have been easy enough to get photographers on the quiet from the RAF, even from Cochrane's group perhaps, there are many ways it could have been devised, then the information slid to Wingate's notice without his knowing whence it sprang. Cochrane, most sensibly, did finally order one of his pilots to take a forbidden photograph – and so the logs, innocently left out to dry by timber extractors, were discovered and disaster averted at PICCADILLY. All praise and thanks to him. Far from being grateful however Wingate apparently had been shouting furiously about this disobedience that night on the strip in Assam when the operation was halted, concerned immediately not about the lives that had been saved but that his order had been violated.

There had been no proper survey of BROADWAY either. It had no obvious lines of logs but there were thirty men killed outright and twice as many injured, many fatally, because of tree stumps and ditches hidden in the grass. We should have known they were there. The obstructions not only caused casualties direct on impact but also left gliders stranded in the paths of others landing, and so there were a number of collisions; in all, including those cast off en route, less than half the sixty gliders that took off from Assam that night landed safely in Burma. It was not a complete disaster, for under Calvert's inspiring leadership the strip was developed enough to let some aircraft land the following night; it was just a minor war tragedy that would never have occurred had humility been amongst Wingate's qualities.

All this happened that first night, March 5th, with us due to fly in five days later. Next morning vague news of the confusion began to float back to us a hundred miles away from the glider take-off airfield, and I was down at our strip actually hearing about it from an American pilot who had been over there when the photograph bombshell exploded – he was describing the Wingate outburst with dramatic detail – when we were interrupted by a Gurkha orderly running up in breathless urgency. The Colonel wanted me at once – '*ek dum*'. I found him outside his tent, a few other officers already with him. He told us that because of the loss of the PICCADILLY site it had been decided that gliders would take in the advance party to CHOWRINGEE that very night. There would be seven officers and about eighty men in

59

the advance party – a few sappers to help build the strip but mostly riflemen to protect the American working party, who would take a grader in one glider, and the tractor to pull it in another. There would be nine gliders only, a comparatively small party because after the lesson of the previous night's landing it was decided not to put too many at risk in that first dangerous phase. The RAF radio group would be among those to go in the glider landing party.

We had only half an hour to pack our kit and get down to the strip whence we would be flown the hundred miles to the glider airfield. The seven of us scattered like a flurry of startled hens, rushing about trying to clear up what we had actually doing, then getting our kit ready. David and Peter had been in the middle of a pay parade; they went back to the table with David thinking about handing over to someone but Peter settled the matter at once by scooping up the acquittance rolls, the thumb-mark pad and all the unpaid money into a haversack then dumped the whole jumble with the adjutant. Tiny Langford had been trying to repair a local map and he just walked away from it on the mess table and started packing. I rushed off to find my sergeants. Horton, young and keen, asked all sorts of pertinent questions about the radio but Sergeant Owen, a phlegmatic type, asked only one:

'What about our rations?'

These were being delivered to us. I ran back to our tent where Tiny was now quietly and methodically filling his pack. We had a canvas bag to hold things we were not taking, this to be cared for by Rear Headquarters. I kept shifting items from my pack to the bag. It was still day, the air in the tent was heavy with glutinous heat, and I was feverish with excitement anyway, so presently my clothes were sodden. No time to change. I left a space for the rations but when a Gurkha turned up with the fifteen packets, five days supplies, I had to unpack everything because there was nothing like enough room. Then I lost my books, the Golden

60

Treasury and the tree book borrowed permanently from Stanley, and was in a panic until my orderly, Lilbahadur, found them. Puttees stuffed into trousers pocket, no time to put them on . . . revolver ammunition . . . water bottle to be filled . . . compass . . . diary and exercise book for notes . . . fill fountain pen . . . kukri sheath to be affixed to webbing . . . blanket and ground-sheet wrapped around the sharp-cornered K ration packs . . . spare socks . . . double-sewn Gurkha hat . . . jungle-green hand towel.

Stanley fussing about – did I have the supply drop notes? The Signal Code? What should he do about my memo copies? Others were thumping past for the trucks. 'Come on, Pat!' from the Colonel – he wasn't going, so could relax and harry us. A singlet and balaclava still on the camp-bed . . . To hell with them! Pack heaved up . . . Let's go!

Down at the airfield we were each handed a hundred one-rupee notes 'in case your glider crashes'. We bundled ourselves into the hot bare fuselage, the engines already spluttering to go, the door thudded shut, the plane wheeled so sharply for take-off that those on the port side were sent sliding across the metal floor, then after the short flight we thumped down at the glider airfield in mid-afternoon. This was over two miles in length, an enormous strip on which the gliders were already lined nose to tail in a long file, with all their white nylon tow ropes laid out to the side like an array of pipelines on the deck of a great oil tanker. At the end of the first rope the line of Dakotas started, they were parked broadside on to the strip, a shivery row stretching away into the heat-hazed distance; when a light plane took off the Dakotas all disappeared within a churned-up cloud of pallid dust, and you dreamed up a towering genie to materialize from it and ask your wishes.

We were given a waiting area in the paddy fields beside the strip, pens with rope barriers, and there we sat down in our glider-groups to do last checks and await our call, while all around the tumult and clamour of the fairground continued.

Like many others I took out all my kit and did a careful repack, and to the base officer who was standing by to provide last-minute aid I gave one pair of socks from the pack, reckoning two would be enough. I wrote up the diary and note book complete to the scene on the strip. Loudspeakers had been set up along the edge of the field facing our pens; we were located according to the loading plan, each group with a number code to be called when our turn came, but meanwhile staff officers were using the loudspeakers to find other staff officers.

First off were to be the planes that were going to land at BROADWAY where the strip was now apparently completed; once they were gone it would be our turn in the gliders. Around four o'clock the planes began to move and at once the bright sun and the cloudless blue sky and the busy scene with the great line of machines all disappeared in a swirling gritty cloud of pale dust, within which a dull orange ball kept glowing fitfully from the west. The noise was so loud we had to shout for speech – the loudspeakers were blaring for units to assemble, plane engines were roaring and thundering in take-off, and behind us there were trucks revving up furiously as they crossed the dry ditch.

The announcements on the loudspeakers were indistinct – coarsened by the massive dust cloud? – but presently you learned to listen only for the code-number concealed in the distorted speech. That was your starting gun. The chap was probably saying that all those allocated to K23, say, should advance to the check point, but what you heard was something like:

'Wah-wah wah-wah-wah K23 wah-wah wah.' So once you got the hang of it you just waited for the triple-wah that led immediately to the vital figure.

It took over an hour for all the BROADWAY planes to get clear. Some mules clattered past us at one stage, presumably to fly in there, so you felt 77 brigade were already veterans; they had had their fateful initiation the previous night, those now leaving were going to a blood-won landing ground where reception parties were waiting to welcome them. For us it was to be the sort of blind plunge their advance party had experienced the previous night, and as if to stress this a captain from Force HQ spent some time with us telling in a sombre voice about the gliders that had crashed into hidden obstacles, leaving BROADWAY littered with broken bodies.

'But you'll be all right,' he said, without producing an atom of proof for such reassurance as against the powerful evidence he *had* adduced for disaster. 'Good luck,' he added, then went on to spread despondency to the next corral.

In the fading light I wrote a last letter to Timmie (in the old Blenheim days I used to write these farewell letters every week or so), rewrapped the rations in my pack, went for another pee, and had a fruitless hunt for my ammunition pouch before taking a substitute from the base officer. The first glider was called and groups began to move off into the tumult about the strip. Powerful lights set the dust cloud aglow.

At last our number was called, just after David had started off from the nearby pen. We stumbled off in his direction, passing by Peter's group who were already formed into neat marching lines (not a gaggle like the rest of us) and found ourselves heading towards the red and green wingtip lights flitting about in the dust. We were stopped at a checkpoint, then led by a guide through the brightest area of lights and into the noisiest spot of the glow, to what seemed like the centre of the swirling dust-cloud. The loudspeakers went on blaring, engines roared, voices shouted, our number was called again and the guide went towards the call. We passed close by one glider where a Gurkha was being pushed in backwards through the door, stumbled over nylon ropes, a searchlight swept across the strip and lit the dust like a flash of lightening, then the guide shouted:

'Here's yours. Load up.'

In we went.

5

You gaze in delight at a glider soaring away from a sunlit hill, free as a seagull floating along the cliff edge, silent and smooth, almost poised in mid-air as it wheels on wing-tip against the blue. You think you could sail across the country-side with never a whisper from the buoyant air, so quiet you would hear the bark of a dog from the earth down below, so light you would keep bouncing gently on faint eddies of the air. But not in the WACO. The WACO was more like a noisy wallowing barge than a glider.

When the tow-plane revved its engines the settling dust boiled up again furiously, the white tow-line shivered taut, we started forward with a jerk that knocked me back in the co-pilot seat, and there was a high-pitched scriek that painfully pierced through all other sound. The pilot had the stick jammed forward, the nose of our glider was scraping along the harsh surface of the strip and I would not have been surprised had the cockpit floor begun to smoke from friction. The dust cloud was so thick we could not see the nylon tow. The pilot – and I too for that matter – had abandoned the outside and was head down to the instruments. He suddenly heaved back the stick, the screeching pain stopped, then we had the roaring sound of a WACO sliding and wallowing about in full flight. It was a composite sound, a violent wind nearly double hurricane force beating against the frail struc-ture, a creaking and whining and crackling of that structure under stress, and the roar of the labouring aircraft now visible in the clear moonlight a hundred and fifty yards ahead of us. We seemed to be attached to a long white cane, being stirred about by swirling currents.

'That's the easy part,' the pilot shouted.

He had to shout to be heard. The noise was as loud as in a light aircraft. The moon was full, shining obliquely into the cabin, and I turned and saw the Jamadar's lips moving, hand cupped beside his mouth to amplify the sound, but could hear nothing intelligible. I waved back at him and he seemed satisfied. They were packed so tightly we had been unable to pull the door shut and men outside had had to ram it closed. They were not strapped in; if we crashed then the ten men together with radio, batteries, motor charger, petrol cans and ammunition would be hurled at about 150 mph against the pilot and myself seated at the controls just in front of them.

The pilot tried to keep the tug aircraft steady just above us but the WACO was so sluggish in response that from time to time the line would slacken before the elevator corrected. You waited then for the fearsome penalty. The line would tauten, there would be a savage jolt accompanied by a thunderous clap as it slammed against the fuselage under our feet and you felt sure the flimsy structure must be smashed apart. No one had a parachute.

It was far too noisy to talk in comfort so we gave up the effort. He flew and I map-read. It was a brilliantly clear moonlit night, with the milky way a glittering trail of stardust streaked across the equatorial constellations – the twin diamonds of Centauri, and Antares glinting red in Scorpio – so bright that the mountains threw shadows and you could pick out the palisade of tree trunks along a ridge. There were silver flashes from the up-moon stretches of the Chindwin and it was easy to get a pinpoint – after the disasters of the previous night when so many gliders had been cast adrift, it was prudent to mark our track. Beyond the Chindwin it was easy: first the straight dark railway across a pallid swathe of the plain blotched with villages, then the long wide bone-

65

white stretches of sand lining the Irrawaddy, and finally the vital checkpoint – the junction of the neat and narrow Shweli river with the untidy sprawl of the great Irrawaddy. Within the curve of this junction, amid a huge dark blot of jungle, there was no mistaking the pale pear-shaped scar of CHOWRINGEE clearing. The pilot looked across at me and nodded towards it. I nodded back as having seen it.

We were already descending when the clearing came in sight, and the tug then banked wide to give us a good look at our target within that U-curve of the Shweli. There were several small paler patches on the landing area that worried me; I had no idea what they were, but they were a distinctly different shade and therefore suspicious. I called to the pilot:

'White patches?'

He just shrugged. I hoped he was going to try for a line which would avoid the larger ones at least. We continued the turn and then caught the best view of the site up moon. I could pick out two gliders already down, and looked across to see if the pilot had seen them but at that moment he suddenly dropped the tow-line and we were on our own. He pushed the stick hard forward and we finally came out of the diving turn heading straight for the long central line of the pear and at an alarming speed, over 140 on the Air Speed Indicator. Even then, with the aircraft away, the WACO was still making a great racket as it rushed towards the ground, the noise making the speed seem even more fearful. He brought us in low over the trees, so low you could pick out branches, then the moment we had clear ground ahead he straightened out his arms and dived the thing straight down at the ground. A terrifying approach. His line-up was perfect though, straight between two paler patches at the near end.

The landing speed was far higher than I had expected, we were just above the 120 mark on the ASI when we first made contact. There was a distinct crashing sound when we flew into the high grass and almost immediately afterwards a crackling thud against the ground, squashing us into our

66

seats, then we zoomed up clear on rebound for a moment before he once more rammed the stick forward and slammed us into the grass again. This time he managed to keep us down. I lifted my feet and crashed them into the instrument panel, head down and hands over face as we tore through horse-high grass, jerked clear then in again, a tremendous crashing roar that went on, and on, and on. Plenty of time to think, and think clearly . . . 'Tree stump – logs – boulders.' The tearing sound stopped abruptly . . . floating clear for an instant over a depression . . . brace for crash. We hit the far side with a hammering thud, were slung sideways and forward as the glider slewed around broadside, a loud crack when the starboard wing smashed back. Then we were still. Solidly still – and alive.

'Thank Jesus!' the pilot said.

And from me, too.

The perspex above the instrument panel was smashed, also at my side, and the pieces had come into the cockpit. My boots had gone through the bottom of the instrument panel and someone's pack had been hurled jammed between the pilot and myself. But we had arrived without a scratch on any of us.

The Jemadar could not open the door. I clambered back over the huddled figures, and discovered it was jammed, the fuselage probably twisted in the crash. Holding the catch open I told him to slam his feet against the panel. He did, so explosively that the door burst open with a force that almost yanked me out of the glider. I tumbled out anyway, on to ground that was superficially firm but slightly springy, an uneasy first contact with Burma.

The explanation came quickly when I stood up. We had finished on the far side of a muddy saucer, a wallow used by buffalo or elephants, and with a surround of that tall 'kaing' grass – the stuff that comprised those paler patches we had seen from the air. There was no water left in it, just mud that had the consistency of dough and was covered by a brittle dry layer which caused that unsteady sensation underfoot. I penetrated the crust once before reaching firm ground and the others following had successively worse luck. They emerged in a soft whispery clatter, dropping packs and going back to help with the radio and other equipment. I was just about to reach down to pull the chore-horse clear of the edge of the wallow when I was struck still by a nerve-shattering report; it split the silence and trailed off into a terrible crackling sound, the snapping of many branches and crumpling of glider structure, a violently destructive sound that stopped as abruptly as it had started and chilled the hearts of all who heard it. Unlike an aeroplane crash this had no visual impact, you looked towards the noise expecting to see the usual fire-ball associated with airfield crashes but there was nothing to be seen in the black trees at the eastern end of the clearing into which the glider had plunged, nor any further sound. Hushed further by the crash we continued unloading, more urgently now as if under threat ourselves but it still took ten minutes or so to get everything out, and then ourselves clear of the stinking mud. The stink stayed with us as we moved off through the high grass.

Our map rendezvous was on the southern side of the clearing, where the pear widened out, and it had been arranged that the first party to arrive there would show a light. We could see no sign of a light nor, when we stood absolutely still for a moment, could we hear any sound except the desynchronized throbbing of an aircraft overhead and a regular strident noise like that of a cricket somewhere nearby. The two gliders which we knew for certain were already down were no longer visible, for there was still a lot of the kaing grass about our position, but a plane had just passed overhead and another was circling with its glider. Of the nine gliders our particular one had been about the middle so there were probably more than two down already. Just as we moved off towards the trees another landed in front of us – we didn't see it come in, just heard the loud crashing impact then the long-drawn SHHHH diminuendo as it hurtled through a wide patch of the kaing grass into silence.

We were clear of the tall grass and heading towards the suspected RV area when I saw a dim light, swinging like a pendulum, off to one side of our aiming point. We turned towards it and at that moment another Indian file emerged from the night. A hoarse whisper:

'Where's the bloody light?'

It was Tiny Langford. I pointed out the light and we joined up together, he with his bulky figure clearing a pathway through the worst patches of grass – this varied in height, mostly about the ankles but occasionally breast-high. All the gliders had probably landed by this time; one of the pilots – Jackie Coogan, of the Charlie Chaplin films – had laid out a few smudge pots as a rough guiding line to the later arrivals. As we neared the trees another file joined us, led by Peter Wilmott; he had also seen the light and was angry because it was not at the actual RV nominated on the map. As one would expect, Peter had gone to pains to orient himself on landing then start off on compass course to the proper RV.

The light went out again as we neared the trees but then we were guided by the sound of whispered voices towards a darker patch at the edge of the forest and there we found Colonel Alison, the senior American of the party, and two of our Gurkha groups – a firefly went winking past between us as we came up to them. The other two joined us presently, and we heard that the crashed glider had made its approach too high; it seemed the pilot had tried to swoop up and turn back to land in the opposite direction – an almost invariably fatal manoeuvre in which, as one might expect, the aircraft had stalled on the turn and then crashed down into the trees. A party had been sent down to the scene and they returned shortly with bad news. Not only were the three men, all Americans, dead but the vital cargo was lost. The glider had been the one carrying our caterpillar tractor. Without it we had no machine to build our airstrip.

I never did discover why we had split this vital piece of equipment into two interdependent units – they had sent just a bulldozer in to BROADWAY. The chance of us losing a bulldozer on our casualty figures was one in nine, but the tractor-grader set-up doubled this risk chance to two in nine, and for no advantage. Had we lost the grader it might not have been so bad, at least the tractor could have been driven to and fro to flatten some grass, but as luck would have it we had lost the essential one. Without a tractor to pull it our grader was useless – immobile as a glider without a tug.

Alison asked me to send a simple message in plain language back to base. It read:

DAY AND CAT LOST.

I was dubious. Day was the name of the engineer who had been killed, 'cat' was the caterpillar tractor: that might be perfectly clear to Cochrane but a signalman might think it corrupt and hold it for checking back, not recognizing its importance. I discussed this quietly with Alison but he was convinced there would be no problem so I told the sergeants to send it – they had already slung the aerial and opened up the set. As a back-up I sent a coded message elaborating on the plain one.

During this period the Gurkhas had gone back out into the moonlit clearing to start hauling gliders into cover under the trees, the plan being to get them hidden before daybreak in case a Japanese patrol or passing plane happened to sight them. Apart from the fatal crash we had three others, including ours, damaged beyond repair, but all had to be moved under cover. The other men who had come in with us were the twelve Garwhalis of the Sapper platoon; their designated task that night had been to help build the strip, but Alison had now abandoned that plan completely.

The loss of the tractor had been catastrophic for Alison. To him the whole landing plan was lost without machinery to build the strip. It had been intended to fly in a hundred aircraft the second night, all Morris Force in fact, but this was now impossible. Until we had a replacement tractor or bulldozer, Alison said, there was nothing we could do. His attitude illustrated the difference between the American approach and ours. He knew what machines could do and so rejected as worthlessly trivial the substitute we offered; we however were ignorant about the machine's capabilities, and to us the substitute of twelve men with kukries and four spades did seem to be a genuine alternative. I discovered his lack of interest from the Sapper officer, who had been waiting to start work, so I left the radio and went back to talk to Alison. He was resigned to delay however, repeating that we could do nothing about the situation except wait for a bulldozer the following night.

'We can get *some* done tonight,' Cheetham muttered rather brusquely.

He was our Sapper officer, energetic, practical, and confident – he had already dug his foxhole, been out to organize the groups pulling in the gliders, now wanted his Garwhalis to start building the strip. He was impatient with such apathy. His natural reaction to the loss of a machine was to build an alternative, if that were impossible then to improvise; and, like me, he was provoked by the disparaging rejection of our capability. We decided to go ahead anyway, collected the men together and went out into the clearing. That Alison had so little faith in our spades and kukries made us all the more determined to prove our point in the remaining hours of darkness. We had, after all, practised the job often enough and felt confident we could achieve something useful even with the primitive tools we had – in fact, after that slighting rejection of our offer, we would have started the job with our bare hands.

It must have been about eleven that night when we began and we reckoned we could work safely out in the open until five in the morning. Perhaps six hours – and I recalled we had once built a 1,200 yard strip in an hour. That had been in

71

daylight in India however, with two full platoons, plenty of tools, and on crop-garnered empty land – just a matter of aligning the strip then knocking down the bunds. But in Burma that night I had first to discover a wallow-free line through grass which in places was up to our shoulders, we had had a long day already and would have to work through without sleep, and we had only four spades.

We had been enjoined to keep voices down to a whisper so the mark-out took time. I set eight men kukri-cutting the low grass and clearing the surface about a hundred yards from the western limit, the estimated touch-down for a DC3, then Cheetham and I and the other four walked towards a v-shaped gap in the trees at the eastern end of the big pear-shaped clearing; we kept about four yards apart and so covered a swathe of some twenty-five yards. Constant checks and stops were necessary to ensure there was no tree stump, log, or other obstruction between us, for even where the grass was only knee high, it was clumpy and threw such shadows in the silver moonlight it was difficult to distinguish between illusion and substance. After about an hour we had found a thousand-yard line which avoided all the wallows and depressions – the quick rough guide laid out by Coogan was all right for gliders but it had at least one sharp dip that would have troubled a loaded aircraft. Our line still included quite a few ridges we would have to smooth out somehow, and several patches of the very high grass which would have to be cut; these would make the task much tougher than we had hoped – but still, it could be done.

Cheetham then went off to help the glider-pushing group, and I returned to Alison and told him how we planned the strip. He could not raise much enthusiasm for our primitive effort but in a goodwill gesture did come out a little distance from the trees to approve the line; he then rejoined the other pilots who were grouped close about one of the damaged gliders that the Gurkhas had already hauled into cover.

Out in the clearing we slashed and dug and pulled until the

72

stars began to fade from the eastern sky and the air grow clammy with approaching dawn. We worked in silence but heard occasional thuds and clanks from the men toiling with the gliders further up the area. From the trees nearby a jungle cicada kept up a monotonous sound all night, like a saw going backwards and forwards interminably through a board, and faintly in the distance you kept hearing the ascending call of a brain-fever bird. When I cried halt we had not only marked out the full projected strip with border lines but actually cleared the first four hundred yards. The surface was rugged but clean enough to allow an energetic man to run more or less unimpeded – as Cheetham proved when he returned from the glider-trundling crowd to join us in the last hour. We made our weary way back to the command post beneath a sliver of mist suspended at tree-height, and found that apart from a section on guard the rest were now sleeping after their equally exhausting efforts. The message about the glider-crash had apparently been significant, for base had replied that a bulldozer would be glided in that coming night. Having heard this I crawled into the slit trench Lilbahadur had dug for me and managed to sleep despite the ants that went tickling over my face and hands in the next few hours – and the dew so trickling cold we all curled up under our blankets.

About four hours later, unable to sleep any longer in the gathering heat, I climbed out of the narrow trench and started on a K-ration breakfast, my favourite of the three packs, then after a drink of coffee felt able to have a look around at our Burmese world. The jungle was not what I had expected, it was more like Australian bush than tropical forest. This was indaing, the deciduous trees were as thinly leaved as eucalyptus and just as stingy in the shade they gave. There was some teak, pointed out by Tiny Langford who also explained their markings. They actually had an identification mark on each tree, so men could be sent out with detailed instructions which particular trees to kill or to cut

73

down; they did this by the Australian method of dealing with unwanted trees on pasture land, the teak was ring-barked. However this was not merely to kill, but also to prepare it for transport. Teak will not float at once, being too full of sap, so the ring-barked trees are left for three years to dry out before being felled, then dragged to the river by the elephants. Each ring-barked tree carried, in addition to its original identification, a blaze showing the year it was ringed – they died gradually to a ghost-gum colour.

What surprised, and alarmed, me was the noise associated with movement near a teak tree. The major leaf-fall is in spring, and when the great leaves drop on the dusty floor of the forest they become crisp-dry; walking on them is like treading on a floor covered in poppadums, a loud crackling sound accompanies each footfall. Impossible to avoid it. Treading softly only makes it worse. There are teak plantations, deliberately cultivated, and there it must be like walking through a cornflake factory. We were so preoccupied with noise in those first anxious days, voices kept low, no cutting of timber, that the crackling uproar as you chanced to pass under a teak tree made you feel guilty – you would stop, look about with a helpless shrug of apology, then go tripping through quickly on tiptoe in a vain attempt to reduce the clamour of your passage.

Our column major, Ted Russel, had sent patrols around the whole perimeter of the clearing by the time I awoke and they found no sign of any Japanese. In fact they had not met a single human being of any nationality, so it seemed we were safe for the moment. Though the trees were thinly leaved it would have been difficult for an aircraft to spot us in the jungle; the only danger from the air was the possibility of an inquisitive Japanese pilot pausing to circle the myriad dust trails percolating through the canopy. The dry jungle floor was so caked in ashen dust that when you crackled through a teak leaf the trodden fragments merged with the powder to create a mosaic of a footprint, the joints in perfect harmony.

The dust was fine, it hung in the air long after it was raised, and made you thirsty. And this was unfortunate.

The shortage of water was a problem. None of the wallows in the clearing had any water left, nor had the patrols so far discovered any. We had only our water bottles, and one extra can brought in with the gliders, so we rationed ourselves to half a bottle a day – not a generous amount in such heat and mouth-drying dust. This water problem was another unfortunate consequence of Wingate's obsession about aerial reconnaissance; we should have known where to go for it. Had that glider crash not delayed construction of the strip we would have had fifty or more mules coming in that very night with no idea where to water them.

That afternoon I went out on a hunt for water to the forest area near the start of the strip. We did a square search on compass for a couple of hours without success. The jungle there was thinner, most of the teak seemed to have been cleared and dipterocarps predominated. One was in fruit and every now and then in the still afternoon a flicker of wind would send a shiver through the leaves and the winged fruits would be set free. They came twirling down, spinning and vibrating, like huge insects in a fluttering dance. Another type, the soaring kanyin, was in tiny flower, impossible to discern the shape some fifty feet up above amongst the leaves, just that pale pink gossamer trapped and held in the tangle of branches – and down below the wispy tendrils of their fragrance. The air was vibrant with the ringing of cicadas. We saw two hornbills, orange-headed, go gliding past overhead; they kept repeating a loud sighing sound, like the swan makes with its wing-beats and about the same tempo, but the curious thing is that their wings were rigidly still as they planed down towards the smoke-blue hills of China away to the east.

During this period David had also ambled off in search of water, and Peter marched forth in search of Japanese, but neither had success. When darkness fell we still had between two and three hours to wait for the bulldozer so we continued with our primitive construction work and finished another hundred yards, now giving us about five hundred in total – should there be another glider disaster we would at least have some sort of strip ready the following night. However the replacement glider landed perfectly, touching-down on the actual cleared section, so we sheathed kukries and let the US engineers get on with it. Their speed was impressive. We had only just reached the trees when the bulldozer began to roar.

That was a nerve-shattering experience, too. It is difficult to convey the impression of the shocking magnitude of the bulldozer engine noise to us when it first opened up. It ripped apart the cover of quiet under which we had been living for the previous twenty-four hours. We had been speaking to one another in lowered voices, never a shouted call, the cutting of wood had been banned and even the breaking of a branch had caused heads to turn and brows to frown; the loudest sound we had made during the whole period was the crackle of footfall on the china-saucer leaves of the teak trees. There was little natural noise to disturb our quiet, any wild life there may have been in the little corner we had appropriated had been scared away, so even a flock of green parakeets pausing to chatter near our position that morning had caused sharp disapproving looks from below. Then into our muffled community came this lumbering engine, starting off with an explosive roar, followed by a continuous thunder as it warmed up for a few minutes, then clattering off to start work at the head of the strip. It became worse after that, because it kept revving up every now and then against an uneven patch, as if deliberately clamouring for notice; it seemed inconceivable that the nearest Japanese commander would not immediately assemble a massive force to march into the area and determine what sort of machine was out there shattering the quiet of his Burmese night. I went back out to watch them for a time, picking out the bulldozer not only by sound but also by the cloud of dust it was raising in the moonlit sky, and marvelled at what it had accomplished in an hour or so. It was no wonder Alison had been so lukewarm about our efforts, knowing as he did the capabilities of a bulldozer. In less than three hours it had completed a good eight hundred yards, including a thorough re-working of our hand-made stretch, and it then drew clear to allow the first batch of planes to come in to land. They came throbbing out of the western sky a few minutes later.

It was hoped to land about seventy aircraft that night, getting in enough men to give a good chance of holding the strip against any force the Japanese could bring up next day to investigate this provocatively noisy activity. Among the first aircraft to land however came Brigadier Old, the US Air Force commander, and he decided for his own mysterious reasons the strip was not long enough – despite the opinion of Alison who had sent the signal to say it was. He barred further landings and ordered back to Assam those already en route. Only the first wave of six landed, without any difficulty, before his edict took effect. So we had created uproar for about half an hour, aircraft circling, landing, revving engines in taxying, taking off again, raising a great cloud of dust that could have been seen from Tokyo one felt, telling the world where we were and what we were doing – then flying stopped for the night and we were left only two platoons better off than when all the row started. The circling lights disappeared, the sound of the aircraft engines faded away into the distance, the bulldozer awoke with a roar and began charging backwards and forwards furiously to complete the strip – and to guide the Japanese patrols, one felt. Also Colonel Morris had arrived with gloomy effect, for he immediately banned all fires and so deprived us of the coffee that had been such a promise. I pointed out that the American pilots, not under his control, had fires still going but the Colonel was adamant. No fires – that was the end of the matter.

I went over to join the Americans. I didn't actually ask for a coffee, just commented at length on the delicious aroma, so Alison duly offered me a cup. He began to chat about the operation, wanted to know how many men we now had and how they were disposed. No one was very happy about our exposed position that night. Alison himself made no comment in my hearing about Old's decision to stop flying for the night but some of his pilots were harshly critical.

'It may have been too short for that bastard,' said one, 'but the others landed with plenty of room to spare.'

The general feeling was that the landings should have gone ahead, the bulldozer lengthening the strip between the waves of aircraft. We had created uproar to little purpose, drawn noisy attention to our presence without landing troops to defend it. When I mentioned we did not even have the full five platoons anyway, one was out on a water search, Alison began to worry about the position of his men. They were actually outside the rim of our small defence area. He came back with me to Morris who, much to my surprise, agreed to extend our tiny perimeter to include the crashed glider, drawn into friendly alliance perhaps by mutual disapproval of Brigadier Old. Outside in the moonlit clearing the bulldozer continued roaring furiously up and down the strip.

All of us felt fearfully exposed that second night in Burma, but we of the glider party suffered most, for we had been counting on solid protection and, as always, disappointment enhanced the lost prospect and exaggerated its effect. I moved as near geometrical centre of our position as possible, dug another trench and tried to get some sleep in what remained of the night. It was not easy, despite my weariness, for the trench was so narrow it was difficult to keep brushing away what was either trickling sweat, gathering dew, or crawling ants. And once finally asleep I was awakened by a sudden onset of silence. The bulldozer had completed its twelve-hundred yard assignment and had crawled back under shelter to rest.

Day was about to break. In the eastern sky the orange glow

flared into golden flame as the sun rose clear to blaze out the last of the stars, and overhead the black silhouettes of leaves quickened into green translucent life; I was grateful for the excuse to climb out of the trench, flick off the dew, get dressed – which meant putting on my hat – and stroll over to inveigle another coffee out of the pilots who had kept their privileged fire going all the night. They had an ample supply of water in the crashed glider, some of them actually washed in the stuff that morning, so I felt no qualms about the cost of water for a coffee.

From dawn that morning we made a sustained effort to find water, sending out about half a dozen patrols. I took another group across to the far side of the strip where we walked more or less on compass for over an hour until we came to a dense patch of elephant grass, a couple of feet taller than me and with feathery tops, the ground soft like a wallow but without trace of surface water. We abandoned the hunt there. On the way out we heard a distant hallooing, a sort of joyous chorus you felt sure could not possibly be a threat, it was too delightful a sound; it was made by a troop of gibbons, we heard them again several times during the campaign, usually much earlier in the day as an awakening chorus when one group would start and others in the distance respond until the valleys rang with their joyous calls. Coming back that day we passed one area where the cicadas were shrilling so loudly it was like being inside a bell; some of the men looked startled for a moment, never having heard them before apparently.

There was some luck that day. Tiny Langford had also been out on a recce, and I was sitting near the Colonel, writing a note, when he came back through the grey tree trunks, rolling along with all his pack and webbing and pouches and map-board and water-bottle flopping and flailing about his bulky figure – he reminded me of one of those loaded prairie waggons you see in films about the opening up of the West. He reported a nil finding to the Colonel but had

79

surreptitiously signalled excitement to me in his approach, so when he made his sober withdrawal from the Colonel's presence I followed quickly.

'Food! Glorious food!' he whispered.

He dumped his kit then led me with conspiratorial casualness along the edge of the jungle until we came to another of the wrecked gliders where he opened the door with a flourish. I saw at once a box of the 5-in-1 rations, already opened. There were two other untouched boxes of these magnificent rations, filled with delicacies as high above the K scale as the K itself was above the old Indian Light-scale. We stuffed our huge pockets and shirts with chocolate, dried fruit, toilet paper, coffee and a tin each of pineapple and rice, a rich and glorious ambrosia that was to become an obsessive dream with me in the next few months. We made a wide detour to come back to our trenches more or less unnoticed, our figures pregnant with loot, and stuffed it away into our packs. Once that was done we passed the word quietly to the others and presently they began to drift away back into the trees – except Peter Wilmott who refused the temptation, and the Colonel who was never offered it. That afternoon I slipped back to get some matches which I had stupidly not taken at first but by then the glider was bare as a cat-lapped saucer.

Cheetham, out on a water hunt that afternoon, had success. He found a fair supply, enough anyway to water the mules which we expected that night. It was not conveniently located – we had to march east from the strip and the water hole was five miles to the west. But it was water, so we were grateful for it. It was exasperating, two days later, to discover an even better supply within a mile of the strip and in our proper direction – again, something we should have known about before landing. Water was to be a constant worry during the first few weeks of the campaign, then later an occassional annoyance as rain, and finally a cruel and relentless enemy when the monsoon reached us up on the Chinese border.

6

On that third night in Burma the Wingate magic worked. The airstrip by midnight was like a fairground at its extravagant peak, wheels of coloured light circling about in the moonlit sky, cones of brilliant landing-lights flashing across the trees and the strip, red and green beams from the signal lamp near touch-down point, aircraft rumbling in, taxying, taking off, fiery red of roaring exhausts, clouds of dust whipped up to float across the stars, files of clanking men following blue guide lights, asthmatic calls of devocalized mules, a jeep scurrying about with headlights blazing, shouting men and clattering mule ramps and thumping doors and squealing brakes. Alison controlled all this blaring, glaring activity superbly from the cockpit of a grounded C47; he used me as a sort of trouble-shooter, sending me hurrying up the strip to check the flarepath, help marshal aircraft, clear blockages and harass the unloaders, but as pressure developed he began to rail at me because pilots were not getting away quickly enough, so I then settled down to avoiding him. Easy enough to do that in the melee. Then suddenly there appeared out of the dust the smiling face of Stanley Mayhew – such a transparent character, Stanley, completely ingenuous, you never had to wonder how he felt or what he meant.

It was typical of his friendship that the first thing he had done on landing was to ask my whereabouts. He was carrying a canvas chagal of deliciously cold water – our plight seemed to have been dramatized back at base. He took over my dogsbody job at once, with some misgiving about its lack of definition but set on relieving me of duty. Free of all responsibility, I went back into the trees, feeling secure enough now to lie down not in the constricting slit trench but on the open ground, with that comforting uproar all about, and to sleep in peace.

But not immediately. First I had to move position because a mule path had developed across it, so I shifted to the base of a nearby teak tree, blanket wrapped about midriff ready for cold dawn, head on the crushed Gurkha hat – softer than the pack – eyelids sealed for sleep. Almost at once a torch blazed them apart again. I swore. The unforgettable voice grated:

'Where is Colonel Morris?'

I knew it was Wingate even before he stopped trying to blind me with his torch. I told him the Colonel was back beyond the crashed glider, about fifty yards away, and pointed there. He paused, so I began to get up to lead him over there but made such a business of yawning and stretching and groping for things that he finally said:

'All right. Go back to sleep. I'll find him myself.'

He strode off in the direction of the glider. Considerate or just impatient? What did it matter anyway? – I was too tired to puzzle it out. I lay down again surrounded by all that reassuring noise and fell into solid sleep.

It was another world next morning. All about under the trees and along the edge of the strip were men and mules squatting and moving and stamping, shouts and laughter, crackle and smoke of fires, you could now see the strip in stark clarity because all the grass our side had been flattened by the intense traffic of the night. Lentaigne with his 111 Brigade HQ had been among the arrivals, we now had our two full columns of Gurkhas, two others were due to land the coming night. I still wonder to this day why Lentaigne's group had come across to us when on the western side BROADWAY was now functioning like an airport; their two columns and Brigade HQ now had the laborious and dangerous task of crossing back over the Irrawaddy by boats to join those who had actually landed there. I spoke to Masters, the brigade major, who was sitting on a log refolding a map – the large patches of fluff on his cheekbones had caught the pale dust, giving him a koala-bear look; he said they had come to us because BROADWAY had more traffic than it could handle, but didn't seem entirely convinced by his own explanation. Nor did Lentaigne seem pleased with life that morning – he looked harassed, fretful, nothing like the relaxed brigadier of training days. Peter Cane, the enthusiastic commander of 94 column, then came striding past and scooped me up in passage, saying we would be moving out in an hour's time.

The plan was that Peter Cane would take both sapper platoons with all the river-crossing equipment – boats, engines, lilos, and so on – straight to the Shweli to prepare a crossing point for our arrival. The rest of us in 49 and 94 columns, encumbered with all the mules and equipment, would spend that night at the water-hole then meet them in two days' time at an RV by the river. Two platoons would stay at the strip that night as protection whilst the remainder of 111 Brigade were landed; then all would join us at the water-hole where we would have the final separation, our two columns going on east to cross the Shweli, Lentaigne's group going back west to tackle the Irrawaddy.

Our recce platoon had already left to find us a night harbour, and Cane's group set off as we in the main party were preparing to move. Now we had our mules and equipment it was like all those other morning starts on training days in India. There were the clattering, clinking, stamping sounds of mules being loaded, drivers cajoling or shouting at the stubborn ones, men crouching down and stuffing things into packs, doing up boots, clicking rifles, tightening pack and webbing straps, standing upright and giving that last spasmodic heave to get the monster settled comfortably on the shoulders, then wandering about to find the column line and preordained position within it; we had been given this at 'orders', also the map identification of the Shweli rendezvous.

There was a sense of melancholy on leaving CHOWRINGEE, an airfield which we had started that first night with our own hands, then seen grow from emptiness to a town-sized community. It seemed sad that all the intense activity of those days and nights, the thousands of men who had milled about the clearing, hundreds of animals, great machines, all would soon disappear; grass would grow over the strip, the dust and leaves and saplings cover our minor traces, and of the great days when the base was young and crowded and noisy in vigorous constructive life, no physical trace remain. But in future years perhaps a Burmese forestry worker might suddenly pause there beneath the trees one moonlight night, catching an echo of our passage – like the stranger on the Sussex Downs hearing the echo of the boy Belloc's song:

> . . . For native ghosts return and these
> Perfect the mystery in the trees.
> So, therefore, though myself be crost
> The shuddering of that dreadful day
> When friend and fire and home are lost
> And even children drawn away –
> The passer-by shall hear me still,
> A boy that sings on Duncton Hill.

Our unwieldy force of some six platoons together with all the animals of both columns – about 140 mules and 10 horses – finally left CHOWRINGEE in mid-morning. Patrols had been out since dawn and still no Japanese had been contacted. We started off on compass course through the indaing and presently picked up a forestry track which we followed at a gentle pace for the few miles to our planned harbour at the water-hole. I walked with Tiny Langford who told me about teak extraction, working elephants, and the songs of Burmese birds. He introduced me to the air 'There is a lady sweet

84

and kind' and perhaps regretted it before the campaign was over, for I found it a haunting melody – and image also; I taught him 'Waltzing Matilda' and he in turn was fascinated, not by the melody but by the Australianisms in the lyric. So as we walked through the Burmese jungle that day we talked about fair maidens with beguiling smiles in the English countryside, and swagmen by the billabongs and coolabahs of the Australian outback. We came to our water-hole, which had little in common with a billabong – it was a wide shallow depression, almost completely covered with bullrushes and shoulder-high kaing grass. There was no trace of our recce platoon.

The water, when found within the reeds, had a rank smell and looked filthy, but the mules seemed happy enough – they are quite fastidious drinkers and have refused water we ourselves had drunk. They rustled and snuffled and splashed about in the reeds, for the water was in several pools, and five large swallow-tailed butterflies with irridescent mallard-green wings came fluttering along slowly in line astern and landed on the back of one of them; they spaced themselves so evenly apart that the mule seemed to have assumed an iguana skin, with green ridges along its backbone. We took up a normal bivouac defensive position about the area, had a cold fireless meal and prepared for sleep.

Some of us chose shelter. Three old wooden huts stood by the edge of the bullrushes, just plaited walls and open doorways, roofs of thatched reeds partially collapsed, dirt floor. There were a number of small round holes in the floor, about thumb-sized and precisely fashioned, which reminded me of the trapdoor-spider holes on the playing field at school in Australia; at another time I might not have stayed there for fear of what awful creatures would emerge from the holes in the dark hours, but the prospect of a dry sleep after those dew-sodden nights was too enticing to resist. All night the constant roars of activity from the strip could be clearly heard when wandering fleas woke me, but whilst they were gorging

85

quietly on some luscious patch of flesh I slept soundly, finally having to be awakened at stand-to by Tiny Langford who had also preferred fleas to dew.

Stand-to and stand-down were daily drills. The assumption seems to be that the enemy always attacks either at dawn or dusk (a 1914–18 war hangover, I wonder?) so just before dawn and dusk every day we all went to our allotted fighting posts – mine was with the Colonel's HQ – and waited, armed and ready to repel the attack. After about half an hour or whatever, at the Colonel's whim, we would be stood-down; at night the sentries would remain in position when the rest of us bedded down, and after dawn stand-to we would usually eat before assembling in column-line for the onward march. This particular dawn we stayed at the water-hole after stand-down, awaiting Lentaigne.

We seemed to have lost our recce platoon, and Lentaigne's group had no news of it either. They spent about half an hour with us at the water-hole; all but the four wrecked gliders had been hauled back to India, the damaged DC3 also flown out, and nothing of value left on the abandoned strip. We had to pass it going back to the Shweli and Lentaigne advised we keep away from the clearing in case the Japanese did finally decide to investigate all our noisy activity. We parted after the short meeting at the water-hole, 111 Brigade columns marching west towards the Irrawaddy and India, we going east towards the Shweli and China.

There were flank patrols out each side of the jungle track, a logging track for clearing teak along which little dabs of colour kept catching your eye – a scattering of violets, rust-red primula, and white flecks of some kind of fallen blossom; you rarely saw flowers on the jungle floor, not enough light perhaps, there you had to look up into the foliage for an occasional glimpse of colour relief from the infinite range of greens. We moved too fast along the easy logging track, and the column began to elongate.

We were passing within a few hundred yards of the strip

when I heard the throb of approaching aircraft. Japanese Zeros, swinging around in a gentle dive when I saw them, three vics of three. We halted, faces fearfully upraised. Although I was intellectually confident we would not be seen, despite the scanty foliage in the thin deciduous jungle, I felt that the long line of dust-puffing mules on the track was an unnecessary risk and was about to call to the muleteers when they scattered anyway, of their own anxious volition. As they were moving aside the menacing throb changed pitch suddenly, the aircraft passed almost directly overhead with a roar, red circles clearly visible. At the same instant they opened fired.

I thought they had actually seen us, just at that opening burst, but the sound faded so quickly you knew they were attacking the strip. They would certainly have seen the wrecked gliders. They attacked with bombs as well as guns, the explosions close enough to shiver leaves overhead. It went on for about five minutes as they made repeated attacks in line astern, turning almost directly over our heads, and we could see smoke rising from the strip area. The shooting stopped and then just as on that final day in Java two years earlier when they finished us off so methodically, they assembled into tidy formation before departing. The throbbing sounds died away, leaving many of us standing there grinning at our astute success in fooling the enemy. Another point of view was expressed however by the adjutant, temporarily caught back with us in the rear.

'One thing is certain: they know exactly where we are now,' he said. With that dampener he left us and went on ahead to rejoin the Colonel.

It was a sobering thought – we had a river to cross, as did the others, to be effected mostly in daylight too. In subdued mood we began to collect the mules and finally got them sorted out again on the track. To my surprise however we then stood there waiting. Five minutes. No movement at all. On a clear level track there seemed no reason for such delay.

Then I heard in the distance, so remote I had to call for silence to catch it, the rallying call of the bugle. Beginning to feel uneasy I told the sergants and muleteers to stay put, then hurried up past the long line of mules to the head of the column to find out the cause of delay. The cause was that there was no head – just the first mule cropping grass by the track, and emptiness ahead of it.

The muleteer looked at me in obvious relief.

'We go now?' he asked, picking up the lead.

He had no idea where the riflemen ahead had gone, nor when. The Colonel had bolted off with most of the rifle company leaving us with over a hundred mules, all the equipment of both columns, and just the rearguard platoon as protection. David Anderson was in charge of this, he came strolling up to query the delay, and I wasted a few precious seconds cursing the Colonel before telling him the position. David always gave the impression of being imperturbable but on this occasion even his equable temperament was under pressure. He brought up half his men to the van, then we both led our ungainly group hurriedly along the track in the vain hope of catching up the unencumbered fighting platoons led by the fleeing Colonel.

They had moved off the track however, this was clear presently from the clean condition of the teak trail, so we simply continued in the planned direction and hoped they would presently send out scouts or sound the bugle. We kept pausing hopefully, stilled in listening, but the only sound heard was the echoing whistle of an oriole, that liquid pure cadence *pyup-pyup* that pierces so clearly through the matted screen of the jungle, so after two hours we abandoned the chase and stopped for a long halt and to discuss the situation. There was nothing we could do except go on to the Shweli rendezvous. David had persuaded himself into a sort of nervous optimism by this time, as if determined to encourage the men, but he was so positive that to me at least his own doubts were only too apparent. The Colonel would stop early to bivouac, he said, to make sure we caught up with them before nightfall.

'Would you bet on it?' I asked, unfairly, as we started off again.

He looked pained at this outspoken scepticism. We marched on towards the river until it was too dark to see the track under the trees and then we were forced to stop where we happened to be. The track had by now dwindled to a path and we drew off to one side of it and made some sort of bivouac in the waterless glade; there was a large thinly-leaved shrub of some kind on which the fireflies were dancing and glimmering in such numbers that the mules shied away with a jerk, violently, refusing to go near it, so we gave them their way and moved on a little. David set out some sort of defence position but without any great conviction – the sheer bulk of all those mule bodies around us was a better defence than anything twenty riflemen could provide.

If the Japanese had found us at this time it would have been a total disaster for Morris Force – and bloody for us personally. Had it been carefully planned to put the soft underbelly of our force, the whole carrier group with our equipment, into the most vulnerable position a treacherous staff could devise, no one could have improved on our situation at that time. We were not alone in confusion either. David and I that night dwelt moodily on the state of affairs, just four days after we had landed with such promise. Morris Force had now lost its recce platoon, the rifle companies were somewhere in the jungle without mules or ammunition or equipment, another group was somewhere by the Shweli also without any mules, and we with the machine guns and ammunition and mortars and all the mules were abandoned in the jungle somewhere about ten miles east of the airstrip. Not one of these four separated units knew where any one of the other three were, nor did they have any means of communicating with them.

Without radio contact it was difficult to reassemble all

these disparate units and the problem was compounded by the inaccuracy of our maps. It was all very well to have an RV in the distinctive right-angled bend of a track marked clearly on the map, but if nothing like that theoretical landmark existed on the ground then the location of the RV became a matter of opinion. And opinions varied. Not only were the maps inaccurate with roads and tracks and rivers, but even with villages. This may not have been entirely the fault of the cartographer, many Kachin villages have the same names, some change the name from time to time, and whole villages often move themselves completely to a new site many miles away from the original one with its exhausted rice-clearings, so the map-maker has an impossible task. Having worked with accurate maps in India it took time for us to learn that the maps of Burma had to be treated as if sketched from vague memory and rumour, not compiled from precise and recent survey.

We who were stranded with the mules spent all the daylight hours next day still in search of our column. We had run out of track by this time so David and I led the group on compass bearing towards the river RV, with occasional scouts ranging for water – the mules were restive after going without water for more than twenty-four hours. By this time we were out of the indaing and travelling through thin jungle in which there were frequent thickets of bamboo and patches of cane grass with pale feathery tops where we kept hoping to find water but had no luck till late in the afternoon. We took a long halt then while the mules drank their fill.

David and I sat on a little hillock, a bamboo clump behind us, waiting for the animals to finish. The sun edged slowly down over the indaing in the west, changing from gold to smouldering red, the light faded, the mosquitoes began to whine – and still David kept trying to reassure everyone, including himself. We made fire, had a meal, then decided to move away from the mosquito-water to a spot a couple of miles further back where we had passed a possible bivouac.

Once there into the trees the mules were unsaddled, loads set out, and our scanty force split into four outlying posts. David and I were checking one of these when a man came running from the next position calling:

'Colonel sahib! Colonel sahib!'

We had found the Colonel's party. One of their harbour outposts was within a few yards of the position our men had just gone to occupy – discovered, happily, without exchange of fire. So we picked ourselves up once more, saddled the animals, loaded up, heaved on our packs, and staggered over the rise and down through the trees to the steep-banked nullah where the Colonel and the rifle company had been waiting all day. We were safe at last within their protection, so at least two of our disparate groups had merged. We still had no idea however where Peter Cane was with all the river-crossing equipment; the Colonel asserted he was now at the correct RV, presumably Peter reckoned the same, their reckonings just didn't happen to agree. And our recce platoon was still lost without trace.

Unfortunately for us the Colonel was in a restless mood, a characteristic he was to adopt for most of the campaign. All that day from their hideout in the nullah he had been sending out scouts looking for Peter Cane, for the recce platoon, for us and the mules; we were only a few hundred yards from the Shweli, and a local paddling past had apparently seen a group of our men, so the Colonel was concerned the Japanese might now have learned where to locate the enemy force which had recently landed. This concern overpowered him finally a few minutes after our arrival when he abruptly decided we should move somewhere else – march in ten minutes. David Anderson in his usual diffident manner made a mild suggestion that the muleteers, the mules, and the rest of us who had been walking most of the day were tired, but the Colonel waved him off to duty. I pointed out we had just unloaded the RAF set and the charger, after spending all day looking for his group, surely it would do no harm to give us half an hour.

'You want to stay, Pat – you stay,' he snapped. 'The rest of us will march in ten minutes.'

We didn't march in ten minutes however. This was the night I mentioned earlier, when we had a repeat of the explosive disintegration of the column as in India. This night it was certain that tension played a strong part. We had all been under stress since leaving the massed security of CHOWRINGEE, and fear had had much to seize upon . . . the raid showed the Japanese knew we were in the area . . . they would be looking for us nearby . . . vital we keep quiet on the march and in harbour . . . no fires, no charging of batteries, the enemy would see, would hear . . . prolong the stand-to at dawn and at dusk, they attack any time . . . extra sentries posted . . . constantly stay alert . . . enemy all about us.

After such a regime since leaving the strip we were all spring-loaded, and when we assembled in the dark nullah at last, moon obscured by the arching trees, waiting in tense silence for a move to God-knows-where, waiting and waiting in one of those inexplicable delays, someone or something must have made a sudden movement way back in the rear . . . a man stumbling, a mule stamping, a pack dropped. It's strange how the mind can so quickly recall a menacing sound. The moment I heard that rising clatter in the distance I scrambled wildly up the bank, pack still on back even before being consciously aware of what was happening. The panic swept through the column like a physical force, as though a dam had burst upstream and a solid wall of water was rushing down the dry nullah bed, hurling everything and everyone aside, kicking hooves and flailing arms, loads crashing into the side of the bank, men grunting and gasping, all in curious vocal silence, no shouts nor cries of pain, just this furious turmoil of mute men and animals gone berserk. Then it passed us, sweeping onwards down the nullah and sending other men and animals swirling against the bank like flood debris, and we who had been left scattered behind began slowly to return to our positions, to hunt for mules, resettle loads and packs, and wonder what strange and terrible force had possessed us in that dark fury. No one was seriously hurt but I was grateful for the experience in India, and the reaction that had shot me up the bank into safety before the surge had swept through our section. It is a disturbing experience being caught up in such a shock wave, you wait tensely afterwards lest it strike again. Not until you start moving do you feel safe – even then, as I discovered later, you are not immune.

It was inevitable that we should march for less than an hour and then settle to bivouac on the same bamboo-covered hillock which we of the mule-party had left some two hours earlier that evening. The Colonel set up his headquarters in a small crispy-dry clearing almost completely surrounded by bamboo and gave out orders. No cutting of bamboo, no fires, stand-to at such and such a time, a new RV somewhere or other, sentry duties . . . any questions?

'Can we charge?' I asked.

He refused, as expected. The need was not great, fortunately, we had done little transmitting the previous two nights. The big 1086 RAF set was the only reliable means of contacting base and this increased my personal involvement in *all* signals, not just those dealing with air matters. It had the problem of battery-charging, the motor that did this job was noisy even when dug in, and in those early days any noise alarmed the Colonel; transmission became difficult when batteries went down however, and he soon learned he had to pay a penalty if he wanted complete silence in bivouac – the charger had hunger as its ally.

The delay in crossing the river also created a food problem. It had been planned we would cross the third day after leaving the strip, then have a supply drop the next night at a site I had chosen from the map. However on the third day the column was still in three separate segments, none of which knew where the others were, and those of us who had come in

93

by glider that first night were theoretically on our last day's rations. When the following day passed still without us finding Peter Cane's river-recce group the Colonel decided we should ask for food and boats at once. I went off late that afternoon with half a dozen men and picked out a site a mile or so back from the river.

This was a comparatively clear space we had passed during our Colonel-hunt, on the perimeter of the indaing and with a trace of bunds suggesting it may have been cultivated at one time. Now it was littered with secondary growth, a variety of shrubs and saplings, the tallest being a ten-foot high crab apple covered with a frothy layer of white blossom and also, surely unusual on the same tree, a branch with four hard little jelly-green apples; they were savagely bitter at even the most cautious attempt to taste. Having checked the site I sent out a signal asking for a standard supply and river-crossing drop. By some freak we not only got through at once but also had a reply within two hours. It was a sharp reminder from Wingate of our time-table for crossing the Shweli. Decoded, the important sentence read:

NO SUPPLY DROP UNTIL YOU HAVE CROSSED THE SHWELI

They just ignored the request for river-crossing equipment, assuming perhaps it was an error, for they knew we already had that equipment. Some thought this method of jabbing the Colonel into action was just what the situation required, typical of Wingate's perceptive judgment; others, less worshipful, might think that if a general considers one of his commanders at fault he should punish him personally – not the innocent troops who have to obey his orders. Anyway, although the Colonel had his faults like the rest of us, the failure to cross the river on time was caused partly by the inaccuracy of maps provided by HQ, and particularly by Wingate's refusal to allow precise photographic survey of the area before landing us there. The unfortunate effect of the signal however was to galvanise the Colonel into convulsive activity, he declared we must cross that very night, even though we had only four lilos and a few life-jackets between us. Luckily, he was dissuaded from this panic reaction when it was pointed out there was no suitable take-off point nearby – the river bank was about twenty feet high. His final compromise that night was that a recce party must select a suitable take-off point early next morning, and the crossing begun by midday at the latest.

I spent a little time after this with Peter Wilmot and Tiny Langford, both of whom had been up to have a look at the river. They reported it as being some four hundred yards wide and with a current of about five knots; neither of them, nor any of the others who discussed the plan in whispers that night, thought we had a chance of getting our mules and loads safely over such a formidable obstacle with the equipment we had. We could build rafts of bamboo, but what use were they without propelling engines? It was madness to attempt such a feat with a few lilos and our lifejackets. Peter Wilmot was determined to get his patrols off at dawn not to select a crossing but to hunt down Peter Cane who was waiting somewhere along the bank with powered boats and completed rafts and mule-ramps all prepared at closely-studied crossing points. We had to find him to stop the Colonel hurtling us into a desperate crossing in which we risked losing most of our equipment and not only rendering our force largely ineffective but putting its very existence into jeopardy.

That was our muddle on the night of March 12th. Later we discovered that on the same day Lentaigne's group was also having problems tackling the Irrawaddy, being forced to abandon the attempt when only half done – one complete column, many of the mules and all the heavy equipment of their other one, had to be left on our side of the river. This group had to return past our abandoned airstrip and try to catch up with us. We also discovered that Dah Force, a small group supposed to be already stationed on our side of the Shweli raising Kachin guerillas, had been delayed and was still back in India. Let's look at the summary:

1. Only part of III Brigade has managed to get back over the Irrawaddy. During the next fortnight they will be marching north, trying to link up with those of their group who landed on that side.

2. Those who failed to cross – 40 Column plus some bits – were starting to look for us. (They took no part in any action for the next four weeks as they hunted for us.)

3. All the mules of our two columns, together with 600 men, were going to try and cross the Shweli equipped with only four lilos.

4. Our sapper platoons under the command of Peter Cane were somewhere else on the Shweli grossly over-equipped with boats and rafts – but with no radio, and no idea where we in the main body were.

5. The Recce platoon of our Column was lost.

6. Dah Force, supposed to be helping in our area, was still in India.

That was the actual position. And now here is part of a signal sent that very day by Wingate to London for the attention of Churchill:

'. . . III BRIGADE NOW CROSSING IRRA-WADDY (to attack) ROADS AND RAILWAY . . . TWO COLUMNS (Morris Force) NOW CROSSING SHWELI TO EAST TO BLOCK MANDALAY-BHAMO COMMUNICATIONS. A SPECIAL PAT-RIOT FORCE (Dah Force) IS RAISING KACHINS . . . (and has) ALREADY ENCOUNTERED AND AMBUSHED SUCCESSFULLY SEVERAL ENEMY PATROLS . . . SITUATION MOST PROMISING IF EXPLOITED.'

I couldn't have lied better myself. After all, you could hardly expect him to send:

DEAR WINSTON,
I AM AFRAID THERE HAS BEEN AN AWFUL COCK-UP OVER THE FAR SIDE OF THE IRRA-WADDY AND I HAVE NO IDEA WHAT IN HELL IS GOING ON OVER THERE. SORRY.

YOURS TRULY,
ORDE WINGATE.

7

I have a clear memory of Colonel Morris one day near Myitkyena when we were moving up a road for an attack and the enemy suddenly opened fire. We hurled ourselves clear of the track, for the machine gun fire was so close you could see bark and white splinters flying from a nearby tree-trunk – when you dared look up for a fearful instant. And in such an instant I saw the Colonel start walking straight on up the road to discover what was happening. I stayed close to the ground, blessing the fortune that made me not a platoon commander but an RAF officer whose duty it was to stay under cover at such times.

This incident however was months ahead and bore no resemblance to his behaviour in the first weeks of our arrival. During this period he gave the impression of a man frantically anxious to avoid contact with the enemy who, one would gather, had massed his force in murderous concentration all about Morris Force. There were signals sent that must have betrayed a sense of insecurity bordering on panic, and I half-expected Wingate to descend from the skies in awesome fury and shrivel the poor Colonel to smoking ashes. It became clear later we were not alone in this sense of fearful apprehension in the early days; III Brigade split at the Irrawaddy was almost certainly unnecessary and due to excessive caution by Lentaigne, and 40 column's delay in catching up with us was caused by over-anxiety to avoid discovery. It was natural that commanders should wish to guard their forces from enemy contact during the settling-in period but the precautions, for us certainly, were so obsessive as to affect morale severely in those early weeks.

The night after the Colonel had been dissuaded from launching us all into a mad midnight dash across the Shweli we moved on immediately after dawn stand-to and then halted five miles away for breakfast on a little mound dominated by four large mango trees then in flower – a dull tawny blob, like mimosa when the bright yellow fluff has browned. It was a calm morning, the mountain ridge on the Chinese border merging imperceptibly into the pale blue sky, and you could pick out the hidden river a mile away by the sashes of mist which wound a low sinuous trail across the landscape leaving occasional tree-tops jutting through like barrage balloons. From the indaing behind us a Burmese cuckoo was calling with that sad reverse note, oo-cuck oo-cuck, we were to hear almost every day in the next two months. As we ate our cold breakfast, still denied fire, the climbing sun dispersed the mist so rapidly in front of us that the mule officer was caught literally with his trousers down, squatting by a bush in the centre of what had abruptly changed into a large open arena. He had a round of applause.

About mid-morning, close by the river, we halted in a shadowy nullah whilst a group was sent to the bank to select our crossing point. Then we struck it lucky. A Peter Cane search-party found them groping about the bank, so we were saved from our desperate crossing. When he heard the news the Colonel rushed off instantly, led by the discovery group, and we with the mules floundered along half-dressed half-packed trying to catch up before he escaped again. We stopped a mile or so further along the bank where Peter Cane had been preparing the crossing for two days. The column halted a little short of the river, on a knoll covered in bamboo, with thin jungle stretching right down to the bank. A cold sweet smell kept wafting intermittently from the river. I went down to have a look at it once the radio was set up. The track narrowed near the bank, passing under a vault of alder-like trees, then came out to a little clearing and there was the river in full view.

It was blue. I had never before seen a blue river, only dark colours or muddy brown, and I gaped at it in astonished delight. It was a pure cobalt blue, the blue of the Pacific beyond the foam-white line where the reef drops down to the abyss of the ocean floor. The flat surface stretched broad and clear across to a sandy strip as white as a crushed coral beach, near which was a single tall coconut palm leaning over the strand, so completing the fantasy of return to the Pacific Islands. The mirrored surface concealed the force of the current, but just below the steep bank the twigs of a fallen branch were wriggling and vibrating under its power, and when a swallow in front of me swooped low for a fleeting sip, and the water sheared up in a tiny bow-wave from its beak, the ripple raced away downstream. A pair of teal, disturbed by the sappers further down the bank, suddenly took off from their hidden nest and flew upstream so low the tips of their wings kept flicking the surface, and I saw a fish jump silver-clear through the line of eddies. I went along the bank through tangled bushes and wispy trails of a delicious freesia scent, and came to the ramp from whence the mules were to be launched; some twenty yards further down was the clearing from which the rafts would be loaded.

The two boats had already been launched and were close-hauled under screening trees by the bank. There was nothing in the clearing itself, but fifty yards back where the bamboo cover started there was a long line of packed mortars, ammunition boxes, sacks of fodder, yakdhans, saddles, all the rest of the paraphernalia stretching away far into the shadowy distance. At the head of this lumpy line were the lilo rafts, bamboo-supported, and already inflated. Now and again there would be a dull heavy 'boom' like distant gunfire, a sound that made the more nervous look about anxiously; it was just the collapse of a division between the inflated compartments of the lilos, caused by the air expanding in the hot close morning and putting too much pressure on the glue-binding. The sappers had made solid-looking rafts and though the beautiful Shweli was about four hundred yards wide just there, and flowing at an alarming speed – we reckoned it was about five knots – I was confident we and our equipment would have no problems. The mules were another matter.

We had been without fire for two complete days by this time and that evening the Colonel finally risked a concession – we could have fires for an hour. By this time he had set out positions covering our rear, our front, our flanks, the mules, the equipment, and the river, we were all concealed in either dense bamboo thickets or riverside undergrowth, and we had the complete force together at last except for the lost recce platoon, so he felt secure enough for this brief relaxation. But the permission had to be qualified after only a few minutes. We had moved the radio away from him up the hill by then but I was with him checking on the map a planned air-drop site when there was a sudden sharp explosion, like a rifle shot; we were stilled for an instant, then when another followed the Colonel rose quickly to his feet and was instructing his runner to go down and find out what had happened when Tiny Langford called:

'Bamboo.'

The voice of reason – as one would expect from Tiny. We had burnt bamboo in Assam and had heard often enough the explosive report made by the trapped hot air when it expands to burst the stem and should have recognized the sound but fear had seized upon the more threatening interpretation. The sound however was far too disturbing for the Colonel and word was sent out that all bamboo must be split before burning – slit quietly with a knife, not crashed open with a kukrie – and so many of the fires had hurriedly to be dismantled and rendered silent.

Up on top of the hillock the sergeants were having trouble contacting base. The colonel had asked for 'continuous air cover during daylight' and I had been unable to persuade him to drop the word 'continuous'; I feared he was asking for too much and so might get nothing at all – as eventually occurred. But just then base would not even answer. We went on trying, chatting in low voices against the background of the clicking morse-key and the soft chirruping of crickets, then suddenly our quiet night was ripped apart by the explosive start of an outboard engine. As with the bulldozer earlier the noise was terrifying after our prolonged regime of silence, almost as if we were again clamouring for attention. I went down to have a look, stealthily by-passing the Colonel who was certain to be most fragile under the assault of that uproar, and came out of the dark tree-tunnel into the moonlit loading point.

Here there was rush-hour activity. Gurkhas of 94 were clambering down into the reinforced lilos, others were massing up behind them with Stanley helping sort them into prepared groups, and equipment was being manhandled up to the bank ready for loading. Across the black water on the far side I could see a faint light flashing on the spectral-white moonlit sandbank – 'Over a quarter of a mile away, you know,' Stanley said in a worried tone. The launch started off below us, burst of white foam from stern, the three rafts were pulled out straight behind it but after just a few yards the current caught them and they swung away quickly almost parallel to the bank, so the launch went sidling across crabwise downstream towards the distant sandspit. Stanley was in too much of a fret for chat so I went back uphill but the Colonel caught me trying to sneak past. Had his message got through? I told him not.

'Keep trying. All night if necessary. It's vitally important.'

Every message was vitally important to him. We had already discovered how inefficient were the signal arrangements for our distant area. Rear HQ kept urging we use the 22 set – traffic on the RAF set was heavy – and this was infuriating. We knew from practical effort that it was out of range. We contacted base only once on it, and that was from the airstrip. Peter Cane, who never let seniority deflect him from expressing an opinion, filed a sharply critical report to which Base in reply pontificated:

THE 22 SET CAN, HAS, AND WILL OPERATE AT 300 MILES RANGE. EXPERIMENT WITH THE LENGTH AND POSITION OF YOUR AERIALS.

Peter sent them the following reply:

HAVE EXPERIMENTED WITH EVERY LENGTH AND POSITION EXCEPT ONE POSITION. LEAVE THAT EXPERIMENT TO YOU.

Had the Colonel seen that exchange he would have had apoplexy.

That night even the RAF set had difficulty making contact, for the ether was clogged by a Wingate message to all columns. It carried the illegal priority of 'Most Immediate' – widespread abuse of priorities was stupidly common in the force – and told at picturesque length about us now being implanted in the entrails of the enemy, or the guts of the Japanese, I forget which, and how we had smitten or smote him with the sword of destruction. There were several other messages – we spent most of that night receiving and decoding. It was a pleasant session however, I was still feeling lively when we finished near dawn, so instead of curling up at once under the bamboo I went down to the bank to watch the clamorous crossing.

The launches were unloading over on the far side and for a short while it was comparatively quiet. There was no mist that beautiful morning, overhead was a limpid daffodil sky and then as you looked down from the zenith towards the east it shaded through deepening yellows to a warm orange glow on the horizon, as if the embers of a vast fire lay behind that deep violet ridge of mountains on the Chinese border. I kept shutting my eyes and counting slowly to ten then opening them again to see if I could discern the difference as the eastern sky lightened from orange to flame red and suddenly at last to a flashing gold so painfully bright I didn't actually see the rim of the sun itself appear over the mountain range that bordered Yunnan. There had been a sleepy warbling of birds along the river bank but as the sun rose there came the loud ringing call of a woodpecker, clear and resonant in the still air, and at once the others all along the bank livened into liquid song. Then the launches started back up against the current towards us, the explosive clatter from exhausts blasted over all other sound and I went back into the dim shadows of the bamboo and slept.

Three hours later I was awakened by order of the Colonel. He wanted me to contact Stanley on the far bank by Aldis lamp. This was a capricious decision, dragging me from sleep for no good reason, messages could perfectly well be sent across by the launch which took less than half an hour between trips. In sour mood I took the Aldis down to the loading point and flashed it at some figures on the sandspit across the river. In due course one of them waved, then ran across the sand to the palm tree. Presently from that area, a lamp began to flash at me and I recognised Stanley's touch – he sent each letter at the same speed, and always gave a lengthy pause between words. His morse was far more accurate than mine, he used to practise occasionally; I hadn't practised since back in the Cambridge training days of 1940, would slap out easy letters like 'E' or 'A' rapidly then have to pause and think at something like a 'J' or a 'Q'. The Colonel had written his request out on a message pad; it asked at length if any of the patrols sent out since arrival had yet discovered anything about our missing recce platoon. I was not going to plough through all that waffle on the lamp, and cut it down to:

ANY NEWS OF RECCE

I got the 'W' wrong, tried to correct but only made a hash, then I scrubbed out everything in such a temper that I yanked the lamp lead off the battery. Once the cursing stopped and it was plugged in again I flicked the switch a few times to check the connection and all this incoherent flashing so confused the painstaking Stanley that he became cross. What happened next was so surprising that I burst out laughing. Stanley called across the sandspit to Peter Wilmott who was just about to leave to come back to our side:

'Tell them to put someone on the lamp who knows morse.'

Every word was distinctly clear across the flat blue water of the Shweli. I called back:

'Oh, Stanley! Don't you love me any more?'

He was as startled as I had been, 'I can hear you, Pat,' he cried.

I passed the Colonel's message and heard – even above the engine row – that our recce platoon was still beyond ken. But the Colonel must have heard too, for he came hurrying down himself to stop our simplified contact. When I pointed out that the engines were making much more noise than our occasional shouts which, as far as a Japanese was concerned, could be from locals he said he wanted no argument about the matter – we were to use only the Aldis for communication. I packed in the job and gave the lamp to the sergeants.

By this time all the men of 94 column were over but most of their equipment still remained on our side. Peter Wilmot, in control of despatching, had become impatient at the leisurely haphazard manner in which rafts were being unloaded on the far side so he had taken over the helm of a boat and was now rushing over, hurling loads on to the sandbank and pelting back, all at about twice the speed of the Garwhalis. But now, without him, our bank was not so well organised; his job had been taken over temporarily by his orderly, who was piling such vast loads on to the rafts that there was threat of disaster if any difficulty arose in the crossing. I took over, settled Peter's immediate tow, then once he was away began to make adjustments in the raft-loads prepared for his next trip.

About the same time Cheetham appropriated the other launch for the formidable task of towing the mules across. He had devised a mule-towing apparatus during the days awaiting our arrival; it was a twelve foot length of bamboo, tied with stays to form a triangle behind the boat, and carrying leads for four mules. He had several made up with quartets of mules already attached to them and waiting their tow-turn. I saw the operation start. Cheetham was a determined officer so a battle of wills was joined, for the mules naturally refused to co-operate; it was hard enough to persuade them across a placid little pool, they always preferred to swim parallel to their entry bank and return to it, and here they could not even see their landing point over a quarter of a mile away, so had to be hauled and pushed and slapped and shouted into the water. Then however their opposition became violent when they found themselves faced with the shattering uproar and stinking exhaust fumes of an outboard engine just a few feet from their faces, and men had to go into the water to force the animals out of depth, so allowing the straining tug to gain advantage in the test of strength.

Cheetham and the muleteers managed to get the first three groups over successfully. We could hear them up beyond the bushes laughing and chattering about their success but we down on the nearby loading point were not so excited; we were only twenty yards downstream and were swamped each time the launch went past with its pole-load of thrashing mules: a box of medical supplies and a saddle had been sent toppling into the water which shelved down steeply at our take-off point, and we had had to dive to retrieve them.

Trouble occurred when Cheetham became ambitious. He decided to double the tow, take eight mules across at a time, so finish the whole job by nightfall. The ramp, which I could not actually see from our position, suddenly became the scene of a fierce struggle between mules and men as

Cheetham tried to put his plan into effect and the noise was such that I went up to see what was happening. It was a wild and violent scene. A horde of Gurkhas were screaming at the mules, pushing and hauling them down the slope in the endeavour to get the double load into the water – the boat could not drag them in, only when they were buoyant did it have the power to pull them away from the bank. Cheetham was recklessly standing in the launch yanking at leads, men in the river up to their chests were hauling at ropes attached to the first pole, the outboard motor was roaring at full throttle, the four mules in the water were thrashing and splashing mud and kicking violently, and about the second four on the slippery ramp was a seething mass of Gurkhas shouting and pushing and slapping at the beasts – and jumping aside from the flying hooves.

It struck me that our position just a few yards down the bank was in great peril, and I ran back to warn the men to haul all lilos in close. We were just doing this, even unloading some, when Cheetham won his battle – apparently. The roar of the motor was muffled as the boat pulled clear, the mules swung around in the current and started drifting down towards us. Previously at this stage the propeller had managed to grip and thrust the boat sidling across the current, but it was only a 5 hp engine and the double tow of mutinous mules was too much. When the animals glimpsed our slope of escape, the eight of them turned as a team and began to swim furiously towards us, wild eyes white and stained teeth bared in a determined bid for the shore. They fought every revolution of the thrusting propeller, we screamed at them, jumped up and down, waved our arms, hurled mud and sticks and anything we could grab, but they fought on stoutly through our offensive until the back four managed to get a foothold just below us. The battle was lost then. They put such a strain on the tow-pole it slipped lengthwise, drawing the other four into the bank, leads slid off the pole and the whole lot of them ran amok. They trampled over our prearranged loads on the path, knocked us aside, and bolted off through the bamboo pursued by screaming muleteers and sappers and riflemen; and on the path were punctured lilos, crushed panniers, saddles and ammunition boxes scattered all about when the plunging hooves were gone. Cheetham accepted the lesson with a shrug and then went back to four mules per trip.

I made a crossing with Peter Wilmot, trailing a hand in the cool water and became involved in an impassioned discussion about the nature of courage, prompted by the actions of the Colonel. Peter was loyal, but judicious in his assessment; he felt that the Colonel was trying to run the operation too precisely in accord with headquarters directives – all this concern about noise and the covering of tracks was to ensure we arrived not only safely but also secretly at our objective. True perhaps, but even he admitted that this obsessive concern could at its kindest be interpreted as fear of making a blunder and so attracting Wingate's terrible attention. The Colonel had been a regular of the Indian Army all his adult life, he lived by its conventions, and to him Wingate was a mad foreigner whose actions were incalculable.

'I still think he'll be a good man under actual fire,' Peter Wilmott said. 'I wish I could be as sure of myself as of him.'

This self-doubt was surprising. He always seemed so completely sure of himself. He never strolled about with the aimless air of David Anderson, who would pause for a chat and wave vaguely to his jemadar to get on with things; Peter always marched with a purpose, knowing exactly where he was going and how to get there. He was intent even in relaxation, studying you through his large horn-rimmed glasses, lips firm, blue eyes never wavering, as he listened. When I told him that day in the boat that he was a model of self-confidence compared to the rest of us he dismissed this as superficial, he had never experienced enemy fire and was most unsure how he would react. To my astonishment he referred to an incident when, he declared, I had shown courage and he had failed the test. He had to tell me about this great feat; it is worth recalling as a good illustration of the misconception about the nature of courage.

It had happened during training in Assam. We were out on a march, had stopped for midday halt and were squatting about the Colonel for orders when a runaway mule suddenly came charging at us. It was carrying a pannier on one side only, had bolted whilst being unloaded, lead reins were flailing about its head as it charged into our midst. We barely had time to move, scrambling aside to leave a gap for its hurtling passage, and I would normally have been first to get clear – but on this occasion I actually jumped towards the beast. It was an involuntary action. The whipping lead had been tied into a ball at the end, just about the size of a cricket ball; I had captained the school team my last two years, always fielding at first slip, it was the most natural thing in the world in that instant to leap forward and snatch the flying knotted-ball with both hands. To save myself being dragged to the ground I jerked back the catch solidly enough to stop the mule almost in mid-stride, he hauled me only a yard or so as he swung around in a semi-circle, sending the pannier flying into the bushes, and then stopped still, fluffing froth all over my face. Everyone gave me a *shabosh* and we settled down again to listen to the Colonel. All forgot about it promptly except Peter and myself – I pleased at the sharp catch, Peter apparently filled with shame that he had bolted, leaving a mere pilot to deal so bravely with the danger.

This is a typical misunderstanding, one that always provoked me. I told him heatedly that he was talking nonsense, my action had had nothing to do with courage, it was merely a test of skill, a challenge. People will confuse this with valour. We were hit by a shell once in an attack on a Japanese task force and the elevator cable was severed but I managed to fly the aircraft back to Singapore and there land it just on the trimming tabs. Everyone said this was a most courageous act, saving a precious aircraft instead of baling out, and the

CO put through a recommendation for an immediate award – it was lost in that lost campaign – but like the grabbing of the mule reins, it was nothing more than an exciting test of skill. It may well have been a unique feat in aviation and I was proud of it, exhilarated, just as I would by evading the charge of a bull or diving a plane under a low bridge – but fear was not involved, so neither was courage. For courage has no independent existence. It is a resistance *against* fear – not its obliteration. Once fear is suppressed one's subsequent actions have no relevance to courage.

That is why medals for gallantry have no validity. No comrade, no commanding officer, no committee can assess the courageous value of another man's action, because he alone has experienced the life that determines that value. Without its precise setting in the imagination the act itself, however well observed, is no more relevant to such an assessment than are the letters of the alphabet to the works of Shakespeare. As a commanding officer I wrote many recommendations for awards because they do serve many very useful purposes within a fighting unit; the fine words that went into them however were pragmatically chosen just to gain approval – the citations for medals that I myself was awarded were equally false. Well intentioned, but false. Spectacularly impressive acts are nearly always just thrilling tests of skill, exciting challenges to be overcome, you might even perform such deeds for sheer fun; the real glittering gems of courage are usually hidden in dull routine tasks that disclose not the slightest hint of their secret treasure. The bravest thing I did in the war, perhaps in my whole life, was to walk along a jungle path one day a few weeks later when there was not a single enemy soldier within miles of the place; we were far away from any possible menace, in no danger whatsoever – but imagination had decided otherwise.

By the time we had reached the opposite bank of the Shweli that day Peter must have felt sorry he had ever raised this touchy subject. One reassurance however I did offer him; it was that when we came under fire I was certain that he, probably more than any other man in our column, would be sure to get on with the job in hand. What I recall most vividly about that launch trip was not the passionate discussion with him but the words of Peter Cane who must have noted our serious manner as we grounded on the sandbank.

'What's the old man been telling you, then?' he asked.

Old? His words shook me. I was twenty two at the start of the war, two years younger than Peter Cane himself, and although my hair was now turning grey, and much had happened since leaving the Solomons, I had still thought myself the same young man who in 1939 had rushed away from the Islands in pursuit of death or glory in a distant war. But suddenly that day he was no longer me. Those words on the river bank on March 15 cut him off abruptly into a separate life, gone forever beyond recall – like the youthful Houseman:

> The pence are here, and here's the fair,
> But where's the lost young man?

It was a sombre day after that, as we completed our crossing of the Shweli River.

8

We lost three mules in the crossing; in each case they broke clear in mid-stream and swam down with the current to finish miles beyond possible redemption. We also lost a lilo of mule fodder, one of the big batteries, a case of mortar bombs, and – most important of all perhaps – the goodwill of our sister column. The original plan had been to let 94 go on while we took over the protection of our own crossing, for they had further to go to their first drop-site; by holding them back until we were clear the Colonel condemned them to a third of normal rations for at least a day longer than us.

'It's not fair, you know,' Stanley said, with a most reproachful look.

Food was already a preoccupation, and during the next three months scarcely a day passed when it was not discussed at one time or another – how many packets do you have left? . . . swop a breakfast for a supper? . . . dare you eat two packets and rely on the drop tomorrow? Food, apart from sweets, has no great appeal to me so I did not suffer as acutely as someone like Tiny Langford who would describe favourite dishes with such passionate detail his suffering was poignantly clear, but I did treasure a fantasy in those months, of slowly opening a tin to see again those golden cubes of pineapple protruding through the luscious white pebbly surface of the creamy rice. We passed through 94 that night in a long resented file that gave them plenty of opportunity to express their hope we recover not a single parachute from our stolen drop. Their prayers were not entirely unanswered.

In the clear silver light of a full moon we followed a track through the sparsely wooded area of the river bank into jungle where the tall trees cut out nearly all light. Once in the gloom the track faded away and we were crashing and blundering through darkness with the man or mule immediately in front as one's only guide. I had a strong temptation to use my small reading torch but the Colonel had specifically forbidden it at an earlier exposure and he was too close to risk it. Happily we came to the edge of the jungle presently, and there halted. In front of us was a wide stretch of open paddy-fields, dry and clear, with two small wooden huts, black doorways, at one side. Apparently they were suspect. Whispered instructions were passed to assemble in line well away from the huts and all cross the clearing together.

We shuffled into position, then were held there, poised. It was infuriating. You felt at times there was a deliberate conspiracy to arouse in the column a high state of tension. Finally we started to move and had covered about half the distance when I heard a faint humming sound; it built up rapidly to a roaring crescendo as three aircraft came thundering out of the moon, bearing down at tree-top height towards us in the moonlit clearing. Panic! Everyone bolted madly back for the dark jungle, packs were shed, muleteers abandoned their animals, platoons split up, all order vanished in the wild scramble of some five hundred men and eighty mules for the safety of the trees. What angered me most was that I recognized the aircraft almost at once, even started crying out:

'They're ours! Dakotas! They're ours!'

But there is a psychic force about mob panic that is irresistible, it engulfs reason, and I was borne away with the rest even as I was calling the protest. The aircraft thundered low over our terrified heads and went on serenely about their innocent business, which was to drop river-crossing equipment to 40 column on the far side of the Shweli – as we discovered weeks later. We spent fifteen minutes at the edge of the jungle, plenty of time for humiliating self-reproach, while mules were caught, loads repacked, gear collected, and the segments of the column fitted together again. The huts on the far side remained silent and lifeless throughout our chaotic performance.

Dawn was beginning to seep through the jungle before we finally halted on the precipitous side of a running stream. Fingers of mist trailed through the tree trunks just a few feet above the ground and gave clammy strokings to the body as we removed our packs and prepared for a rest. We halted for an hour, without fire or battery-charging, time enough to get drowsy before stand-to, when the sun's rays seared through the mist and we could see it rising like steam from the trees the other side of the valley. Then on for another hour . . . bivouac . . . sleep till early afternoon . . . on again.

This was to set the pattern for the first ten days or so. We acted as though the enemy were hot on our trail, just waiting for us to settle so they could pounce, we kept hurrying away from fear. We dare not stay still for more than eight hours at the most, we halted late at night where we happened to be when the Colonel decided it was safe, then pushed on quickly after dawn stand-to and stopped later for a meal, usually without fire. Scarcely ever were we allowed to start the battery charger, conversation in bivouac was controlled down to little above whisper-level, we seemed not so much to be heading purposefully towards a site of planned operations as trying desperately to shake off a demon pursuer.

That morning after leaving the Shweli we came to a patch of thin evergreen jungle, just a scattering of cassia, alder and other recovery types on flat land which had once been cultivated, and the Colonel decided to break our trail there and so confuse our phantom pursuers. We had practised the exercise frequently. It is inevitable despite all the care in the world, that some six hundred men and animals will leave evidence of their passage when they march through jungle in snake-formation . . . broken branches, tree-trunks white-scarred by pannier blows, hoof and boot marks, trampled manure and – despite all the warnings about it – scraps of paper and metal and leather and cloth discarded by men and mules. To shed this distinctive trail we stopped in column, turned right on command, then set off on compass bearing on a front almost a mile wide. The huge band of us moved in a wide wobbly line across this open secondary growth for about half a mile and then I noticed we were coming into shadow where the old clearing ended abruptly, and looking ahead you could see the wall of ash-grey trunks of the tall dipterocarps, and the dapple of thin shadows through the canopy. The first tree I came to was a slender-trunked padauk draped invisibly with the sweet sent of its tiny orange flowers and I was sniffing around to catch as much scent as possible when I became aware of a loud crackling noise. Explanation came quickly as my own feet began to crunch on the fallen leaves of teak and other noisy deciduous types, all of us suddenly making such an uproar that we halted, looking along the line, waiting for the inevitable order. Yellowish dust which lay like a coating of mustard on the big fallen leaves rose in a listless haze that crumpled your lips dry in an instant. The order from the Colonel took only seconds to reach us. We had to retire on our tracks at once. Reassembled presently at the edge of the teak-infested indaing we set off in column line once more, keeping just clear of the big brown shattering leaves in the tall grey-shadowed forest on our right.

We stopped about midday just short of a clearing covered in shoulder-high reeds, but although the mules sniffed water and were restless the Colonel decided it was too risky to take them into the open, so the poor things had a tantalizing halt. He discussed with me the plan for our drop that night, and agreed I should go ahead to prepare the site. I had picked it out on the map before we left base but it could be unsuitable. The mountainous area into which we were heading was marked as jungle-covered but a few patches were marked with sparser forest and it was one of these areas I had selected.

We started off at once. Peter Wilmot was in charge of the ten-man escort and he insisted we move in the approved manner of a scouting party, with a single man leading about fifty yards ahead – the principle being that he is the one who gets the bullet, and the others the time to scatter. It was not that he thought there might be Japanese in the area but he wanted the men to get used to the drill. Peter never missed an opportunity to further training, was always eager to put theory into practice. As one would expect he himself took the first lead, then later on each of the ten men had a turn in front. After the nervous stuttering progress of the column under the Colonel's direction the crisp efficiency of Peter's small group was a relief, he inspired confidence, his men were alert, yet relaxed. It was an easy march along a contour line of the foothills, packs now almost empty of rations and plenty of black cool shadows from the gathering jungle. The path kept crossing ridges, opening up views of little valleys to the next slope, and nearly always you would glimpse a touch of colour somewhere in the vast green background. It is no wonder nature uses colour in such variety to attract insects and birds; when surrounded by all those interminable greens even the faintest smudge of colour at the periphery of vision jerks your head around into compulsive attention.

We halted for a break by the edge of a tiny stream that was making pleasant chuckling sounds down in its deep rocky bed as we chatted about the Colonel's sense of insecurity (Peter striving for kind explanations) and our lost recce platoon. We were in shade but across the far side of the streamlet the leaves of the trees were a fresh translucent green in the sunlight, all perfectly still except for one quivering branch, and on going down to the edge of the steep bank to investigate this I found the commotion was caused by a weaver bird working on a nest. It had a yellow cap and breast, was about sparrow-size, and flew off when my face caught the light. The nest was straw-coloured and hung on a short tube, the whole contraption looked like a partially deflated balloon draped over the branch and dangling down over the rocky stream-bed. What was particularly fascinating was the height of the nest; it must have been about fifteen feet above the level of the bubbling streamlet at that time but from an undercut on the other side you could see where the flood height of the water reached and the nest was only about a foot above that. Safely clear when the monsoon rains arrived. How on earth did the bird work that out so precisely?

In mid-afternoon we came to the map-planned site and found a small taungya. Taungya were our salvation in the hills. They are patches of jungle cleared on the slash-and-burn practice common in South-East Asia – where rice is grown on the burnt-out clearing for a year or two until the soil is exhausted, then the site is abandoned. In the autumn when the monsoon rains have ended, the Kachin starts preparing his new taungya, cutting down or ring-barking the trees until the whole chosen area is covered with the dead material, which is then left to dry right through till late spring. The clearings then show up like suede-leather patches sewn on the mountain slopes.

Flying over the mountains of northern Burma at the turn of the year you see these brown patches lying everywhere on the green waves of the jungle, huge bonfires now ready for the torch. Just before the monsoon rains arrive the fires are lit and then at night the blobs of flame are visible from fifty miles or more upwind, monstrous flares dropped from the sky, scattered about in the darkness without pattern but each delineated clearly in its block shape and streaming smoke. Once the fires have reduced most of the dead wood to ash the Kachin clears the easy debris, leaves the intractable stumps, waits for the rain to start, then plants his rice. The site is used for only a few years until the crop falters, then it is abandoned and a new taungya prepared. The old one remains clear enough for passage for only a year or so before the secondary growth develops into an almost impenetrable tangle – this is 50-yard-per-hour jungle, where a parachute load can be little more than arm's length away and still be invisible. Ten years pass before the tall trees begin to emerge and capture the light, so regaining control of the floor and allowing the slow recovery to climax jungle once again.

The taungya we found for our first drop was a rough square, about four hundred yards across. Several tall black skeletons of trees had been left standing, and in practically no way at all did the site conform to the requirements laid down in our manual but I reckoned it was good enough – anyway, by then we had no alternative. The column harboured by a stream a mile away but unfortunately the Colonel decided to come forward to look at the site. I was with Peter on the far side when I saw him emerge with Tiny Langford and a group of Gurkhas from the track near the first fire-pile. He seemed to be talking and kept pointing towards the next fire. Then he began to move with slow deliberate steps towards it, it was like the march of an automaton. I suddenly realized what he was doing – and swore.

'He's measuring the bloody distance,' I said.

Peter wanted me to wait but I decided to get in with some story or other before the Colonel committed himself to ordering the fires reset. He saw me hurrying across and waved me aside as he continued his slow deliberate pacing to the next wood pile. He stopped, but I got in first:

'It's short. I want to keep aircraft well away from the ridge.'

This was claptrap, there was plenty of room for a circuit, but I hoped to confuse him with technical expertise. The manual specified six fires spaced at hundred yard intervals, but I had simply divided the six into the available space – 'only seventy-four yards apart,' the Colonel said severely. I tried to shrug off the shortfall as unimportant, hoping he was in amenable mood. At times you could manoeuvre him on to your track without any effort, just express a vague doubt about a perfectly reasonable decision and he would hurriedly amend it; at other times you would present an overwhelming argument, based on fact (or indisputable lies) against some quite irrational decision and he would become bristly at once, and wave his rank at you:

'That's an order, Pat.'

The imperious state was often the result of an impetuous decision placed on public record, making it difficult for him to recant. This particular day he had told Tiny Langford the fire gaps were not the prescribed distance and would have to be altered so when I pointed out that the total length of the taungya was only about four hundred yards he still insisted, though it meant laying the last two fires in dense jungle.

This struck me as such a stupid decision as to be labelled so at once – a blunder I sometimes made in recoil from his preposterous orders. Such instant critical reaction would set him rock-firm in commitment, whereas wiser ones in the column like Tiny Langford particularly would have gentled him into a change of mind. I tried hurriedly to gloss over my charge of stupidity by stressing that we would lose even more to the trees if we put actual fires there, but the damage of my outburst was beyond repair. He interrupted the flow of cover-up with a snapped order:

'Fires must be set out the regulated distance,' dabbing a finger at me with each articulated syllable. Then he left, with the Gurkha section.

Peter wasted no time in recrimination, went off at once to carry out the order. Tiny Langford stood there puffing his pipe, then sighed and shook his head sadly as he pointed out how I had botched it. The Colonel had been in a most amiable mood along the track. I could have had a pleasant chat with him, reached a friendly compromise, and all resolved in a congenial atmosphere; instead I had practically called him an idiot to his face, and as a result we would have to rebuild all the damn fires, and the Colonel had been sent off in a foul temper.

'Not very clever, you colonials,' he said.

The failure of that first drop was due not so much to the Colonel's readjustment of the fires but to his dominating fear of discovery. By dawn we had collected only about half the drop, and had just begun to chop down the first of the trees which held parachutes when the column arrived. The sound of the axe was reverberating about the hills, the Colonel seemed to wince at each blow as he approached – and ordered me to stop the work at once. Naturally I protested, but he said the risk was too great, we must settle for what we had collected and get away from the area quickly. There was a parachute load of 144 K-ration packs dangling from the branch of a blackened tree just by us and Peter Wilmot suggested we blow it up, so at least get that one before leaving. The suggestion shocked the Colonel. Was he mad? The sound would be heard for miles! Peter, suitably chastened, went off to his platoon.

'We'll ask for another drop in two days' time,' the Colonel said.

To ask was not to receive however. That night, before we could put through the request Wingate sent out another one of those threats that did little to shore up the Colonel's confidence. It concerned the situation reports, the Sitreps, we tried to send off every day, and apparently Wingate expected that these would always begin by giving our position. We had not done so. I can't think there had been a specific order about this, the Colonel was punctilious about following to the letter every instruction from above; the first he knew of an offence was when that signal came condemning him for it. The reprimand was accompanied by the usual threat – if we sent another sitrep off without giving the column's position our umbilical cord would be cut. No sitrep, no food. The threat was effective, as death threats usually are, and thereafter Wingate always knew where we

were. It has to be admitted also that the Japanese did not –
and this had been as Wingate decreed before we left, when he
said:

'My intention is to land you where the enemy is not.'

He had done this most successfully. The absence of enemy
troops was surprising. They must have known roughly
where we were but though we walked along roads used by
their transport, left jungle trails that a soft fat financier could
have followed, still no Japanese came anywhere near us.
There were few enough local people also, but amongst our
early contacts with them was one that had fatal consequences, despite Wingate's severe warning – he had failed to
appreciate that the Japanese might use the locals in an
intelligence system far more dangerous to us than any radar
coverage such as he had presumed when selecting landing
sites. Knowing that the Kachins were unsympathetic to their
cause the Japanese used Burmese or Shans to gather information, particularly after the CHOWRINGEE landing was
discovered; although they seem to have assumed that the
bulk of our landing force had travelled back over the Irrawaddy – and that must have bewildered them – they knew
some remained on our side, so they had intensified the
dispatch of Shan spies into the Kachin hills where the
intruders would be harbouring.

The incident occurred when a section of 94 column passed
through a village and noticed four strangers, not Kachins.
The reason the men gave for their presence was so implaus-
ible that they were taken back to the column – the Shans said
they had come to buy a pig, but were unable to explain why
they had only fifteen rupees between them yet knew a pig
cost about fifty.

A Kachin scout with the column however then recognized
one of the captives as the *thaji* (headman) of a Shweli village
who was renowned for his association with the Japanese; he
had rounded up stragglers in the Burma retreat two years
earlier and handed them over to the Japanese, and had

ordered one group of captured British soldiers to be stripped and publicly flogged in the village. Carrying this man and his three associates along with the column was like having a cargo of nitro-glycerine – if they escaped the Japanese would have at once full information about our force, but far, far worse was the terrible threat they posed to the Kachins. These men had seen the villagers welcome us, one young man even joining up as a scout, and if that information got back to the Japanese the villagers would pay with their lives. The Kachins were fiercely partisan against the Japanese, who were well aware of this and consequently were prepared to accept and act ruthlessly upon any denunciation of them by the plains people.

What to do? It was not possible to get them out to India at once, the terrain was too rugged for construction of an airstrip, so Peter had them bound and he warned that any attempt at escape would mean instant death. The Gurkhas guarding them were told to use kukries in that event, not rifles, because the column was close to a road used by the Japanese patrols. That same evening the Shans foolishly decided to make a bolt for it, rushing off down the hill when they thought the guards were relaxed; the Gurkhas may have been temporarily, but they reacted quickly enough to the attempted escape and hurled themselves in pursuit with kukries flailing. They killed three including the murderous *thaji*, but the fourth unfortunately managed to get away without a scratch. A few days later the Japanese went to Sinthe village where the column had stopped, seized the headman and all his family, together with five other complete families – twenty-one people in all, men and women and children – and took them down to Bhamo. There, the next day, they were publicly executed for their crime of offering shelter to us strangers – as custom obliged them to do, and as they had done also to Shans and Japanese.

After that terrible lesson we would all check most carefully to discover if any strangers were in a village before we made public contact with the Kachins. If strangers were found then they were questioned long and anxiously before being released. Some, the discovered spies, were not released but were sent out or executed to prevent them disclosing the Kachin's hospitality; I think a total of seven were killed for this reason, thereby saving the lives of about one hundred and fifty innocent villagers if that tragic count at Sinthe is taken as an average of Japanese revenge.

I never had any doubt that we were not merely justified in such action but compelled into it by the paramount need to protect the innocent Kachins. The Japanese were ruthless in their treatment of locals suspected of helping us – even if they had displayed nothing more than the normal courtesies towards strangers that their custom required. We killed, but only to protect the lives of those who befriended us; the Japanese killed in harsh punishment, then overkilled grossly just as an example. There is a difference. We had to protect those who would risk their lives for us, and though cynics might say that the Kachins served only their own self-interest in supporting us, that it was their hatred of the Shans and Burmese that drove them, I don't believe it. I spent many hours in their houses, talking long into the night with them through a Kachin officer who joined us a little later, and am convinced their friendship was genuine and disinterested. God knows we, the British, treated them badly enough in the end anyway, deserting them after they had committed them-selves so publicly to us, but at least we in the columns did what we could to save their lives whilst we were actually in there behind the enemy lines.

Luckily for them it was a Kachin who found our lost recce platoon. We heard about them towards the end of March, the Kachins got word to us of their hiding place and we were presently able to retrieve this unhappy group. It appeared they had gone to what they thought was the correct RV at the Shweli – and might well have been right, as our experience of those groping days had shown – had waited two days and then crossed, wrongly assuming we were already over and that they had somehow missed us. They had given away all their horses and mules to a villager in exchange for the loan of a boat, an unfortunate bargain, so had had to shed their heavy equipment; the batteries of their radio had gone flat by this time and so they too, together with the radio itself, were abandoned. They had then gone on quickly to hide in the hills and await what fate had decreed for them – which fortunately was that a Kachin should find them. They were taken to a hideout near the village and given food, the locals sent out word about this isolated group sheltering with them, so eventually the news reached us and a party was sent out to collect them.

The episode had a serious effect on their morale however, and long afterwards when Tiny Langford and I had occasion to go off on a recce into China we took some of these men with us and found them most unsettling company. The recce platoon was in fact disbanded, so shattered was the morale of the men, and some were sent out prematurely. They were our first casualties, destroyed by the enemy within and not the Japanese. There, but for the grace of God . . .

9

My first tour of operations was in early 1941, on Blenheim bombers based in Cornwall – thirty sorties, mostly against Brest and other Atlantic ports. We got through safely in seventy days during which time the squadron lost sixteen crews out of a strength of sixteen, so we were statistically very lucky to survive. That was the quickest, and most dangerous, of my four tours and I had imagined the Wingate expedition would be very much like that – a mountain jungle as our base, dashing out on operational sorties when guns would blaze for an hour or so as on a bombing raid, then making or fighting our way back to safe base again. A day or two later we would be out once more, so it would go on, ten sorties or so a month hammering at Japanese convoys and lines of communication until our tour ended – Wingate had promised we would be brought out after three months.

The practice was very different. We spent a far greater proportion of time between operations than in the RAF; I reckon we were in contact with the enemy – under fire, our own guns in use – for only fifteen hours out of nearly three thousand on the operation. An hour a week average, say. The rest of the time we were engaged in the laborious business of moving, chasing after food, preparing for the job, positioning ourselves. Instead of darting in lightfooted like a boxer, quick left and right then out again, we were closer in analogy to a prima donna dressed in regal splendour, train-bearers carrying the long trailing robe; we had to manoeuvre carefully on to stage, do our set piece, then like an ample Wagnerian soprano turn away with slow deliberation so as to keep our train in position as we made our stately departure back to the wings again.

A typical example of such manoeuvering occurred about a fortnight after landing in our first aggressive action. It was on the main road that runs down some six hundred miles from Myitkyena to Rangoon. The column split into four parties: a demolition party to perform the action – the blowing of bridges – a foraging party to go ten miles up the road to see if food could be bought, a drop party to go on to a map-planned site, and a harbour party with all the mules and oddments to go to a safe hideout in the hills. We met up the following day, having left behind us by then not a single purposeful track but four widely diverging ones made by obviously different groupings of creatures meandering about the area – including a buffalo we had picked up en route to the drop site.

Actually it was the buffalo that did the picking up. Again it was Peter Wilmot's rifle platoon accompanying me – very much against his will, he had hoped to go with the demolition party and perhaps meet the enemy. We were now well into the hills but still at no great distance from the Shweli; when we stopped on a ridge that midday we could see down on the plain a broad strip of the river, placid blue surface edged with silver sand, and the occasional palm to add that nostalgic Pacific island touch. It was just after the halt when we came to a small clearing planted with tobacco, then in pale-lager-brown flower, that we met our buffalo. He was domesticated, halter about his neck, and he raised his head to inspect us in that supercilious manner their structure enforces upon them, before ambling over to greet us. He stopped just in front of us, breathing noisily, peering myopically at each of us in turn. He was in beautiful condition, hide like polished ebony; it is said they can smell Europeans and don't like them but this one let me pat his glossy neck and feel his horns – they lay so flattened back that his head seemed to have been forced through a too-small hole. He lumbered along to the site with us, stayed to watch the drop that night, and some locals who helped in recovery took him back next morning to his owner.

The bridges were successfully blown during the night, without any contact being made with the enemy, and next afternoon we had all joined up again. So we had left behind on that occasion not the single purposeful trail of a raiding column but four quite different ones, three of which seemed pointless wanderings – a further curiosity for trackers was that all trails finished in a clearing where dung evidence indicated several types of herbivorous animals had participated in some sort of jamboree.

Two days later we had another animal contact, not so tranquil this time. We had crossed the first low range of hills and were down on the flat for a ten-mile stretch that finished at the base of a big threatening 3,000 feet ridge. Our packs were filled after that drop, there was not a flicker of wind, a scorching sun blazed through the soggy air as we marched along a wide and waterless *chaung* – a Burmese nullah – in fine deep sand that made every step a squeaking effort; blinding white too, painfully reflecting the rays of the sun. After nearly an hour trudging through this rasping sand most of us had ceased to take any interest in the Burmese scene and were head-down with eyes half-shut in a stupor of momentum. The sweat was dripping clear away from my eyebrows, so low was my head, the pack was slithering about on wet shirt-back, and I was counting up to a thousand footsteps before allowing myself to look again at the watch to see how much longer for the halt. There was not the slightest vestige of shade along the wide *chaung*, high dense elephant grass on the left, on the right open ground with clumps of scrub and shimmering heat waves.

The appearance of the elephants shattered me out of stupor. There was a sudden shrill squeal, I looked up startled to see an explosive thrashing of grass, then an avalanche of enormous battleship-grey shapes burst out of the straw-coloured wall and came thundering almost directly for us in the centre of the column. I stood rigid for an instant in terrified nightmare, then either flung myself to the sand or was shaken off my feet by the tremor of the stampede. I saw the monstrous line for a moment, led by an immense beast, ears flared, trunk curled up, flash of red from open mouth, like a great steam engine shrieking past at the head of an express train. The ground shook as if in an earthquake, sand rose in a turmoil, mules bolted and scattered their loads all about the *chaung*, most of us crouched in blind terror against the ground. Then the train had thundered past, crashed through the bushes on the far bank, and we could breathe again. It took us about half an hour to sort things out afterwards, a check-up showed we had suffered nothing but fright which was extraordinarily lucky, for the elephants had charged in a single undeviating line, an irresistible force that would have smashed down and pounded to destruction anything that happened to be in its path. The incident kept me alert, darting anxious glances at the tall grass on our left and now oblivious of my pack, until we came at last to halt-time.

We climbed that first big hill that afternoon, it was the start of our hill travail. The mountains along the Chinese border go up to 8,000 feet, the valleys down to 500, and as we were going across the lie of the land we had no alternative but to climb up and then down again, up and down, in unforgettable anguish. Two or three times a day we might do a straight climb of 2,000 feet, and one wild night we climbed up to 7,000 feet on a slippery hillside with a gale-force wind and slashing rain trying to hurl us back down the mountainside. Occasionally there would be a more humane track, an opium trail perhaps, winding down the side of a hill in an attempt to give an easier gradient for loaded ponies, but we were in Kachin country, they build their villages on top of the ridge and make their tracks straight down to water or the valley plot. Kachins are gravity-proof, they float up the mountain trails as if they have helium in their veins. We had to haul and climb and claw our way up to their villages.

Sometimes there would be a reprieve at the end of the climb. Instead of an immediate drop down to the base of another monstrous hill there would be a string of villages along the ridge itself; then the track would undulate gently along the spine with spectacular views on either side, westward over partially cleared foothills to the immense honey-coloured plain of the Irrawaddy, eastward the high blue ridges of Yunnan with the forest clinging to the slopes like fur. In the crisp clear mornings of these uplands it was no hardship to start off on the day's march, the sun just risen and driving golden wedges into the valleys, up all the slopes the harried spectres of mist fleeting into disappearance, and the melodious chatter of a flock of scarlet minivets in the trees above your head. You would come to a nat shrine by the side of the track, like a nesting box fashioned with loving care, then the village itself with tawny bamboo dwellings and smiling faces of welcome, people engaged in peaceful tasks – a man carving pipe-bowls from bamboo roots, a woman weaving striped cloth with a zigzag pattern, children bringing up water in bamboo stems, a girl in dirt-grey careless lungyi winnowing rice from a broad shallow basket – and about the village itself the non-forest plants, glossy-leaved citrus trees, a sago palm in tasselled flower, banana plant with cool green fronds, and once a tamarind tree with branches radiating from the huge trunk almost as precisely aligned as those of an umbrella. There were relics too of the white man, a dak bungalow with two long-armed deck chairs on the veranda as if waiting for the sahibs to emerge for their pre-dinner stingahs, another time a police post, white as a gull and beside it a huge jacaranda misty-blue in flower.

There was little food to spare in the villages and for a time in late March we were so low on rations we began to try out edible roots – those I tested had the barely discernible taste of bitter turnip – and to collect bamboo shoots which you boiled and then ate only because they were said to be nourishing – I thought of chewed straw when eating them. The animals were luckier, they had a bit of bamboo and even grass on occasions. Then we had a most successful drop and lived briefly on the full ration compliment of three packets a day. This drop was in a taungya beside a village, the perfect combination, for the help the villagers gave could make a dramatic difference in recovery. The Kachins were always eager to help, not only because they are hospitable by custom – and nature also, it seemed to us – but also because they always received some of the parachutes in return and these were prized rewards; they wove their own cloth, usually in the sloped-line patterns you associate with Aztec designs, but much preferred manufactured cottons and these became unobtainable after the Japanese invasion.

Strangely enough we never had a free-fall – mule fodder, say – or a streamed parachute ever hit a house on a village drop. About a quarter of our drop might be free-fall, and about ten percent of parachutes failed, so the drop site could be a dangerous place; on moonless nights even a parachuted load could be a deadly missile, unseen, unheard, in its rapid descent. We had no fatalities, our worst casualties were broken limbs, but I know of at least four deaths in other columns. The free drops were in double bags, the outer one being bigger than the actual container; the inner one would usually burst on impact, spilling the contents into the bigger bag, but it was extremely rare for that second one to fail – I saw a load of boots once ripped open by a jagged stump, and Stanley had an inner rice sack split when it hit a firewood pile. We had each developed a protective plan against these lethal free drops, using a tree or stump as a shield. We operated the Aldis, the most reliable method of contacting the pilots, so had to be out in the open.

It is interesting to see the difference between the instructions issued by headquarters for drops and our practice. This divergence created no problem for Stanely – except his pernickety conscience – because his column commander Peter Cane was himself always happy to ignore regulations which were patently ill-founded or ineffectual, but I had Colonel Morris breathing down my neck, so had to rely on subterfuge or lies to cover all the infringements of regulations.

Here is the precis carried in my note book of the Chindit Supply Drop regulations issued by Force Headquarters:

(RAF OFFICER) X   *   *   *

*   Site: L-shaped,
        500 x 200 yards.

*   100 yard gap
        between
        all fires.

        50 yard gap
        between
*   RAF officer at
        point X and first fire.

        *

        *

1. Summit of a cleared ridge.
2. Nothing 100 feet higher within 5 miles.
3. Preferably moonlight, from 1 hr after rise till 1 hr before set.
4. Light fires 15 minutes before ETA of aircraft.
5. Wait for aircraft to signal first.
6. Essential we reply from point X on plan.
7. Can cancel drop with red verey light.
8. Last aircraft will flash FIN.
9. If site 5+ miles from signalled site, must put out indicators.
10. Transmit homing signal for 10 minutes before ETA (My Wingate disagreement.)

By the fourth week I had deliberately broken every one of these rules except 7 which I never had occasion to use, and no aircraft gave 8. We set our fires within any cleared ground we could find, hillside or valley, even as short as 200 yards – better a drop in which you collect only 20% rather than reject a site and starve. We took the drop any hour of the night, moon or no moon, never lit the fires until we actually heard the aircraft (firewood usually too precious), and the faintest engine sound set us flashing the Aldis continuously and often firing off a green Verey light to ensure attention. I signalled from a protective point which could be anywhere on the site at all, never bothered to put out an arrow if we changed sites (as if 5 miles made any difference to a pilot!) and never *ever* gave the homing signal even when specifically ordered to do so on at least two occasions by the Colonel – he had no means of checking if we carried out his order. We never missed an aircraft that was sent to us.

All experienced collectors took up protected positions when free-falling loads were being dropped. With a tree trunk between you and the plane you could feel fairly secure; when parachutes were coming down however you had to be out in the open to mark them on your chart so you had no protection against streamers. The proportion of such failures was disgraceful; almost certainly the responsibility lay with the packers at base and the types of parachutes used, not with the despatchers – it is no trouble for a despatcher to clip on the static lines in the aircraft and indeed it can be highly dangerous if he doesn't, for he could himself then go flying out with the load.

In a three-aircraft drop we have had as many as six streamers, which is an appalling record. The load could be over sixty pounds, a solid block of K rations, steel petrol containers, a box of ammunition, deadly missiles which would be fatal in a direct hit. Though the army officers gave them unstinted praise, the standard of the pilots varied. You tried to give the pilot a clear run-line and a left-hand circuit that would keep him safe at 250 feet but it was not always possible; sometimes there would be only a short run at a safe height, sometimes a right-hand circuit would be needed to keep low. In such cases many pilots simply stayed very high and carried out their normal drill. This was the worst fault, dropping at excess height. Drift could be disastrous, for if a chute missed you on a ridge you had no chance of finding it five thousand feet down in a nearby valley. Not once did I see a pilot start with a single parachute marker, a simple technique in which all of them should have been trained because it is the only way to ensure accuracy: you drop the marker on estimated windspeed-direction, aligning engine-nacelle say on some ground feature as drop checkpoint, bank sharply to note actual landing spot, then adjust on your checkpoint accordingly for subsequent runs. Most pilots charged straight in and flung out half a dozen parachutes from directly overhead, irrespective even of wind direction. Some adjusted after faulty runs, some did not. The pilots, both American and British, were like any other group of men – some were conscientious, some were not.

Looting on the drop site had to be discouraged; it continued off and on until at the end when we were getting full rations. You can forgive a man for succumbing to such a temptation but what always angered me was the waste associated with the crime. In the jungle periphery of the site you found ration packs broken open, the more tasty items eaten at once and the rest discarded or deliberately hidden; and on the harbour track you would see wrappers and opened tins, evidence that those taking back the loads to distribution point had been unable to resist the insidious temptation of a damaged case. The Colonel applied group punishment but this was wasteful injustice. Three days cigarette ration were collected from all Gurkhas on the first site where looting occurred and these were then publicly burnt; this meant some definite innocents were punished – I could vouch personally for twelve men – and also a commodity of great

133

value as a medical comfort and reward was deliberately wasted.

I argued with him that we could cut down the list of suspects to about a dozen individuals; for Peter Wilmot and David Anderson could also vouch for their groups, but the Colonel declared that all must suffer.

'That's the only way they will learn,' he repeated, waving away argument.

The problem of punishment had been the subject of various recommendations by Wingate, but much was left to the discrimination and ingenuity of the column commander. Wingate recommended that for a serious offence the culprit should be banished from the column with a clip of ammunition; this was almost tantamount to a death sentence, for the Japanese had announced publicly they would not take prisoners from the Chindits because we were guerillas and therefore outside the conventions of war (I have no idea why they bothered to make this announcement, they showed no reverence for the conventions anyway). For the Gurkhas any public punishment was severe; they are proud of their reputation, therefore particularly sensitive to public disgrace for any offence against the martial code. Apart from the so-called flogging – a few gentle swipes on the shirt – we also handcuffed men on the march, and tied them to a tree in a prominent position for a few hours when we harboured, something like the stocks – but the problem of discipline was never serious with us, the offences were of a minor nature, and less than a dozen occurred altogether. An expedition of such a nature seems to band men more closely together so that there is a stronger resistance to any selfish act that makes one's comrades suffer. Looting was an exception to the code however; the pressure of hunger and the cover of a black night combined into an irresistible temptation.

Punishment to some looters recoiled from the loot itself. More than one person unwisely assumed that the lump he managed to prise out of a broken or deliberately cut package was edible. We once found soap with tooth marks, and a discarded bottle that had held hydrogen peroxide and not the foretasted rum. The worst incident concerned gelignite, involved on two occasions to my knowledge. The first was when I myself found a stick in a patch of wild strawberries where, sadly, not a single fruit was yet ripe enough to eat; the gelignite had been bitten through, tooth marks plainly visible on the piece tossed among the strawberry leaves. The brown sticks certainly look toothsome and, more important in the dark, have the feel of an edible sweet of some kind – marzipan perhaps, or a bar of delicious fudge.

On the second occasion some Shans noted that soft malleable feel and they did actually eat the stuff. There were four of them, they happened to pass one afternoon with a pony train as I was lining up the fires on a taungya for a drop that night. They had a cargo of pipe bowls, bamboo cups, homemade dahs and knives, which they intended to barter in China, for salt so they said – far more likely for opium; we decided they were not spies, but felt it wiser to hold them until after the drop. They volunteered to help collect with their ponies, and seemed at the time to have played a perfectly honest and useful part in the collection. We gave them some cigarettes in thanks and they settled down to spend the rest of the night in our midst – we had called a halt to collection about 3 am deciding to leave the rest till daylight. I was sound asleep, wrapped inside the blanket against the cold mountain air, when awakened by agonized screams. I shouted at them angrily, thinking they were frightened about something, but the screams persisted so we went over to see what was wrong. We found three of them writhing in agony, one still screaming, their mouths were foam-flecked and the trouble was obviously something internal but we had no idea what, and the column medical officer was ten miles away somewhere in the jungle. By dawn the three were dead, and it was when we discovered a stick of dynamite nearby that the survivor admitted by signs the others had been eating it; from his grimace he had either found the dynamite distasteful or, less likely, their action immoral. I would not advise anyone to eat gelignite to commit suicide, far better take it with a detonator and be explosively killed – those poor wretches had an awful death.

Most of the Shans we found in the hills were there for genuine trading reasons, Japanese spies were the exception, but because these did exist we had to treat all non-Kachins with caution. Many itinerants were engaged in the perfectly legitimate illegitimate opium trade. One such group had wretched ill-luck in an encounter with us. When stopped they eagerly displayed the cargo in their baskets, it was tea they had just obtained by barter from over the Chinese border. Tea was attractive to us, there was none in the K rations, and when the Shans noted this interest they offered to sell some – thereby proving themselves innocuous traders. To their dismay however we decided to take the whole twelve baskets; it was clear they would have liked to renege on the bargain but the Kachin guides were watching them so suspiciously as they talked that they finally accepted the money and departed. The reason for their sorrowful expressions, and hasty departure, became clear next day when in transferring the tea to mule-panniers it was discovered that the baskets all had false bottoms, and opium secreted within them. Its hill value was over a thousand pounds, the tea-price they received was less than forty.

It was intended that we should establish temporary blocks on the Bhamo-Myitkyena road, and at a Kachin village on a ridge above it we were given detailed information about the Japanese convoys using the road, and the regular daily passage of signal vehicles. This particular village had prepared its own defences against the Japanese. They had only two ancient guns, both of them muzzle-loaders, and the plan was to blast off at the enemy as they rounded a bend in the track just short of the village. There was a five-foot drop into bushes on the downslope, so the tendency would be for the

Japanese to dive down there into cover. But it was a dreadful trap. Hidden in and about the bushes were hundreds of deadly punjis – bamboo stakes sharpened to needle point and fire-hardened, firmly planted in the ground. These are fearsome weapons. Anyone diving off the path into that trap would be punctured by more than a single punji; lucky victims would be pierced through a vital organ straight to death, the less fortunate would survive for an appalling time after the excruciating impact. The Kachins planned to abandon the village once the first group of Japanese had impaled themselves in the punji trap – it would be burnt to the ground anyway by the Japanese punitive party.

Our first ambushes on the road had only limited success. We worked in conjunction with 94 column and the objective was to blow two bridges that were some five miles apart; (Japanese signal trucks patrolled the road daily and it was hoped to catch them passing in that area then blow the bridges immediately afterwards.) Peter Cane with 94 column had the northern bridge, Peter Wilmot the southern one.

The rest of our column went on to a hideout in the hills, but when the Colonel belatedly thought of the possibility that a large convoy might be trapped within the two blocks he sent me back to plan an air strike for such an event. I spent some time discussing this with Peter Wilmot down on the road where he was then preparing his signal-truck ambush. He had put himself up on the bank opposite the planned ambush point, and fifty yards further on was a bend from which the Bren Gun would fire *only* when the truck reached his position. To ensure they did not fire early he sent up a curious marker just below his own position. Growing there was a clump of the thick thornless shrub the Burmese call *bizat*, and this was now in false synthetic flower – from a white-blossomed feathery cassia tree nearby Peter had broken off two flowering branches and stuck them into the *bizat* bush, which now looked like some monstrous bug with wavering antennae.

The outcome of all his careful planning was a disappointment, however. The signal truck came bowling along the road as expected, everyone trigger-tense waiting for it to reach the decorated bush – above which Peter himself was sited with five men – but then it suddenly screeched to a stop. About fifty yards short of him and the marker. We never discovered why (I suggested the driver was a keen botanist, spotted the fake hybrid at once and realized a trap – and Peter actually worried for a time he might have so blundered). Anyway it stopped short, the men began to get out casually, and still the obedient Bren did not open fire. The Japanese seemed about to amble back along the road when Peter, determined not to let the opportunity completely pass, grabbed a rifle and opened fire. He missed. The Japanese scrambled for cover, returned the fire for a moment but when the Bren finally opened up they abandoned the fight and bolted. One Japanese soldier was wounded, as was one Gurkha. The truck was burned. Peter was furious about the confusion.

'We should have killed them all,' he said – not in bloodthirsty relish but in the harsh self-criticism of a dissatisfied professional.

Peter Cane's ambush further up the road also had difficulty opening fire. Their problem was caused not by their signal truck stopping but by everyone being so surprised by the advent of a vehicle that they simply gaped at it as it went past. However they had already planted an anti-tank mine a little further on and it, being inanimately devoid of curiosity, blew up as primed when the truck passed over it. The ambush party then came alive and opened fire, two Japanese were killed and one captured.

We kept the captured man for several weeks. He marched with us in the column quite happily – he thought K rations wondrous things, just as we had at one time – and made no effort to commit hari-kari or escape. Tiny Langford and I later took him on our recce to China to send out from there.

Before he left he gave me a letter of thanks in spidery script which I kept with my note book as a possible insurance in case of being captured alive by the Japanese; to ensure that it didn't say something like 'Kill this bastard – he insulted our emperor' I took the precaution of checking with Corporal Chang, our interpreter of Japanese script, that it was a genuine thank-you note.

Had we remained we could have harassed the enemy for months at these blocks but we were ordered back into the border area to help the disorganized Dah Force. It took a day or two to solve their problems, and then we stayed on in the mountains for a supply drop. This one remains clear in mind for the glimpse of wild life on that particular taungya.

In the warm stillness that afternoon, the preparations complete, I was looking down across the site when a movement on the mountainside across the valley caught my eye. The crown of a big outstanding tree seemed to be shivering, then a dark shape appeared on a long dangling branch and ran straight on down it like a fast-flowing drop of liquid and continued on into the air, a falling curve with a long tail streaming behind in flight, brownish in colour, not a gibbon or langur – some other type of monkey. It fell with a green splash into foliage below and others followed, perhaps ten in all, with the launching branch flicking up and down like an angler's rod as each brown shape flowed down to the tip and fell.

It was often like this on the drop site. There you did have a chance to discover the evidence that a wild life exists in Burma; on the march with a blundering column everything is scared to flight, only the first few in the leading platoon ever catch a glimpse of native fauna. On the drop site however I was often with only a few men of the rifle platoon and many hours I spent quietly in the mountains with the site all prepared, waiting in the still afternoon for the collection platoons to come and join us, or in the moonlight waiting for the aircraft to arrive. Then, as you rested stilly on the site, you would sometimes see the life of the jungle. Lying at the top of a taungya one afternoon I saw a porcupine move across the corner of the clearing, flowing over the broken ground like a sack being pulled on an unseen cord, and I have seen gibbons bounding through the trees with silver tail fur glistening in the westering sun. In the low hills near the Shweli one night a barking deer came so close we could hear its actual footfalls, and that same night I saw a thousand flying foxes go flitting across the face of the moon. East of Bhamo one morning I had a cuckoo settle in a tree almost directly above my head, cock its head and look down at me with ruby eye, then unperturbed begin its sad song, ashy head dipping over the barred breast with each throbbing call. I have seen a golden oriole snatch a caterpillar dangling from a fig leaf and then beat off its fur before consuming it, have watched a dove-grey moth with a wingspan the length of my hand quivering as if in ecstasy on the pale lilac flower of a buddleia, and one afternoon I imitated so well the flutey whistle of a little green parrot that he flew down closer to the tree right beside me and kept answering me back until I suddenly stepped away from the trunk whereupon he gave a startled squawk and shot away like a bright green arrow through the dark fig trees.

Then came the night of 28th March. I had saved my rum ration to drink after the road action and had it that night with the two RAF sergeants as we sat in a little dip in the hills, relaxed from duty, no messages to send. Lying on a blanket, and looking up at a night sky prickled with glistening stars, we were listening to some music on the set, 'Dreaming of a White Christmas' – listened right to the end in sentimental mood before flicking to another station where there was routine news from London, then a single word from the announcer jerked the three of us up into stilled shock. We looked at one another to confirm the unbelievable. He said something like this:

'Mr So-and-so, speaking in the House of Commons today,

referred to the forces under the command of the late General Wingate when he asked . . .'

The *late*!

I told the Colonel and for several hours we tried to get through to base or to any other column, but without success. Then early next morning we had contact with 94 and they confirmed the news. Wingate had been killed in an air crash two days earlier. The immediate response of the adjutant typified perhaps the general reaction.

'What will become of us now, I wonder?' he asked.

10

We were now on the edge of the Chinese border but in that remote and roadless mountain area east of Bhamo the border line of the map has no trace in reality. No differences were marked on the steep wooded ridges that were squeezed together in the east, the tracks coursed up and down the same jungle and taungya and villages, the people were still subtly divided into tribes and not nationalities, they knew nothing of border lines between entities we called China and Burma only the demarcation areas between their village and those of their neighbours. We were lucky to enjoy the friendship of these people, we could walk openly into their villages, secure in the knowledge that they would know about and warn of any Japanese in the vicinity.

On one unforgettable day we had both the best and the worst of the hills. We were heading for the Taiping River where, so a villager told us, the bridge was 'not all destroyed,' and when we started out it was such a perfect morning of sparkling light and fresh new air and glistening dew it made you think of the opening of the Pastoral Symphony, all those lilting trilling melodies running one into the other that Beethoven describes as 'Happy feelings on arrival in the country.' And the going was just as good – a light pack and a track weaving gently down the mountain ridge in a kind descent towards the river.

There were few trees, the breeze was cool on our faces, and at times we could see a flash of sunlight from a bend in the Taiping down where the plain flared out from the foothills to be lost in the haze. The path passed through a fertile little valley with the permanent paddy fields covered in grass and a small clear stream bubbling along beside the wide smooth track. The valley was two or three miles in length, had no concentrated village, but all around on the slopes of the cleared hills were the golden-brown huts of the Yawyins or Kachins or Lisu – I don't know which particular tribe lived there. A little further on we came upon two red and white bungalows with purple bougainvillea now smothering the veranda railings, and between the two were growing banana, papaya and lemon trees, with a white picket fence around the grove, a Police Post now deserted but still able to create the picture of starched uniforms, white-plumed hats and bugle salutes – officialdom in all its Eastern pomp and splendour.

Then, eventually, the Taiping River. It is not one of the great rivers of Burma but the short passage down from 8,000 feet is severely restricted so it is a foaming turbulent torrent in the mountainous area where we intended to cross by the footbridge that was 'not all destroyed'. That turned out to be a fair description. It was an old suspension bridge strung across a gorge some fifty feet above the river which went crashing and bounding through dark polished rocks like an ebullient Dalmatian dashing to greet its master. When the Chinese retreated across it in the 1942 debacle, they had little materiel left and the only way they could destroy it behind them was by firing the wooden planking. They were not entirely successful; only a five-yard length in the centre had burned out completely. The Kachins had since filled this in with a few logs bound together; this was quite adequate for their casual light-footed passage but for us and the mules it was a far more serious matter. I sat with Tiny Langford watching the column make the crossing, a long process because the bridge would only take three people and one mule at a time, even then it swayed and dipped in a manner that clearly alarmed the mules and also, covertly, most of us humans.

Tiny and I were sitting in a car during this observation, a battered old 1930 model Essex open tourer, part of the detritus left by the Chinese or civilians in the retreat. How the cars – there were three of them – ever got there was a mystery; they could never have travelled over the hill tracks we had just used, we could only assume that the track leading down to the plain must have been widened temporarily to get them up there. Why they had ever made such an effort was equally mystifying, for the bridge in its original state had never been wide enough for a car, and certainly there was no road on the other side, only the most precipitous track we were to meet in the whole campaign.

The magnificent morning had ended – now we had the appalling afternoon. When talking afterwards about the cruel hill climbs we had endured everyone would at once point to that immediately after the Taiping as our worst punishment. We had been higher, the climb was only about four thousand feet, but it was by far the steepest and there was little respite. By the time we had reached the top that day more than sixty men had been left by the track because they could go no further – the majority did not rejoin us till the following morning.

The animals suffered too. Time and again that awful afternoon we had to unload when the passage was too steep for them, haul up the charging-motor or the radio by the loading straps, then load up again and set the mules at the slope once more. There is an axiom that a mule can take its load up any slope a man can climb without use of his hands, but at times that day we had to use our hands and we were far too maltreated ourselves to let the mules escape on such a mere technicality, so we drove them beyond theory. Many of them achieved the breakthrough. They would do it by bounding – first resisting the pull of the muleteer by crouching back on their rear legs, and then as if suddenly released from a springhold they would hurl themselves upwards with a thrashing and clattering of hooves and legs and harness, the driver jumping aside as he flung away the lead. And in the column ahead we listened for the warning shouts, and however exhausted we may have been we still jerked around to check and then hurled ourselves aside to let the breakaway go bounding past, dilated nostrils, mad wide eyes, foaming flanks and flailing lead. I saw one fall with its load, the slope so steep it toppled almost directly backwards on to the load, somehow regained its feet and then waited patiently and unhurt whilst we reassembled the load on the ground and dragged it ourselves up the bad patch. And there were many bad patches.

You could not see the end of the mountain, even in the open stretches, for if you tried to raise your head that much the weight of your pack would topple you backwards. Near the end a misty rain enwrapped us for a time, enough to wet the track thoroughly and so give a final turn of the screw; you would lunge forward a step then slither back to lose half your hard-won gain, and then you would curse the rain and the mud and the fate that had landed you on that awful mountainside. When you fell it was sometimes preferable to stay down on a bad patch, you could make almost as good progress by clawing at roots and rocks, hauling yourself up on all fours till the slope eased slightly. It was hard to beat down the despair that surged as you raised yourself upright after such a beastly clawing effort and look up as high as you dared to see the track still continuing straight up to block out the sky and you had to keep saying to yourself 'I'll beat the bastard . . . beat the bastard . . . beat the bastard' as a driving slogan, over and over again the words throbbing in your brain, until at last you won through to the top. And on arrival there I stayed upright for a moment, leaning against a tree, breath rasping through parched throat, just savouring the victory, before easing off the pack at last and then crumbling down to finish cruciform on the muddy ground.

The next afternoon there was an unusually sharp disagreement between me and the Colonel. The selection of drop sites had by this time become a constant source of friction, for our interests were at variance. His primary concern was to avoid discovery by the Japanese, mine was to try and collect every item dropped by the aircraft; his ideal site would have been impenetrable jungle where we might collect a single parachute or two, mine would have been open paddy fields down on the plain where Japanese forces might well have been able to get to us before we had collected anything at all. So we each had to compromise. The trouble was that the Colonel would not adjust to a compromise once made (and to be honest I would, where possible, cheat on mine). He would rush away so quickly from what he thought a dangerous site that half the parachutes would be left dangling in the trees, he would shift the DZ at the last moment from open hillside to the valley below and so force the pilots to drop at a height that meant half the parachutes floated away far beyond recovery, and he would sometimes have the fires doused the instant a drop finished to leave us stumble about all the black night trying to collect.

So I was always having to devise stratagems to bypass his orders. I lied to him once about the true location of a site, another time when he rushed away he allowed a group of us stay behind and wait for what I had said was a special call from base – which never arrived, of course, as we hunted down seven more parachutes – and for on-site problems with him we would carry out his orders on the rare occasions he was actually with us but then stop doing so the moment he left – only very rarely was he on the drop site during actual delivery, so the risk of being caught out was very small.

On this occasion I had gone ahead as usual with a rifle section to decide upon a site, and the best I could find was a black patch on a western slope where the taungya had been fired very recently. I saw it first in the late afternoon and felt sure that if the Colonel visited it we would have a problem. It was nakedly exposed. Standing on the crest that afternoon I had a magnificent view of the plain spread out like a coloured map below, white stitching of a tree-lined road, grids of fields, green pasture, mirrors of flooded paddy, and the dark horizon-line of the Irrawaddy with hazy blue hills against the pale western sky – all quite innocent, but also in the picture was the flecked blob of Bhamo about thirty miles away which I felt sure the Colonel would descry instantly if he visited us. So, to stifle possible objections, I sent the signal to base at once committing us to the site. He did come that day. I rushed over to meet him and babbled about the problems caused by the heavy deposit of ash, how it would force us to take loads off site to break them up – did he think we should move the loads complete back to harbour? I could not distract him however. He kept peering across at the plain, and finally the inevitable question came:

'Where is Bhamo, and that Jap airfield?'

I pointed out a smudge that was a good bit further to the north than the actuality but he was no fool with a map and corrected me quickly. There it was! Far too close. The site would have to be changed. I told him we were stuck with the selection, the signal had been sent, anyway there was no alternative that I had been able to find. And did it really matter if anyone saw our fires? I asked. At this time of the year, with the rains now imminent, there were fires all over the hills as the taungyas were burnt off, so even if the Japanese were able to discern our tiny fires from 'fifty' miles away they would obviously ignore them. The argument penetrated, but he still kept peering towards the distant threat of Bhamo as he questioned me about the search for an alternative site, then finally he asked the time the drop had been arranged. I told him midnight.

'Then send out a signal for Direct Air Support against Bhamo airfield at midnight tonight.'

This was preposterous. It was the sort of order he would abruptly produce and shock you into incredulous response, the result of which was to lose the argument out of hand. But it was difficult not to ridicule such a nonsense. We had two types of air support for offensive operations; Direct Air Support was an attack by fighters or bombers on the same enemy force we were engaging at that moment, and Indirect was against an enemy target which might interfere with an assault we were launching – to ask for DAS against an airfield thirty miles away from where we intended to have a supply drop had nothing to do with either of these categories. I tried to discuss the subject calmly, to win him over, correcting first what I called a slip of the tongue in asking for Direct as opposed to Indirect Support.

'No, I want DAS,' he insisted.

'But they'll think we are attacking the airfield.'

He was quite happy about this, saying it would ensure the field would then be bombed. But it was crazy. We had never, even in training, planned for DAS on a night operation – even the daytime ones required markers and identification and timing particulars, all sorts of planning details. When I protested at such a deceit he said:

'Let them think what they like so long as we get the air attack.'

This was the same irresponsible attitude as shown towards signal priorities. The result of such disrespect was that genuine calls for urgency or action lost their value, and as with the boy who cried 'wolf' we too may well have suffered ourselves a little later when we had a perfect target for air attack but could not get any response to our calls. That afternoon I persisted in argument, pointing out that it was part of my job to advise him on air support; perhaps because he knew he was on a rickety base he did not immediately lose patience but tried to justify his action on the grounds that the Japanese might send up aircraft to bomb and machine-gun us whilst the drop was actually in progress (he ignored the peril to the unarmed supplying aircraft in this fantasy.) I told him the RAF knew far more about Bhamo airfield than we did; they would be covering such targets by aerial reconnaissance practically every day of the year – anyway it was most unlikely the Japanese had even a single fighter aircraft at Bhamo, for the field was far too vulnerable to attack. But it was waste of talk and temper, he was impervious to reason, and the argument ended with the same old closure:

'That's an order, Pat. You get on to it now. And tell me their reply.'

Unfortunately the radio was working, messages were coming in as we talked, so the obvious evasion was not open to me. What I did was to adjust the standard message with a preamble:

'COLONEL MORRIS HAS ORDERED THIS RE-QUEST FOR DAS ON BHAMO AIRFIELD WHILST WE ARE HAVING A SD TONIGHT . . .'

and then followed the standard DAS request code. The only reaction I can think for the surprising reply is that the staff were skilled at diplomatic handling of such differences in the field, for they sent back a signal to say they would give us 'strong air support' – without saying where, when or the type. The Colonel later flourished this message at me triumphantly, accepting it at its face value, but certainly no aircraft bombed Bhamo airfield that night. And we had a placid supply drop from which we collected all but three parachutes. We even recovered our mail that evening.

Stanley never had this sort of problem with his supply drops – luckily, for he would have worried himself to a breakdown in obeying such freakish orders. Peter Cane, the commander of 94, did not subscribe to the belief that the Japanese forces were always massed nearby in readiness to attack, were scanning the hills for the wisp of smoke that would betray our position. When 94 had a supply drop they would not leave the zone until they had collected every possible parachute, often blasting down trees to complete a recovery; had they been threatened by Japanese interference on the site then Peter Cane, far from abandoning it, would have rejoiced at the convenience of having the enemy come at him rather than being forced to hunt about on the plains searching for him.

This difference between the sister columns reflected the difference between the two commanders; we in 49 column, commanded nominally by Russel but in effect by the Colonel, always seemed to be withdrawing into the wings, whereas 94 were always rushing into action led by the energetic and spirited Peter Cane. A typical example of this difference in command occurred in the week after we crossed the Taiping, when we met together in the mountains north of the river. Immediately down below us on the edge of the plain was the village of Myothit, where there was a bamboo bridge over the wide shallow mature-version of the Taiping River, and two miles away to the north along the road was another village called Kunlow where the chief was a notorious Japanese agent who had been responsible for the execution of at least six Kachin headmen and their families. It was decided that Peter Cane's column would attack Myothit, and we would deal with the Japanese and their allies in Kunlow. I happened to make contact with Peter's column the afternoon before the attack, for I was off looking for a light-plane strip, and we chatted about their part in the operation; the plan was that they would move in at dawn, deal with the dozen or so resident Japanese troops, then destroy the rice mill and the bridge. They intended to put a block south of the bridge so as to stop any Japanese reinforcements which might attempt to come up from the big garrison at Bhamo some twenty miles away but they had no need to worry about the northern road as we would be up there attacking Kunlow. We had arranged for Direct Air Support – but in the event it never came.

So at dawn on 9th April Peter's column moved into the village and captured the place at the cost of only a few rounds of ammunition. The resident Japanese troops happened to have left the night before and the few Burmese levies surrendered after token resistance of a single burst of fire. The bridge was destroyed, the machinery of the rice mill wrecked by explosives, everyone crammed their packs and pockets with as much rice as they could carry and the remaining ten tons was spilled from the bags and the villagers told to help themselves. In the midst of this mayhem there came the sound of firing from north of the village, up towards Kunlow, and it was assumed our column was meeting rather more opposition than they themselves had encountered. In fact, we were miles away in the hills. We had never launched our planned attack on Kunlow.

Fortunately Peter Cane had not entirely ignored that northern road. Either because he had doubts about the Colonel's strength of purpose, or thought it possible some Japanese might try to bolt south to escape our assault, he did decide to put a section of his own men up there just in case. This group set up a perfunctory block and waited for the sight of fellow Gurkhas from our column to come marching down the road to contact them, but in fact the Japanese troops up there in Kunlow were having a peaceful day; there was a garrison of about twenty men and they had no worries at all that morning even when the telephone line to Myothit went dead – cut by 94 column. They assumed that the signal truck would deal with the fault in due course. But later the sound of the demolition explosions did seem to call for investigation so they sent down a lorry with a dozen men and a machine gun crew. This group ran straight into the astonished Gurkhas at the road block. Their lorry was their doom; on foot they would surely have been mistaken for the expected Gurkhas of our column and may have escaped. The lorry however was hailed with fire. Within the next few minutes ten of the Japanese had been killed and the remaining two escaped into the bush.

When I rejoined our column at the rendezvous I learned that the Colonel had changed his mind about attacking Kunlow just the previous night. He was not the least upset when I told how 94 had believed we were covering the northern flank, telling me I was mistaken about the plan, or had been misinformed; the two operations had been entirely independent, he said, and the fact that 94 had put out a road block on the north showed they had understood this. It was one point of view. Another interpretation of course was that the northern road block was established because 94 had no faith the Colonel would comply with our part of the joint plan. It seemed to many in our column that the Colonel should at least have got a message through to Peter Cane telling him of the change of plan. It has to be admitted that 94 column had reason to feel aggrieved about the unhelpful behaviour of our column in that first month . . . it was only by good fortune, and the bad aim of our Vickers machine-gunners, that we did not kill many of them about a week after this incident.

We did finally move down to the road again to establish a block, but although we waited a full five days not a single vehicle appeared. The destruction of the bridge at Myothit would obviously have stopped anything moving up from the south but it was surprising that none of the Japanese garrisons to the north came down to challenge us or repair the telegraph lines. They must have known we were there, must have known about the action at Myothit. But no one came to molest us.

I spent most of one day down the road with Peter Wilmot, and nothing could have been more peaceful – much to his impatience. He had established a position on a bend where the hill jungle thinned out, with patches of scrub and bamboo taking over the spaces. It was noticeably hotter than up in the hills, the vegetation was drier and crackled underfoot, and the road was bordered with many of the common flowers you saw in England – some honeysuckle which seemed to be without scent, white-flowering convolvulus, violets, and a scattering of willow-herb. The heat was accentuated by the pinging of a coppersmith bird from the nearby hillside, a sound that always reminded me of the blacksmith's shop down below our home in Australia, when as a child I used to hear the ringing sound of hammer on anvil all through the still heat of summer afternoons. The only birds I actually saw down on the road that day were two of the ubiquitous bee-eaters, the green Burmese variety, which kept flitting up and down the dry *chaung* in that strange flutter-and-glide flight; then in the early afternoon when we were sitting up beside the gun-post a column of jungle fowl paraded past us along the edge of the road, the cock strutting proud with his metallic blue thighs and orange tail, the dull hens following untidily behind and scratching at the earth to chase after the roused insects then having to scurry to catch up with the rest of the brood.

The death of Wingate had resulted in Lentaigne taking over command, being duly promoted to Major-General for the job. His job as titular head of our group passed to the most senior Colonel of the brigade – who turned out to be our own Colonel Morris. When we came back up empty-handed from the road to rejoin the head-quarters party the Colonel had little red tabs of Brigadier rank already attached to his shirt. Apparently he had got hold of a piece of red parachute and chopped two shoulder tabs out of it which his orderly had affixed to his shirt. He had now become 'the General Sahib'. It was gently amusing, for a while, to see how much he enjoyed his new rank and began to act the role – calling Staff Conferences, poring over maps, despatching imperious signals to the other columns and to base. Portentious decisions were announced about trivia. Rank had to be utilized.

He brought back to mind the action of a Group Captain during our escape after the Far East campaign. There were several hundred of us in a cargo boat with just two lifeboats, Java and fallen, and the likelihood was that we would be sunk before we even got out of sight of the coast. The senior Group Captain, having assumed command issued an imperious decree to solve the insoluble – how to survive an enemy attack. Every officer was given charge of a group of men in a particular section of the hold and immediately after our ship had been bombed or shelled to destruction he was to join his men there in the hold and (to quote the memorable phrase exactly): 'supervise the construction of rafts from wreckage which will then be available.'

Our new Brigadier did manage to conceive a need for such a wild contingency plan from me. He asked me one day about this time if I had considered the possibility of an aircraft crashing on site during a supply drop. What would I do? I told him I had no idea. How do you know what you will do in an emergency until you have done it? He went on about it however, so I quickly agreed it was a most important subject. I promised to give it studious and urgent consideration . . . some day.

It was now mid-April and the clouds were beginning to pile up every afternoon against the hills, great turmoils of cumulus which from the ridges you could see swirling and writhing in violent activity as they surged upwards in the peak heat of the day, sometimes bursting into rain and so blocking off our aircraft lifeline. We were now back again to a third of the proper scale of rations, just one pack each day, plus an occasional cup of rice when we managed to buy any from the Kachins, but this did nothing to remedy the deficiency in our diet. The strain and privation were now beginning to take their toll – nine men had already died on the trail. We were tired, hungry, filthy – and above all, lousy. Every night you would feel the faint tickling movements of lice coming out of the seams and starting off in transit for the foraging grounds of the midriff; however hard you tried to hunt them down during the day you never killed them all. Many of us had developed a good growth of beard by now and some, particularly the heavy smokers, had yellow stains about the lips that added to the general seedy appearance of the whole column. The first showers of the imminent monsoon – called the mango showers – hit us one night at 7,000 feet where there was no escape from the cold driving rain on the bare exposed slope, and two men died during that black night. Next morning I watched the bedraggled column pass along the muddy track under the pregnant grey clouds, the faces of the men were as gloomy as the sky, and when I joined in finally with Peter Wilmott in the rear platoon even he, whom no circumstance seemed to dismay, merely nodded in silence as I fell into step beside him.

Next morning something occurred which nearly brought an abrupt end to my own part in the campaign. That previous day had turned out as bad as the gloomy start had presaged. It rained intermittently, the radio mule kicked me in the ribs when we were re-loading after a fall, and the radio itself had landed edge-sharp on my foot. I was limping with pain all that afternoon up the muddy slippery track and, though there were precious few rations left, the rain had soaked so heavily into the canvas pack that the load was as cruel as ever, a physical incubus weighing down the body as well as the mind and the spirit. We lost our way and finally stopped where we happened to be when resolution wavered, the search for the planned bivouac was abandoned and we slept under dripping trees in mud and cold blackness. At first light I went to a bush on the perimeter for a morning squat; I moved away afterwards to stand erect and was just clipping my belt when the sky went black. I had collapsed.

When I recovered I lay still for several minutes trying to discover my identity and situation. I tried to get to my feet but found my right leg almost useless. A Gurkha rifleman saw me in difficulties, helped me back to our position and there presently our Doctor Bannerjee, a genial and excitable Bengali, decided I had had a stroke and said I should be sent out at once to hospital. Fortunately this was not possible, I had to stay until such time as we could prepare a strip to get out our sick and wounded. The Brigadier said that in the meantime I should travel on a horse. This treatment however lasted only one day, then I refused to mount the beast again. I have never been attached to horses, we kept one at home in

Australia when we were boys but although my brothers were fond of dashing about on old Binghi I preferred to stick to the bicycle – it never pigrooted me off and sent me crashing on to the paddock fence as Binghi had once done. Moreover for an unskilled rider in my wretched physical condition a horse offered pain, not comfort, we were all so thin there was little cushion of flesh on our buttocks and my skin was wobbled red-raw against the haunch bones by that first day's ride. I rejoined the marchers, but allowed the horse to carry my pack. However, as I continued to feel and look just the same as before the incident the talk about me being sent out was presently dropped, and a week later the pack was up on my back once more: not by order, but there were so many men who were really unfit and totally unable to carry their packs that it required a far tougher hide than even I possessed to insist on the continued right to this concession.

I never did discover what went wrong with my body that day by the stream.

II

In mid-April Lazum Tang, a Kachin officer who spoke perfect English, joined us for a time and came with me twice on site-hunts. Lazum Tang did not have the usual stocky build of the hillmen, he was tall and slim, looked like a clean-shaven suntanned Errol Flynn. He had come in with Dah Force, the group of a dozen or so which was supposed to raise a guerilla force to work with us, but their trials with the Japanese kept dragging us back into the hills to assist them instead of getting on with our planned task of attacking enemy convoys on the road.

The day after he joined us I went off with Lazum Tang on a recce, and that afternoon we finished in a village where for the first time since leaving the CHOWRINGEE area I slept under shelter. It was a typical hill village, situated almost on top of a ridge, about a dozen houses in all. Just before the first house, by a small patch of tobacco, was the usual nat shrine; this one was a bamboo tripod about five feet high, and on top was a little wooden cage containing a ball of cooked rice and some white tobacco flowers as an offering. The nats are guardian spirits whose influence is apparent throughout Burma; it is important to keep them happy with homage and gifts, for they are capricious spirits and can do great harm if irritated.

The headman had been warned of our advent and he met us near the shrine, obviously dressed for the occasion. He was wearing over his tatty grey lungyi a long cerise-coloured Chinese coat, richly embroidered, and there was a large ornamental dah in decorated scabbard at his waist. When Lazum Tang introduced me I said the only Chingpaw word I knew: 'Kaja'e' (it means something like 'Good-day'). I think he smiled, but it was not easy to discern his expression because he had a huge scar on his cheek that kept one eye partly closed, and gave him a permanent conspiratorial leer. He led us up through the village, past two girls pounding rice with large staves in a shallow canoe-shaped trough, and a pig ran squealing across in front of us chased by three small children, scattering some chickens in a squawking flutter.

The chief took us up to his house where five women greeted us briefly, the younger ones with giggles, the older pair more sedately. The Kachins rarely, if ever, wash their bodies or clothing, there is a sort of genial scruffiness about their appearance that is attractive because so artless, but on this occasion the older women had obviously prepared themselves in special dress, smocks of some coarsely woven cloth; one had a triple-row of those silver cupolas of hammered rupee coins around her neck, and the other a string of rough jade pieces, mostly the prized pea-green colour, hanging down to her waist – the famous jade mines of Mogaung were only about fifty miles away. The younger women wore home-woven skirts with the Aztec-type zigzag patterns of orange and scarlet and yellows, the colours dulled from lack of water, their heads uncovered and hair twined into pigtails. When we entered the house they produced bamboo cups and one of them filled this with cool *sapa* (or *zaku*, the Kachin rice-beer) pouring it skilfully from a four-feet length of bamboo almost as wide as her own waist.

The house itself, raised above the ground, was about sixty feet long. It had a heavy thatch roof, floor of plaited bamboo which bounced and squeaked when anyone moved, and along one dark side were four alcoves like horse-stalls, separated by head-high plaited screens; these occupied about a quarter of the floor area, the rest was clear except for two separate fireplaces. The interior was blackened with the

158

smoke of years from head height up to the gloom of the thatched roof, and in the rising smoke the festoons of soot waved lazily like seaweed responding to subtle underwater currents. Family treasures were strewn about the walls, barely visible in the gloom – long strings of amber beads, a leather shield, muzzle loader and powder bag, copper pot with lid attached by a metal chain, crossbow and quivers of arrows, two monkey skins and a large willow-pattern china platter. At each end of the house was a porch under the overhanging eaves, the rear one covered a pen in which hens and pigs were kept. The house itself and most of the things within it were derived entirely from the bamboo plant.

The bamboo and the coconut plant must surely be the two supreme botanical gifts that nature has provided for humanity. No other plants, not even the cereals, approach the range of benefits these two can provide. For most people in the Far East life without the bamboo would be inconceivable. The Kachin makes his house out of it, he makes knives, forks, spoons, cups and jugs, twine, flutes, weapons, hats, ladders and needles. He eats the young shoots, uses the stem as a water pipe or fuel, feeds leaves to his buffalo, uses strips to grill meat, weaves them into baskets and he can write with them on paper made out of the plant. Life in the hills would be hard without bamboo.

This particular village chief was a man of some importance, a *duwa*, one who ruled over six villages in the area. He was in his fifties, lean and wiry; one of the elderly women was his wife, the other the wife of his dead brother, the three girls his daughters. We squatted on the matting floor and continued drinking sapa, talking about the war as the women prepared the meal. They boiled the rice in an iron cauldron and added pieces of chicken meat; they showed me other ingredients – these included ginger and chilli and tamarind – and the whole rice dish was then put between leaves on the fire embers. They had prepared separately a tuber that looked like the taro I knew in the Pacific, called *panyu* – it was

sweeter in taste than taro, closer to a yam. When they finally
served the meal it was as a pressed mound of the rice dish for
each of us, and beside it on a large leaf was the *panyu*. It was a
delicious variation from the K rations, and the cool sapa was
kept flowing to douse the chilli fires.

Our party went on until after midnight. We drank much of
the gentle sapa – the chief must have got through over a
gallon – as we talked about the hazards and the delights of life
in the Kachin hills, and it was when we were talking about his
dead brother that I made a surprising discovery. His brother
had been killed by a fall from a tree just after he had come
back from the 1914–18 war and I asked, through Lazum
Tang, where he had been fighting. The chief replied to me
direct, as if assuming everyone in the world would know the
famous battle.

'Kalee-kalee,' he said.

When I looked blank he repeated it, distinctly, as if to
insist I must know of it. Lazum Tang was equally mystified. I
kept repeating aloud 'Kalee-kalee', but the sound struck no
response in memory. The Chief suddenly called out and
presently one of the girls came over with a scrap of rough
paper, flicked off a strip of bamboo from the firewood and
burnt the end, then wrote out the mysterious battle in capital
letters:

GALIPALI.

Gallipoli! She had been to a mission school, and then
pronounced it recognizably closer than her father. I had
never heard of Kachins fighting at Gallipoli, but they must
have done so, for both he and the girl pounced on the word
'Turks' as they realized contact had at last been established,
and the chief also produced the war medals carefully wrapped in a piece of that striped cloth. I never discovered where
or how a Kachin regiment became involved in that Anzac
battlefield, but assume they were probably attached to the
British group that landed at Suvla Bay.

The drink and the talk and the pleasant company that night made me oblivious of the crippling effect of sitting cross-legged for several hours. When I rose to go to the toilet, which was the wide outside, I promptly collapsed, and this caused great distress to the chief who thought I was already drunk, and so incapable of continuing our party. He was relieved to discover it was merely cramp, and when I returned he had filled my cup to the brim again and we had to drink another toast to 'Kalee-kalee'. I managed to stay sober however, and the party broke up when Lazum Tang persuaded the old man it was time to rest. We slept that night in the warm big room with the fire glowing in the blackness, chickens cawing sleepily and pigs snorting and snuffling in comforting domesticity just outside the doorway to the stars.

The day after our return from this jaunt we were engaged in another action down on the road. The main staging post on the Bhamo-Myitkyena road was at the village of Nalong, about halfway between the two towns, and there the Japanese were reported to have taken over most of the houses and to have built a small barracks, with about a hundred men in the garrison. The road runs along the foothills of a thickly-wooded 3,000 ft high ridge that slopes steeply down to Nalong, and beyond it a small river crossed by a wooden bridge. This bridge was a vital link for the Japanese convoys; we intended to destroy it after the direct attack on the Japanese garrison. A two-pronged assault was planned, our column would sweep down from the steep slope on the northern side, Peter Cane's column would approach across the bridge from the south. We had arranged for air support, which I was to direct, using smoke bombs as markers.

We left our mules and non-combatants ten miles back in a safe harbour among the hills, and set off in the dark pre-dawn hours of April 22nd. It was about six-thirty in the cool clear morning when we crossed the final ridge and a few minutes later, at a spot where the track was exposed, we had our first sight of Nalong. We took a halt there, looking down at the village. The picture is cut into memory with the indelible clarity that shame always contrives for any action in which it is involved.

It was the exciting vision of air combat that had drawn me into the war. It seemed to me that to remain in the Solomon Islands in 1939 would be to miss the chance of a lifetime, the chance to hurl myself about the skies in flashing deadly duel with the enemy; as with Yeats' young Irish airman 'nor law nor duty bade me fight,' it was just that same 'impulse of delight that drove me to that tumult in the clouds' and made death in the skies such a romantically attractive alternative to dull peace in the far Pacific. So, at twenty-two I abandoned the plantation company, tried to join the RAAF on arrival in Sydney but when told there would be at least six months delay sold my birthright for the fare to England – who cared for money and stodgy security? – and joined the RAF the day of arrival in London in December 1939. Nor was the reality so very different from the vision. True I did not get on to fighters, but the Blenheim light bomber was close enough in style, and on that first tour of operations we were always near enough to death for the excitement to be sustained. And the second tour, starting out against North Sea shipping and Dutch airfields, then leading the flight out to doomed Singapore until finally being blasted out of the skies by the Japanese, had always been in the face of furious opposition – streamers of coloured flak, orange bursts that made the aircraft shudder, daylight tracer flowing past as you dived on the ship, explosions of black cloud and stink of cordite, once at night the fiery trail of a friend shot down, and in daylight the scattering of twirling metal when the plane in front was hit by a shell. The fight was fierce, life at risk, the enemy always resisting violently – all just as you had imagined with such tingling anticipation when you came rushing from ten thousand miles away to join the fray.

It was nothing like that at Nalong that day in April 1944 however. When we stopped at that clearing on the ridge and looked down towards the plain the scene was one of idyllic peace. The last remnants of the night mist were being swirled away by the rising sun, and soon the trees emerged clear along the bank, so still they looked like models set down on the edge of that glassy curve of placid water. The thatched roofs of the houses were pale gold in the sparkling light of the morning, a few columns of cigarette-blue smoke rose vertically in the still air above the tranquil village, shivered on meeting the faint breeze at ridge-line and then trailed vaguely towards a zenith of limpid blue sky. I could hear a cock crowing from somewhere in the village, could see a man outside the nearest house cutting wood and only hear the soft thud of his dah when he was halfway up for the next stroke. A woman in the classical pose of arms upright to a terracotta pot on the head moved back towards us from the river then veered away to a figure crouched by an open fire, the smoke swirled about them for a moment before once more it resumed its quivery climb. Not a sign of a Japanese anywhere.

This was the tranquil scene we were about to desecrate, the village we were about to bomb. This was never the sort of war I had dreamed about back in the Pacific, nothing like any target I had ever known as a pilot. When you thought of the death-loaded aircraft now thundering towards the peaceful village you wished you were back in the hills with the mules, miles away somewhere, knowing nothing of what was about to happen. You wanted no part of this sort of thing.

The operation was not only morally disturbing, it was also militarily inept. The air strike was due to start at 1000 hours and when we moved off after that halt on the ridge we still had three hours to get down into our positions, less than a mile away. It should have been plenty of time but unfortunately the Brigadier was with us and in charge, and when we stopped at last to settle the details he took almost two hours

163

coming to a decision – he sent out two separate groups to report back before agreeing to the final positions and allowing the groups to move. He went with the machine-gunners and mortars to check their site but still would not allow me to go, though I was supposed to be actually directing the air support. When finally he did send for me to join them by the mortars I found they were far too remote from the target for my purpose. I had said we would mark with smoke the actual target, the Japanese barracks building, but the mortar officer told me it was well beyond range. He waved impatiently towards the Brigadier, about twenty yards away in his command post:

'He says this will have to do,' he said.

I went over to the Brigadier and told him the mortars would have to go down closer. Moreover I could not see the approach line of the aircraft from the position he had chosen for me, only just a narrowed glimpse of the village itself, and that was not good enough to direct the pilots. By this time he was in brittle mood and did not bother to argue but just snapped rather petulantly:

'Then go and find a better place yourself.'

'I will,' I told him.

But where? There was precious little time left. Luckily, Peter Wilmot had just come back up to ask something and he signalled me with his head to follow him. He took me down by a precipitous game track to his own post, a rocky promontary, just a few low bushes as cover, a perfect site for the job. I hurried back up to the Brigadier but he then turned perverse and said he would have to check it himself before allowing mortars to be moved, even though I told him time was now almost finished. But he insisted, then dawdled on the way down, argued about the exposed nature of the site on the way back before finally agreeing the mortars might go, by which time I knew it was too late. The planes would be over before we could get everything set up in the new position and when I told him this he instructed the mortars to stay where they were. We had not even finished packing the radio for our own move down when the planes arrived. We never did contact them.

We did send down some smoke bombs – well short of the barracks building – but they were ignored. Because most of the houses had been taken over by the Japanese the pilots had been briefed, as I discovered later, that the whole village area was their target. The P51 fighter-bombers came in first of all on a bombing run over the centre of the village, then afterwards they each did attacks with 75mm cannon-fire. The destruction of the peaceful village was a terrible thing to watch. After the bombing run, when the fires started, you could see the houses splinter and shiver under the cannon fire, and when it was all over there was no more blue smoke rising gently from the scene but black clouds of it churning up into the sky and spreading over the plain to the west. There were crackling explosions of bamboo, people screaming, and most of the village was now hidden in smoke and hurling flames.

Then our mortars began to thump shells down into the conflagration, and the two heavy machine guns near the mortars started a deadly chatter. The Brigadier was beside the guns, madly excited, shouting instructions:

'More left . . . up higher . . . another burst . . .'

I had abandoned the useless radio by then, had nothing to do, and was actually looking beyond the village to the paddy fields on the far side of the river when a long file of Gurkhas emerged from the trees and began to move obliquely towards the bridge. Just as I had noticed them so too must have the Brigadier and he shouted for the guns to switch on to this target. I was astounded, I had felt certain it must be 94 column but assumed the Brigadier must be right. Yet the plan had been clear enough, they *were* to come from that direction. I fumbled wildly for my field glasses as the machine guns began to bang away at their new target. Once focussed however I knew he had made a mistake, the troops were definitely Gurkhas, the hats were unmistakeable. I shouted across at him:

'It's 94 column. For Christ's sake! It's 94.'

He seemed to have lost reason, he kept urging the gunners on, but as I ran across still shouting the Support Platoon officer had also begun to have doubts. It was he who actually stopped the guns. Then the Brigadier had a closer look himself, realised the blunder, and he gave a curious little giggle:

'Doesn't matter,' he said. 'We didn't hit anyone.'

When we descended into the village we met only a few short bursts of rifle fire, the reason being that there were practically no Japanese in the place after all. Half a dozen or so of the garrison were all that remained, they bolted once 94 column got to the bridge, some being wounded by the rifle fire that followed them. We found masses of documents and stores, and discovered later that the main body of troops had actually gone up into the hills the previous afternoon in our direction. Luckily for some of us in both forces there were two different tracks coming down from the ridge; we had used one of them, the Japanese another, so bloody contact had been avoided.

The village had not suffered as badly as had appeared from above; there were only about twenty Burmese there, working for the Japanese maybe but certainly not combatants. I saw one old man who had been badly injured by a shell fragment in the shoulder being attended by one of our medical orderlies; and two small girls clinging in fear to an old woman just outside the doorway of one house looked at me blankly, eyes wide and lips parted, when I tried to smile at them. There was a buffalo with red blood gushing down its black hide, squatting mutely by a partially collapsed shrine, and a litter of piglets started out of one dark doorway in a squealing burst that stopped me cold for an instant. The rifle shots of burning bamboo also had me gripping my carbine convulsively as we moved through the shattered village.

We set fire to all the Japanese-occupied houses as well as the barracks, burned down the bamboo bridge, blew up the anchors of the wire-ferry, took what we wanted of the Japanese supplies and burned the rest, set fire to their personal belongings (including a large collection of porno-graphic photographs), smashed their radio and telephone installations, and took away what documents seemed to us might be useful to Intelligence. My final memory of that afternoon was of the Brigadier beating a young boy furiously about the head – it seemed he had been telling a pack of lies under questioning and when the Brigadier discovered this he suddenly went berserk and lashed out at him. The beating was effective. The truth he did then glean from the unfortu-nate child was that the Japanese were heading for the old fort where Dah Force was recruiting guerillas, and this informa-tion was to cause Morris Force to miss what could perhaps have been the single most destructive action on the Japanese that any of the whole Wingate force could have inflicted, for instead of waiting by the road for the Japanese convoys as originally planned the Brigadier retreated at once back into the hills with us in 49 column – not only to protect our own harbour party from the Japanese force which had just sallied out to find us but also to aid Dah Force. So we withdrew, hurrying up towards the Chinese border once more, and left Peter Cane's column alone to deal with the road oppor-tunities.

It was not enough. The Nalong road, running along the lower part of the ridge through thick jungle, had one particu-lar bend above a ravine which might have been designed for the perfect road block, a good charge of explosive at that point would leave a sheer drop of over fifty feet and take weeks of manpower to repair. So the perfect target con-ditions were there. Then the Japanese obligingly proceeded to ensure they were filled. It took them about a week to patch up an alternative to the burnt bridge by which time a huge number of vehicles was waiting to cross. They finally got over

167

the river and into Nalong on 28th April. That night there was a total of at least 318 vehicles – that was just the number the scouts actually counted – in Nalong. They, and the thousand or so Japanese soldiers with the vehicles, were the prize now offered. A small party from 94 column thereupon blew up the bridge again just south of the village, and a short distance up to the north a demolition group used their last explosives to drop the road into the ravine. So the trap was then closed.

At this stage Peter Cane called for a major air attack on the trapped vehicles, sent a message to the Brigadier to bring back 49 column to join him in finishing off what the air bombardment would leave, and called base for a drop of more explosives to ensure the ravine block became a permanent one. In response to these separate calls he received nothing. No explosives were dropped. No men were sent from 49 column. No aircraft came to bomb the target they had created.

I had to contact Stanley about a possible airstrip during this period and so shared in their fury of frustration as they waited in vain for support in exploiting the situation they had created. They alone in 94 could not secure the prize, the enemy was hugely superior and equipped with heavy artillery, they needed another column with them and they needed above all the air support so lavishly promised back in training days; in the meantime small parties of their force were able to harass the Japanese repair parties, delaying their efforts and giving time for the air force to mount the attack. They received signals acknowledging their call for more explosives, and for the air attack, and for the Brigadier to come, but that was all they did receive. Acknowledgments and nothing more. Days passed and the great opportunity was rigorously ignored. Peter Cane was justifiably bitter at the apathy of his superiors.

Despite the harassing attacks the large Japanese force were soon able to get in repair vehicles, including bulldozers, and presently they had a rough track cut above the ravine and a fordable passage across the river. The convoy began to move and so the prize was irretrievably lost. We did have minor successful attacks on the road by both columns before and after this, destroying very many vehicles, but never again were we offered such a massive target as that at Nalong – and one which could so easily have been destroyed had the effort been made.

The achievements of Morris Force against this vital road link to Myitkyena were considerable. The block south of Nalong was never repaired, all enemy supplies had to be manhandled across the damaged section and a thousand Japanese were tied down in this task. These troops were held back from the northern front, and other troops and materiel were blocked and attacked in subsequent minor actions along the road, so we did have an effect on the battle around Myitkyena even before we ever reached that area. But these were minor achievements in comparison to what might have been.

Had we utilised that opportunity, employed the full three columns available there in those last days of April 1944, we could have blocked the road permanently, taken a full regiment of Japanese out of the campaign, and destroyed a thousand tons of arms and ammunition and supplies. Had that happened the fighting at Myitkyena might have ended weeks earlier, the ordeal of the major Chindit group and of Merril's Marauders on the other side of the Irrawaddy would have been far less harsh under Stilwell, and have endured far less time.

But the air support never came – the Air Commando should not be blamed perhaps, for it was Force Headquarters who decided priorities (but remember that bright-eyed confidence that we only had to call for aircraft and the bombers would come at once?) And Force Headquarters did not drop even a single stick of dynamite despite the repeated and anguished calls (remember that Wingate promise that you only had to ask for arms and the 'sky will deliver them to you'?) But it was not only Force Headquarters who were guilty by default in missing the opportunity. Our own Brigadier Morris also, wandering about the hills on the Chinese border in a pointless (or evasive?) effort to help organize Dah Force, was also heavily to blame; he should have ignored that advice from headquarters and joined in the road action, he had the rank to argue – there were many other commanders even of lesser rank who would have done so. But he lacked the will.

The only group who came out of the whole episode with credit was 94 column under Peter Cane. They had battled, and suffered casualties, to create the opportunity – and they it was who were forced to watch it being slowly and in the end, irrevocably, wrenched from their grasp.

12

_____

The day after leaving the road we rejoined our mule party which had been hunted and harried by the Japanese force but escaped contact, then went on to the fort where Dah Force had met the enemy group. The area was said now to be clear of Japanese but we were to discover presently this information was incorrect; a small party had remained, they were watching us from the ridge, waiting for the chance to pick off a straggler.

The fort at Nahpaw was not unique along that hazy border in the north-east of Burma. In practice the border there is a strip about twenty miles wide, it is only outside that strip that in normal times the respective governments showed official presence. On the Burmese side this was usually manifest by a police outpost, or in the more dangerous reaches of the country one of these wooden forts. These were not all occupied all the time, only when trouble threatened, but whenever the Commissioner set off on an official tour the fort would also then be ornamentally manned to supply the panoply of government.

The typical one at Nahpaw was like one of those cavalry outposts of the American army in the last century, a wooden stockade with watch-tower in one corner and firing balconies within – the gate at Nahpaw was now gone, as were most of the interior wooden fittings. It was about ten miles from the cartographer's border line, and about 5,000 feet above sea level; the hillside south of the fort had been kept cleared in the past, not as taungya but to open up fields of fire should it be attacked by Chinese irregulars when minor officials were in residence with the treasury box full of silver rupees – Tiny Langford found a treasure that afternoon when we arrived, a raspberry bush at the bottom of the slope, and we had plucked it clear of every trace of colour within a minute or so of discovery.

The Dah Force group had been scattered after the Japanese attack but there were only a dozen or so in the party and they all turned up finally. Their problems were sorted out, they shared a supply drop with us, and the Brigadier came to some arrangement about the role they could play in conjunction with us. Meanwhile we had a signal from base about a possible airstrip in that remote area which might provide a safe permanent link with them, so the Brigadier ordered me to go off on a reconnaissance over the border into Yunnan, the most westerly province of China, to examine this potential development. Tiny Langford was to accompany me, also Corporal Chang of the Hong Kong Volunteers, a Chingpaw-speaking Gurkha, and ten of the Gurkhas from the old recce platoon which had become so demoralized after that early misfortune – their morale had still not recovered, and they were only a tiresome responsibility for us throughout this operation. We took our Japanese prisoner so he could be sent out from there.

A primary and secondary rendezvous was arranged with the column as usual. As mentioned earlier, the maps of Burma thereabouts were often inaccurate, but in those we had of that corner of Yunnan the cartographer had even abandoned guesswork in some places; there were areas without any brown contour lines at all, just a white space with a dotted line across it joining a river or track from the known world on one side to that on the other, and a series of question marks beside this hypothetical line. Even the village of Sima'pa itself was followed by a question mark, querying perhaps not just its location but its very existence. We had to pass through about five miles of one of those white unknown areas just inside the technical border with China and I was disappointed to find it was just hill and jungle like anywhere else; you have a right to expect strange and wondrous things in an unexplored land.

It was early morning when we left the others at the fort, crisp and cool, the blue sky not yet cluttered with the cumulus clouds that now kept frothing up every day to herald the monsoon. The track was an impressive width starting out from the fort, wide enough for a wheeled vehicle – although none could ever have been seen in that area – but this was all for show; once it was out of sight, a few hundred yards away into the trees on the eastern ridge, it contracted at once to a humble single-file width. Then followed a gentle climb leading up to the 7,000 ft pass.

For a time after leaving the fort we had been in tropical rain forest, fig trees with vast smooth trunks and clumps of fruit bulging from dark green leathery foliage, aerial roots dangling down like enormous cables, many of the grey trunks with basal roots jutting out as flying buttresses and covered with moss and lichen. As we gained height however, the scene changed. It was a subtle alteration, you sensed a difference before you recognized what was happening; there were fewer fig trees and aerial roots and palms, you began to notice a few European-type trees like oaks and chestnuts and maples, and these became more and more frequent the higher we went. There was still plenty of bamboo but not the common types of lower levels; here were clumps of a more leafy variety through which we walked on damp brown leaves and were assailed by a heavy scent of lavender that came from a glossy-leaved parasitic plant that twined loosely about the lowest culms of the bamboo – the only place it could get a grip. There were some trees in flower, a chestnut with spikes the colour of parchment, and an acacia with sweet scented tiny orange flowers about which masses of bees were humming – throbbing like a giant dynamo. It was an easy march, smooth path and gentle gradient, and we had no cares; Tiny Langford and I started a game with one of us quoting a verse and the other having to produce a new quote somehow associated with it, and justifying that association; but I got stuck almost at once and began to cheat, fabricating a Flecker line, and got away with another one before he detected the fraud and joined in what developed into a bawdy variation of the original game.

Once over the pass and into China the terrain was undulating, a plateau with curving hills and occasional small streams; nearly all the forest here had been cleared, not only for hill-grown rice but also for more regularly cultivated plants. There was a green sheen of new rice in a few of these cultivated patches, but most were given over to the opium poppy and nearly all of these had already been cropped; from the late-comers you could see that the majority had been the white flowering type but there was a scattering of the purple and crimson, and one uncropped patch was covered almost entirely with the purple flowers. There was no one working in any of the fields however; in the distance ahead we could hear the ominous sound of sporadic gunfire and this was probably the reason no one was out that afternoon. Later I saw women working in the poppy fields, scratching the green capsules with little forks of bamboo so that the milky fluid began to ooze out to coagulate into the brown wodge ready for collection. Its use up there is not limited merely to being smoked in a pipe; in some areas they wipe it off with a collecting rag which is sucked directly or soaked in water to make a drink, and some hill people simply eat the seeds – you often saw green capsules discarded, like the wrappings from a K ration delicacy, along the side of the track. The seeds and the liquid are supposed to be prophylactic, particularly against malaria, but I never heard of such an excuse for smoking the stuff. I found the seeds too sharp for my sweet tooth, the pipe made me dizzy, and I never had an opportunity to taste the liquid. The little fields gave a patchwork-quilt effect to a hillside, and even after the crop had been taken the evidence remained, for not all the plants were ready at the same time and they made no attempt to collect late flowers, so where the grass had started to grow again there were these isolated white bubbles bouncing about the lush green carpet.

The first Yunnanese we met that afternoon was an old man who had a good command of Chingpaw and he agreed to lead us towards Sima'pa. By that time the crackle of gunfire and the explosions of mortar shells had come much closer and so he had no need to explain his refusal to go anywhere near the village of Sima'pa. We too hoped we could avoid this. The place sounded dangerously unfriendly. There were reports that an agent known as Edgar – he was OSS or SOE – operated in the area, and fortunately our guide knew of him. More fortunately still, Edgar was out of the village, hidden in the hills to the north. Our guide declined to take us there however, it appeared he had no wish to be caught wandering about the plain with a dozen armed foreigners just then; we were within a mile or so of Sima'pa when he disclosed this, and when a prolonged burst of machine-gun fire suddenly echoed about the hills, we were disposed to sympathize with his point of view. We had halted near a shallow stream and he told us we should wait there in the bushes whilst he took a note from us up to Edgar. We had to settle for this, wrote the note, and off he went. Despite his friendly manner however Tiny and I decided it would be prudent to get away from where he had actually left us, just in case he took the note straight down to the Japanese in Sima'pa. We moved up the stream for about half a mile to where it narrowed in passage through a little ravine; on the rocky ground there was a great bush of flowerless azalea, useful for emergency cover, so we waited beside it, lying on a rock in the warm afternoon, listening to the occasional gunfire and keeping under surveillance the spot down-stream where the old man had left us.

He proved to be trustworthy. An hour or so later he

returned accompanied by a tall lean figure who was clearly not Japanese so we disclosed ourselves. The newcomer was Pete Joost, an American Cavalry officer attached to Dah Force. His job was to provide liaison with Stilwell and he had by chance found Edgar, and so a refuge, when the Japanese force moved into Sima'pa. He reported that the village was much larger than we had thought, with a population of several hundred; it was now crowded with Japanese troops and none of Edgar's trusted messengers were anxious to go near the place – two had already been shot as suspected spies. With so much fighting going on between various factions in the area suspicion was rife, and the Japanese were in such strength they could act with impunity on the instant, avoiding all the bother of trying to resolve doubt. I had no intention of going into Sima'pa but I had to go out into the open paddy fields beside the village because that was the potential airstrip to be assessed. Joost told me a light plane had actually landed two days before but had crashed because the distance was too short; no one knew what had happened to the two men who had been in it. We decided to try and get my job done that same afternoon, before the Japanese had established firm control of the whole surrounding area, so Tiny Langford took the rest of our party back to the little dell with its observation rock, and Joost and I set off down the track towards Sima'pa.

It was a wide track, we could walk abreast with comfort, sloping down gently by the stream towards a low ridge through which it weaved a way to the open ground about Sima'pa, hidden from our view by the ridge but located by the occasional bursts of gunfire. We were now completely clear of the forest, there were little plots of maize and rice and tobacco about the hillside but also uncultivated patches with clumps of rhododendron, some still in pale mauve flower, offering possible cover. We had only gone a few hundred yards, moving quietly and in silence, when we heard sounds and voices approaching, and we darted off the track into a large tangle of rhododendron, quickly enough to be hidden safely before the speakers came into sight. A single glance was enough to make me relax, even if Joost had not recognized one of them to be friendly. They were an incongruous pair. The one Joost knew was a Bengali, black as ebony, wearing an orange smock and a sort of hooped skirt about his spindly lets so that they looked like two filaments dangling from a broken electric light bulb. The other was a plump Chinese wearing emerald slippers and sky-blue silk pyjamas decorated with silver embroidery; he was, he told me portentously in English, a 'mandarin'. They were both out of breath and obviously scared, kept looking behind as they persuaded us off the track again back into the hiding of our rhododendron.

The Indian had been a sapper in Wingate's first expedition, left behind because he lost himself. He had drifted across Burma and then on through the Kachin Hills, not so difficult at first because there were many Indian traders living on the plain but the further west he went the more conspicuous became his colour, and he was more or less forced to stop just beyond the border at Sima'pa where black skin finally peters out, and beyond is only Chinese tan. Here he had set up in business as a barber, but the occasional Japanese entry made life miserable; he always had to bolt into the countryside, his colour betraying him as a stranger – and the Japanese grabbed strangers. When he heard about the advent of Dah Force he saw a chance of being delivered from this precarious existence and hurried across the hills to the fort at Nahpaw in the hope of being flown out to India. But he arrived just an hour or so before the group was attacked by the Japanese. He managed to extricate himself safely from this tangle and immediately fled back to the hairdressing business in Sima'pa to wait for a safer rescue party. That afternoon he was on one of his usual hurried exits when he met the mandarin engaged on the same exercise; he said the Japanese force had been attacking, and been harried by, isolated groups of Chinese on the plain but had now moved into Sima'pa itself. There were a thousand of them, and they carried heavy machine guns on their mule train.

The mandarin in colourful dress was Mr See – he could have meant Mr 'C' when he said it, just an initial as is so often affected by people in clandestine operations, but I put him down in my diary as 'See'. He was the official representative of the Chiang Kai Shek government in the area, but as he had no actual forces with him his position was without authority in Sima'pa. Around that remote area of China the fighting was complicated. The local inhabitants had banded together to form a vigilante group to protect themselves, the Japanese were present in about battalion strength widely scattered, there were marauding Chinese irregulars who were the private armies of various war-lords involved in the opium trade, Communist guerillas visited the place occasionally to pick up food and recruits, and finally there were troops of Chiang Kai Shek based about fifty miles to the north. Mr See had been sent to persuade the locals to be more helpful to these great fighters against communism but this ideological argument cut no ice in Sima'pa, experience had taught the villagers that all armed groups wanted only to grab their food; Mr See was trying to subdue this prejudice when his efforts were cut short by the entry of the Japanese who had more forceful arguments to apply. He improved on the Indian's estimate, doubling the number of Japanese troops and saying they had mountain guns. The firing that was still continuing sporadically as we talked was, he told us, between some Japanese and a group of irregulars occupying some huts in the middle of the paddy fields which were to provide our airstrip. There had also been some firing within Sima'pa itself – the Japanese had been executing suspects in a display of force.

Both Mr See and the Indian assured us that the pilot and passenger from the crashed light plane had been picked up by the Japanese who arrived on the scene shortly after the accident. The burnt-out plane now had a Japanese guard.

They recoiled in horror at our request for guidance to the potential airstrip, urging us instead to join them and get away to the north until the fighting stopped. Joost and I let them go and made our own way once more down the path towards the ridge beyond which the occasional crackle of rifle fire and thuds of mortar shells continued. After about a hundred yards however we both stopped; ahead of us the path narrowed as it curved into a shadowed gap made by the streamlet through the ridge – an ideal spot for an ambush. The thought was mutual, simultaneous: we looked at one another, shook our heads in silent agreement, then moved off the track up the slope, crouching low to the ground. Near the crest we dropped right down and crawled on our bellies like scouts in a Western up to the skyline. Then at last I looked out over the plain.

The name of Shangri'la came to mind. After those weeks in hill jungle it was a magnificent sight. The plain is at about 5,000 feet, pressed down between the mountains, the hills rise on three sides for another thousand feet or so but to the west there is nothing at all, the land drops away steeply and all you see is a great misty-blue void that looks like the end of the world. The little stream glistened in the sunlight, meandering along the western edge of the plain to disappear into the blue space. The paddy fields were covered with fresh green growth, uniform as a tennis lawn, and in the middle distance was a small grove of trees within which some straw-coloured buildings could be seen. At the south-eastern rim of the plain, about half a mile away, was Sima'pa itself, with the houses so close together they made a startling white barrier, like a continuous pile of snow along the foot of the distant hill. The shadow of a cumulus cloud was drifting across the paddy fields like a huge grey raft, and the whole scene looked bright and peaceful as a coral-ringed lagoon on a soft Pacific afternoon.

It was in a turmoil however. We could see as well as hear the evidence of violent action. The oasis of trees in the middle

distance must have been the place which Mr See had reported was being held by a group of irregulars because there
was a line of men carrying guns, perhaps half a dozen,
moving quickly back from it towards us along a clearly
defined path; the reason for this withdrawal and its speed,
was suggested by the occasional explosive puff of mortar
shells landing amidst the trees there. The mortar shells
seemed to be coming from near Sima'pa and we heard also a
distant burst of automatic fire from somewhere beyond the
village. Immediately ahead of us the ground was almost level
for a little way before it dropped down sharply, cutting out
sight of the armed men when they came close up to our little
ridge, but we heard them clearly enough a few minutes later.
The sounds came from our right, down below where the
track weaved through that menacing gap, and then they
moved away up in the direction whence we had come –
clattering, clanking, shuffling sounds of armed men on the
march, and a short sharp unintelligible call that sounded like
a command or a warning. We waited very quietly on the brow
of the hill. We were in no hurry to move after them. I was
studying the terrain from a professional point of view by this
time, particularly the obvious line of a possible airstrip
running more or less parallel to the stream, and had already
picked out the mangled shape of the burnt-out plane near
that line where Pete Joost asked in a wary tone if I still intended to go out there that afternoon.

'Not bloody likely,' I told him.

We both relaxed then. I think Joost was a regular US Army
officer, his uniform was still smart, he was clean-shaven and
looked clean bodied too – not like a scruffy, bearded, lousy
Chindit – and he seemed to have felt he was obliged to
accompany me out on the plain had I so decided. He pointed
out the line which Edgar's men had marked for the strip, and
it was clear, even from where I was lying, that it was far from
the best; it ran directly towards the low trees by the stream
and not parallel – it had almost certainly not been laid out by

a pilot. Had that been the only reason for our trip I could have finished the job then and there, simply asking Joost to get Edgar's men adjust the line; but I had to check its feasibility as an all-weather strip and this required nearly double the present distance and a close examination of the terrain. It was necessary to go out there and walk over the ground. No way of avoiding it – but happily it had not to be done that very day.

Having assured ourselves there were no other soldiers coming from the plain we made our way back to our starting point. Joost left me there and went on up to Edgar; we arranged that Tiny Langford and I would follow later, led by the original messenger, once we had our party settled into a safe harbour. I climbed down off the track and made a difficult way up beside the stream to the spot where I had left the others, but on arrival could find not a trace of them. Nor any blaze anywhere to show the direction of their going. After a fruitless search of the area I set off back towards the track so as to make sure I had not missed a guide who might have been posted for me. Luckily I had taken ten minutes or so in the search for them, for I arrived back at the track just a few seconds too late for what could have been a fatal meeting.

There was a little dip with a small bamboo clump stretching up to the track, and I had just threaded through it and was about to climb up on to the track itself when I heard men approaching from the plain. They were very near, I just had time to ease back quickly under the arching foliage, only a few steps, and to stand rigid between two bamboo stems. As they scuffled past about five yards away I could see them only up to waist height . . . drab green trousers . . . non-British rifle held at the trail . . . a black scabbard . . . hip haversack . . . legs moving across one another . . . and flickering of shadows on the far bank . . . then gone beyond the rim of vision. Perhaps six men in all, following the direction of the others, silent, purposeful in pursuit. Slowly, the scuffling tinkling noises faded, I let my breath burst clear, and the blood started to pound mightily through the arteries.

I waited, listening, there was not a sound to be heard, no more shooting, no bird song, no rustle of leaves, nothing but that faint high-pitched tuning-fork sound you get in your ears when you strain hearing to the utmost. Cautiously then, I climbed up on the track. Even after seeing them at such close range I could not swear to their true identity. I felt sure they had been Japanese but could not find the proof – their rubber-soles have a zigzag pattern that leaves an unmistakeable track but the path was stony and showed no trace of their quiet passage.

It was understandable that I should think afterwards about Peter Wilmot, and how he was going to react to the story. I could imagine his keen military approach . . . Couldn't I have opened fire – after them, say, along the track? . . . Or followed the group for a better opportunity? . . . and I would ridicule his professional commitment: 'At six to one! Not bloody likely. I leave those odds to keen types like you.'

Tiny Langford eventually found me hunting about the track. His face lit up when he saw me and he hurried up to greet me in obvious relief. They had had to move, there had been a misunderstanding with Lilbahadur about waiting for me – a typical language confusion – he had subsequently followed them and so Tiny had himself come hurrying back to retrieve the mistake, luckily arriving just a few minutes after the Japanese group had passed. We returned, light-hearted at our escape, to the new bivouac, organized look-outs, then went off with the guide up the steep hill path to meet Edgar.

We found him settled in a little basha hut on the far side of the steep bare hill, his hideout approached by a precipitous path on which he kept a constant lookout-man. He was a British army officer – 'Edgar' was his code name, I don't think I ever heard his actual name – and he had a rich fruity voice that could have been natural or wrought by long and loving treatment with alcohol; he did in fact have a bottle of rum ready for us when we arrived. We discussed the situation at some length, almost bottle length, and decided the sensible course was to wait and see if the Japanese moved out next day, then do the job in safety. We were speculating about the missing pilot and passenger from the crashed plane when his lookout brought a Kachin to the doorway. He was a Dah Force scout, he had happened to contact our column near the fort at Nahpaw that same afternoon, and it was from him that we first heard the stunning news of the death of Peter Wilmot. The details that night were sketchy, we discovered more later on, but there was no doubt about the sickening fact. Peter was dead.

It seems the column was moving in long line down the hillside below the Fort when the Japanese group watching from the ridge started to lob mortar shells on them. Quick action was needed to dislodge the enemy, for there was no shelter for the column on the open hillside. Peter took a section of men across the slope and then up the track, the only possible means of approach; the enemy had laid the ambush well short of their mortar position and Peter, leading the section as he would in such a deadly advance, was hit by the opening burst of machine-gun fire and killed instantly. The death of Peter was a deep personal loss to those of us who had been such close friends during all the long period of training in India and the actions in Burma; it was also a serious setback to the column itself, for he was our best fighting officer, always prepared to stand up to the Brigadier and plead for action when an opportunity occurred, and showing determination and initiative when allowed to take the offensive. Whether he would have continued after the war as a scholar back at Cambridge or made a career in the Army it would have been with distinction in either field, for he applied an intelligent concentration to any task he tackled, and the standards he set himself were severe. I missed his friendly company, his honest judgments and his earnest sincerity, and have always regretted the loss of what he might have become. We spent a sad first night by that stream in the mountains of Yunnan.

13

The failure of Wingate and his staff to utilize the illicit organizations for the landings into Burma was an error these organizations themselves might have minimized were they not so concerned always to preserve their independence. They are well placed to protect it, too. They represent a second dimension in the normal chain of command, on a plane beyond the knowledge of the actual fighting units to whom their assistance could be a godsend, controlled by a remote authority far back where politics provides the ultimate link, away beyond the horizon of humble field commanders. The OSS had its own link back to Washington, the SOE finished back in Baker Street in London, the ISLD back at the Foreign Office as far as I know, the Free French of Indo-China went back to De Gaulle, and even the lesser fry such as Z Force and D Group were linked direct to Army Command rather than through an active division.

The organizations themselves were positively obstructive about interference with these links, they carried their internecine warfare to such a length at times that it amounted almost to sabotage. You would fly an aircraft out empty to Indo-China for a nocturnal pick-up of some French agent and not be allowed to drop supplies en route to an SOE group whose headquarters in the jungle you were actually overflying, and if a reception committee from one group did not appear on the drop site you were never allowed to deliver any of the supplies to a separate group, not even a few uncompromising bags of rice. I have taken just two parachutists to an ISLD site in Siam and been refused permission to drop a few packages to an OSS group nearby. There was far too much jealousy and amour-propre in these organizations, and as a result their full potential was certainly not realized in Burma – maybe they organized things better in Europe, but knowing something of the rivalries involved I doubt it. Our particular reconnaissance into Yunnan was unnecessary; Edgar could have been asked to supply the information direct but he never was, because we had no link with OSS or SOE so as to connect with him (I am not certain to which group he belonged). It was pure luck we discovered him and were able to utilize his resources and assistance at Sima'pa. This was no way for grown-ups to run a war.

The day following our arrival the firing continued about the plain, and in the afternoon we took the Japanese prisoner up the hill and delivered him to Edgar – we were worried we might have to move quickly from our hideout and so lose him altogether. Edgar sent him off into store with one of his outlying agents till the bigger strip was prepared and a plane arrived to take him out; he said it would be madness to go anywhere near Sima'pa at the moment, we would have to wait another day. Joost also advised delay.

When we returned to our men down by the stream we discovered that two strangers, apparently unarmed but dressed in military-type clothing, had seen the Gurkhas filling water bottles and had bolted precipitately in the direction of Sima'pa, so it seemed likely our hideout had now been compromised. We moved about a mile away to the west of the stream, up a slope where there was a large clump of unusual bamboo that had a smooth polished lemon-yellow stem with a creamy ring around each node; it was beside a poppy field that had long since been harvested and on which there was a thatched-roof hut, doorless, windowless, dirty straw on the floor. It was a grey afternoon, low dank clouds trailed mistily about the slopes as if groping for escape, and crouching under the dripping bamboo Tiny and I had fretful conversation about the delay in completing our task. The tapping of rifle fire continued from the plain, there were too many Japanese about, the longer we stayed the more likely we would be discovered, but we could not force Edgar to help; he was only providing assistance out of kindness, was under no obligation to do so, he had his own particular work to do and the security of his cell to consider. But we had to take our report back to the column without undue delay, and could not afford his waiting game.

All next day we waited for his messenger. The plain was quiet. Not a single rifle shot throughout the day. Yet no one came. So finally, when the great orange balloon of a clouded sun had dropped behind the purple ridge, and the bats had emerged to flit silently backwards and forwards over the poppy slope, we set off again for Edgar's eeyrie. There we learned that most of the Japanese had marched out of Sima'pa that afternoon, and Edgar promised he would take us down to the plain next day with a local who could scout ahead and find out what was happening in the village.

Once that was settled we shared a drink or two, then a meal of rice and chopped spam spiced with chilli and ground beans which Joost had procured from somewhere, and finished off with a curious gritty sweet produced by one of the Kachin scouts – it was composed of the dried leaves of a certain wild plant chopped fine like tea-leaves, about which wild-honey was crystalized. They looked like frosted ants, and the leaves tended to clam to the roof of your mouth – the taste was vaguely reminiscent of anis liqueur but no one knew the parent plant of the leaves.

Just after we had finished our meal the lookout man suddenly appeared with the two plane survivors, the Canadian pilot who was shivering with cold, and his passenger who was a cavalry officer called Kennedy I had known from our training days. Whilst they helped themsleves hungrily to the remnants of the food, all of us squatting tightly together on the floor of the little shelter, they told us of their misadventures. It appeared that subsequent to the crash a second light aircraft had come to rescue them but after a couple of passes at the strip the pilot had wisely decided a landing was not possible and had flown away. The two had then gone over to the burnt-out aircraft to check if anything had been inadvertently left and at that moment the Japanese turned up, and they had to bolt for the stream with shots crackling after them. They continued on up the far hill for two hours before pulling off into the trees beside the track and collapsing with exhaustion. They dozed off for a time and were awakened by loud cracking sounds which they discovered to their horror were being made by a column of Japanese who had also pulled off the track and were cutting up branches to make fires, having chosen that spot for their bivouac. They had a large number of mules, one of which was actually within touching distance of the two on the ground. Fortunately for them, cloud had drifted into the hill, the whole scene was cloaked in a misty moisty greyness, and Kennedy said that the Japanese unloading the mule had actually looked at him steadily for a moment then just shrugged and turned away, as if ignoring a local tribesman. The two managed to sidle away at last without being questioned, but for the next two days had been constantly meeting Japanese patrols as they hunted for Edgar's hideout.

It must have been after midnight when finally we three columnists, Tiny and Corporal Chang and I, edged our way fearfully down the steep path in the black night, and then groped for a further mile or so to the hideout in the lemon bamboo. It began to rain heavily just as we arrived and so we moved into the filthy little hut-shelter on the poppy field. The floor was covered in straw which you could feel moving slightly all the time when you rested your hand lightly upon it; it was activated by a host of small creatures, fleas, ticks, ants, beetles, millipedes, spiders and other such tickling and biting insects, all engaged in a vicious struggle for existence, and supreme in this little eco-system before our arrival were the rats that kept skittering and squeaking about our bodies all that long night. Tiny and I had decided well before daylight, in outspoken agreement, that we would not endure another night there and so when Edgar sent down a note in the morning to say he thought it wiser to wait yet another day we rejected wisdom at once. It was a measure of the relationship between Tiny and myself that neither of us assumed command of our little group at any time, the question simply did not arise, we discussed decisions and never had a disagreement. We ordered an immediate move.

The approach was made along the edge of the stream, under cover until we arrived opposite the grove where we had seen the mortar shells landing. It was now all quiet, not a sound of action from anywhere on the plain. We left the Gurkhas in cover by the stream, and Tiny and Chang and I walked along the edge of the plain, having little to say to one another in those first few tense moments. The ground was firm underfoot, covered in stubble from a cereal crop of some kind that had recently been harvested, and the large fields were separated by terracing with bunds only ankle-high. There were two wooden buildings in the grove of trees but no sign of any life there. Two people suddenly emerged from behind the wrecked plane as we approached but after a moment of intense study we began to relax – cautiously, in spasms. They ambled towards us, not at all aggressively, and we could see they were obviously locals, clad in rags and without weapons of any kind. One of them could hold a conversation of sorts with Corporal Chang; he said that most of the Japanese had left the previous afternoon, only about fifty now remained and these were camped with their mules on the far side of the village. I left Tiny and Chang there and went on out to do the job that was the whole purpose of our trip.

Feeling as exposed as an ant on a plate I thought to walk over the projected line as quickly as possible, past the grove with its buildings and on to the far corner then back again, finishing the job in about ten minutes. But there was a snag; I discovered that the course of an old stream, with impossibly soft ground, cut across this line. The soggy dip had somehow to be avoided. When I came back to plan an alternative Tiny was already waiting, anxious to get away into the trees again but unwilling to leave me alone out there.

As so often happens when you are in a dangerous situation, or feel you are, if you have something to occupy your mind you can bypass fear. The pilot is the lucky one in the aircraft; he can go diving down at a spectacularly defended target like a battleship in harbour and be intensely occupied as he keeps pumping the stick forward, jiggling it to swing the wings, slamming feet alternatively against the rudder bars, one hand flicking backwards and forwards from gun-button down to throttles to keep them hard open, probably shouting obscenities into the microphone all the time, no space left in mind to consider the threats of flak streaming up past him, explosive flashes of heavy shells, or probing searchlights. You have a fury of action diverting you in such an attack. It is the poor wretched navigator and the gunner who have to sweat it through, nothing to do but to watch the storm and wait for the terrible impact of violent death.

That day, Tiny and I each had our bad moments – at least I think he had a bad time whilst he had to stand idly by and just wait as I wandered for so long about that exposed area near Sima'pa. It was the only time in the whole campaign that he showed a sort of nervous sharpness with me as he urged me to finish the job – usually he was imperturbable, superior to all this squalid war business. I have no doubt about my own bad time that day; it was later on, in the afternoon, when fear threatened to take control and reason itself was in desperate peril.

Tiny was moving nervously back and forth between me and the locals as I kept trying to work out how to effect the layout. The current strip was faulty because it headed for the trees beside the stream, but there was a line from the far side of the grove that missed the soggy dip and would give a safe run; this measured out at about 500 yards. Good enough. Having checked it both ways I then made a sketch of the planned layout, standing in the middle by the grove near the silent buildings. They were merely two wooden houses built a foot or so above ground level, little more than a good-sized room each and with steps going straight up to wooden doors that were tied shut with bamboo thongs. There were a few azalea bushes, nothing in flower, but amongst the scatter of trees was a magnolia standing in a pool of ivory-white petals from the fallen flowers. Nowhere in houses or trees, could I see any record of all that gunfire and mortar explosions we had seen about that grove the afternoon of our arrival.

I sat down on the grass to finish the sketch, still looking at the houses, when a man's voice sounded behind me and I turned sharply to see he was only a few paces from me. He was wearing a cloak of sacking over dark bottle-green trousers of ankle-length and carrying an enormously long rifle. I had Lilbahadur's stengun and had swung it around as I turned but he approached me with a tooth-gapped smile and was holding out a cheroot so fat that I thought at first it was a sausage. I accepted it and offered him a Hershey bar which he took and began to eat at once, sitting down beside me and making friendly noises as he passed over his rifle for inspection. It was a muzzle-loader with a big bore, a barrel that must have been nearly a quarter of an inch thick and well over a yard long, a Napoleonic piece. It was obviously a treasured weapon, as was clear from the way he himself handled it and his pride in displaying it; the barrel was tied to the ebony-dark stock with close strands of brass wire, the powder was in a cloth bag attached to it, and in a leather bag at his waist he carried the shot – bits of rusty metal and some sharp glassy fragments that looked like quartz.

He pointed to my sten enquiringly but I was reluctant to hand it over for examination, despite that amiable idiotic grin – his two central incisors were missing – and he was still entreating me with his hands for a closer look when Tiny Langford came striding up with his carbine. That distracted him from my simple sten. But Tiny was not at all friendly, he snatched back the gun from the groping hands and his manner suggested he would shoot rather than yield it. He was anxious to get us off the plain so we left the man, still smiling and nodding his head – but both of us kept looking back just to make sure he was doing nothing with that treasured gun of his. When we rejoined the Gurkhas we found that one of Edgar's men, our original guide to his hideout, had joined them, so we gave him a note with a drawing of my strip layout to take back to Edgar; they must have done some work on it because we heard the pilot was picked up a little later, but I never discovered what happened to our Japanese prisoner.

We set off westwards across the stream and up the slope past the poppy fields and clumps of mauve-flowering rhododendron, thence on to the track that led towards the Burmese border. Because of the news about the Japanese group which had killed Peter we decided to avoid the fort itself on our return and take instead a by-pass used by opium runners. It was after midday when we left the plain and we walked for about twelve miles during the afternoon along the same track we had followed coming into China. When we called halt for the day the sun was low in the sky blocked from dazzling sight by a conical cloud mass behind which the golden rays were sprayed out as if from a battery of immense searchlights. We moved away clear of the track down into a grassy glade where we spent a peaceful rainless night.

The next day I passed through the worst hours of the Wingate campaign, perhaps the worst of the whole six years of the war. By mid-morning we had found the opium-runners' track the local had mentioned, the one that avoided the fort at Nahpaw, and were moving down it in the usual fashion with two men some fifty yards ahead of the rest of us, when suddenly we came upon evidence of a recent presence.

There were empty cigarette packs – the little ones from K rations – small round tins, paper wrapping, and then a single Japanese toe-split sandal. Tiny and I discussed it in low voices, and were about to warn the scouts up ahead when we realised they must have seen the evidence themselves; they had stopped and were looking back, they waited until we came up to join them.

'Japan,' one of them said.

He pointed to a pile of similar debris just beside the track, with Japanese fish-tins amongst the K-ration relics they had grabbed in the fort; it was a little clearing which was trampled flat and liberally marked with that herring-bone pattern of rubber-soled shoes. There too a fire had been lit, and recently, for although there was no warmth left in it to my testing hand the ash was still in the precise form of the actual twigs that had burnt, ghostly shapes that a puff of wind or a drop of rain would have fluffed into disappearance. Not only was the identity of the group clear but so too was their purpose. We had just come over a slight kink in the main ridge, and now we could see across to the palisades of Nahpaw Fort half a mile away, and below us was the wide clearing leading up to it on which we had taken our supply drop. We were on the ridge path from which the Japanese had been watching the column for several days, then finally lobbed down the mortar shells that had drawn Peter Wilmot up to his ambushed death. In trying to avoid this Japanese group we had taken the very track on which they had established their hillside position.

The ambush had occurred three days earlier. Were they still there? If so, where? These questions Tiny and I discussed in English, keeping our voices down, while the others in the party also had their whispered worrying conversations. There was no sense in going back; not only would we lose a lot of time but we had no guarantee the Japanese would not be about the fort also. We warned the scouts to proceed with extreme caution, but the warning was either too impressive or gratuitous, for they showed at once they had no desire at all to continue in the lead.

A great deal of nonsense has been written about what is called Gurkha bravery. It is suggested that Gurkhas are entirely devoid of fear and will charge senselessly to their doom like lemmings – just point them in the right direction, give the order, and they will rush forward with kukries flailing up to the brink of oblivion. The eighteen months I spent with them did not persuade me to this much-publicized view. I found them to be normal human beings with as strong a sense of survival as anyone else; when they risked their lives, as many of them did, it was not as Pavlov-conditioned monkeys or automata but as men who had to quell their fear like the rest of us. To believe otherwise is to demean their courage. It is true perhaps that there exists among them a high proportion of men who will knowingly face death if duty so demands, as there is amongst the Japanese – reputation being so precious perhaps, or adoration so compelling – but there are also many like the rest of us who are reluctant to challenge death whatever the cause or the drive may be. The Gurkhas we had with us that day had all been members of the original reconnaissance platoon, the group that had gone astray in the early days of the campaign and finished huddled in hiding, and their morale had never recovered from that ordeal. They should have been broken up as a unit, split among the rifle platoons, but they had been kept together subsequently as a sort of mule-guarding group, non-combatants, and so had never had a chance to recover their spirit and their Gurkha pride. Up till the moment we came upon the evidence of the Japanese presence on the path they had taken their turn as lead pairs quite happily like the rest of us, but when we tried to start off again it was clear at once they were of no further use in such a role. They went at snail pace, kept stopping and looking back at us, poised in fear on the track, and Tiny Langford lost patience.

194

'They're useless,' he said. 'We'll do it. Half an hour each?'

It was the obvious course. I couldn't disagree with it. He went off at once, on his own – no sense in losing two men, he said – striding quickly down the path as though determined to make up for the time wasted. I, however, had been contaminated by the Gurkha's fear, reason all fluttery under its viral infection, and could think of nothing else as we went on past more evidence of Japanese presence but that in thirty minutes I would have to take over the lead. That was why I had such a bad time of it in the end, I suppose – there was nothing for the mind to do in that waiting period but to gorge on fear.

I feel sure that Tiny himself was able to discipline his imagination more effectively than me – either that or he was a far better actor than he had ever suggested before, because he seemed perfectly normal when he finally halted for the change. More convincing still, he had actually taken almost five minutes over the planned half-hour for his lead period. We took a halt at the handover, during which he mentioned a trench we had passed a moment or two earlier, then went on to speak of what seemed a more important concern to him, the possibility of a leech inside his boot. He took it off, muttering angrily, but found nothing. He smoked a pipe, and talked about steamer trips up the Irrawaddy. All perfectly normal.

I took Lilbahadur's sten gun with me – God knows why, because if there were any Japanese waiting on the path their bullets were going to smash me to death before I ever discovered their presence. But the feel of a sten in hand was a comfort – and it *could* reasonably be held in hand; you could not walk along with a drawn revolver pointed ahead, such an obvious display of apprehension would be ludicrous. The track weaved about the top of the ridge, which was sloping down steadily; you kept seeing through the trees on the right the bare hill slope below the fort, and all the time the evidence of occupation was visible along the track – stubs of

195

broken branches, brown waxed cartons and, above all, slit trenches cut so cleanly you only saw them when practically abreast. The ridge was virgin forest of intermediate level; the lighter foliage of upland trees like chestnut and maple and hornbeam was becoming less frequent as we descended, the sombre trees of tropical jungle more common, particularly the dense dark ficus types with black shadows about the alcoves and caverns at the base of the trunks. These solid blocks of darkness, and the occasional clumps of small acacia-like shrubs with delicate pinnate leaves that trembled at the faintest breath of wind, were the worst of the threats; every time you turned a corner of the track there was bound to be one or other of these deadly menaces about fifty yards ahead where the next corner waited. Either the ominous black shadows, or those leaves that were being moved – by something.

You had to force your feet to keep going, not to pause, not reduce speed, or those behind would then begin to close and would know you were faltering. The palms of my hands began to sweat so that the sten kept slithering through the quivering grip, I had to keep rubbing my right hand on trousers to make it hold. As I rounded each bend, praying it would go on turning and turning for ever, the sight of another fifty-yard straight hit like a physical blow, almost blocking me in track . . . one of those acacia bushes ahead at the end, too leafy to see if anything hidden . . . eyes strain to peer through it . . . leaves are moving, but maybe a faint breeze down there, please God . . . another slit trench on the right . . . corner now only about twenty yards away, they would have opened fire by now surely? . . . or waiting to make sure the others had come into line? . . . the leaves, watch the leaves, the leaves . . . and it's over! The breath shudders out, you look at your watch and discover it has not moved in all that time, you turn past the bush that was always innocent and there ahead of you is a straight stretch of forty yards with a towering black-shaded ficus like a monster of doom at the end of it. You pray – and you swear – and you pray.

Twice along that ridge I took the lead, and each time lasted a life. The watch said exactly thirty minutes for me but Tiny Langford, whose time I checked as carefully as my own because it measured the life that was left to me, spent extra minutes up there on both his sessions. Whether because he noticed my suffering – despite the efforts to hide it from him – or whether he had managed to dismiss fear from his own mind I don't know, but I blessed him for each instant of reprieve he gave me. I could never have fired the sten usefully had an occasion arisen, my hands were shaking so much the aim would have been erratic, and when each session ended I had to compose myself quickly, suppress the trembling evidence by flexing the fingers as though troubled by nothing more than ordinary cramp, clear the sweat from face and beard as though merely fatigued, so that when the others caught up with me I could greet Tiny in what I hoped was the same casual manner as he handed over to me. I had never, in the air, had fear threaten as badly as on that day. Even when circling about a heavily defended target at night, watching the flak and deciding upon an attack line through the inferno, there was only a sort of tingly excitement about the impending run, like you feel when waiting at the door of the plane for your first parachute descent. But there was no excitement on the ridge that afternoon. Only a terror never to be forgotten.

One moment in my second session I very nearly did break down. We had come to one of those slight folds in the ridge, the fort was almost out of sight by then and on the left was a tangle of lantana leading down into a little dip. An opening had recently been man-cut through this clump, I could see white splintered wood and broken twigs, was trying to peer through the tangle to discover an associated slit-trench when suddenly I heard a loud crackling behind my head on the opposite side of the track. The body reaction was to swing round the sten – though the heart had stopped – and I should have fired instantaneously but the trigger finger was some-how stopped from the ultimate pressure.

A horse's head in the bushes . . . almost within touching distance . . . enormous glossy dark eyes. I stepped back and it pushed noisily through the leaves and up on to the track, a gaunt bay mare starved to sinew lines, lumpy rough coat and open sores throbbing with flies. Where she came from we could not tell but the probable origin was Dah Force. She was in such appalling condition we might well have shot her at any other time – but we dared not fire a gun that afternoon unless attacked; we left her beside the track, standing mutely on three legs, skin corrugated over ribs, with a prayer of thanks from me – not only for being a friendly horse instead of an enemy soldier, but also for taking several precious minutes off the half hour of my lead.

By the end of that second lead we had passed the worst. There were no more slit trenches, no more track evidence, so that when presently we tried the men from the recce platoon again they kept their space ahead and I had a chance to relax and haul myself out of the chasm of fear. Tiny and I discussed practical matters, such as the distance to the RV, marching rate, and the passing of time. We made our own way into dusk, moving from a clearing where we could see the trees on the westerly ridge silhouetted against a vast expanse of orange sky, and then dropping down steeply into a narrow valley where the tall trees blotted out the sky at once and crickets had already started on their nocturnal chords. We lit fires, had a meal, and discussed action. We still had about twelve miles to go, and as it was by Kachin-type track across the lie of the land we reckoned it would take at least five hours, but we were anxious to get 'home' and still felt reasonably fresh so decided to press on until we came to the rendezvous with the column. Accordingly we sent the Kachin guide ahead to tell the column we would arrive about midnight.

It was night when we started off again, enlivened by coffee

and relaxed from tension; the track was well marked and then presently we had a crescent moon to light our way, so we made good and pleasant time until we were within about an hour of our target. We had stopped for a break by a taungya which had just been planted and were scooping off the ash-black mud from ourselves prior to starting off again when the stillness of the night was suddenly shattered by the explosions of mortar shells, followed by bursts of automatic fire. The sounds kept on throbbing through the hills continuing for perhaps a minute and then stopped abruptly; a moment later they started again but just sporadic rifle fire, and every time it died away there would be a few more shots to keep the echoes flying. The disturbance seemed to be located directly ahead, somewhere down the slope towards our destination.

It was a measure of the different effect the earlier trials of that day had had on Tiny and myself that he seemed quite unconcerned about the action that was going on down there just ahead of us. He was knocking off his pipe on a tree-trunk as he speculated on the causes of the uproar, as though it were nothing more than an interesting problem in deduction; he considered it might be an attack on vehicles trying to use the road or – and this he thought less likely – an attack by the Japanese on the column in harbour. I had no interest at all in these theories about the source of the action, the only thought in my mind was the threat it presented to ourselves. I interrupted his speculations with an abrupt suggestion:

'I think we had better stop here.'

'Here? Why?'

He was genuinely surprised. The thought had clearly not even occurred to him. For the first time it seemed that the question of command might arise between us as I tried to justify my suggestion, pointing out that if the column were being attacked then we might have to pass through the Japanese line to reach them, and they would certainly open fire on us in the darkness. We had no assurance our messenger had got through to the column; even if he had it would be perilous to assume we could walk straight through any action at night, avoiding the enemy and yet being recognized as friendly by the column outposts. To my relief Tiny suddenly interrupted me:

'Of course you're right. I didn't think of that.'

I wished he had. It seemed to me later as we settled down under the trees for the rest of the night, not a sound now disturbing the moonlit stillness, that I had pressed my arguments with almost panic-stricken urgency; his calm dispassionate discussion of the situation had been in marked contrast to my feverish outburst. It had been a bad day for me, and I worried for a long time that night about whether this had been manifest to Tiny. He never mentioned it, never afterwards suggested he had even noticed anything unusual in my behaviour.

A long time afterwards however I decided that he who was me that day had no reason to be ashamed about that attack of fear. On the contrary, he deserved a medal for keeping on walking down that empty harmless track.

14

_____

The rains came stealthily, not in an overt torrent but insinuating through occasional showers until you suddenly realized it was a long time since you had known a rainless day. From the day we rejoined the column on May 3rd until the end of the whole campaign we never saw dry ground again. The tracks on the hills turned dark and slithery, the road was muddy brown and eyed with puddles, your pack stopped drying out and was now always moisture-heavy, your hands stayed wrinkled with damp, and when you removed your wet boots in the daily search for leeches your feet were white and clammy as a frog's belly.

There would be sunshine too most days, and then we could start to dry out for a few hours. Standing on the top of a taungya drop-site one sunny afternoon, the whole column gathering at the bottom of the site preparatory to marching off, I saw a diaphanous cloud rising from the sodden men and mules; like steam from a hot spring it came rolling up the slope carrying with it the smell of sweat and dung and uncovered drains.

The nights could be cruel . . . you would lie on the ground wrapped in the blanket and beg for a rain-free night, but there were precious few. When you heard the inevitable drumming roar on the leaves high above you would hide under the blanket and hope it was an illusion, but soon you would feel a probing chill trickle like a refrigerated louse crawling down your shoulder, and then other patches of dampness from the sodden blanket would begin to penetrate and ooze coldly about your hip bone and your shoulder and your knee, everywhere the blanket touched your shivering body, and the longing for warmth and dryness and comfort would become so intense, the appeal for it so passionate, you felt that will-power alone must compel a miraculous response. I doubt that suffering ennobles the soul but have no doubt whatsoever about its power to ennoble the commonplace comforts of life. Many a night on those wet Kachin hills I swore in vengeful concentration never to forget the misery of that moment, to guard it forever as a precious criterion, and so it has become. One in particular – when I crouched, not lay, shivering all night against the trunk of an ailanthus – I can always recall to ensure blessed appreciation of a bed, a blanket, and shelter, however squalid they may be. Even on nights when sleep comes hard there is always comfort to be derived from the hoarded memory of those nights of undiluted misery on the cold rainy mountainsides of Burma.

The lice became more active – and more difficult to eradicate. You could still strip off your shirt and trousers to search the seams, still perhaps find and kill every one in your clothing, but there would always be a few temporarily outside your garments at the moment of the hunt, searching for new feeding grounds or in transit over your webbing or pack or blanket, so when dressed once more you would be already infested and know about it when they began to move again that night. We had been told that once the rains started we would lose our lice, they would not live on damp cold bodies, but this is not true. The lice may not have liked our cold wet bodies but if that was all they could get then they accepted their lot with lousy equanimity and thrived. I had as much trouble with them when the rains started as I had when sweating dirty down on the plains, and much less chance of washing and drying clothes so as to reduce slightly their numbers.

With the rains too came the leeches. We had met them

occasionally before, but only as notable events; you would pass through a stream or boggy patch, discover one trying to get inside your clothing or see it actually plugged into your flesh, and show it to others with a certain pride before burning it off, rather like displaying the membership badge of an exclusive group. You too had now been bitten. But all exclusivity was washed away with the onset of the rains, now there could have been no one in all three columns, neither man nor beast, who had been exempt from attack. There were days and places certainly when we saw not a single leech, but days and places too where we saw them almost lining the track in wait – a whole range of colours and sizes, gold and olive and mahogany and worm-brown and black, from little more than pin-length up to three inches long, always starting off thin enough to pass through the eye of a boot and slither up the stitched tongue to curve over the top and get down inside, there to suck the blood through your sock until they were gorged to the size of your little finger. They stirred the grass like a zephyr of wind, they wavered and groped for you from the trackside bushes, they swayed upright beside the path as if feeling blindly for you, they would double across the rocks and send up probing tentacles from the seething mud by the edge of a stream, they would fall on your hat and shoulders as you brushed your way through massed bamboo and thence go curving their way down inside your collar, they would fasten to your trousers and enter through the gap between fly-buttons, and they would cling to your dumped pack at a halt and then worm a way through under your belt once you were on the march again. Every time you halted you either spent precious minutes of the rest period hunting for leeches to burn off, or you took your full rest and prayed you were clear, but then spent the next march period worrying about the blood being drained from your emaciated body. The very painlessness of the attack is unnerving – the pain, the itching, only comes later and often not at all. You wondered how many were sucking your life's blood away, unseen, unfelt, stealthily engorging themselves, as you clambered up the slippery tracks in the hills.

We met both rain and leeches that last morning on our return from China, but the first part of the march only lasted an hour or so, for we came to a village and there found 94 column. Peter Cane had water boiling, gave us hot tea as he told about his adventures and frustrations down on the road, and laughed about the noisy confusion of the action we had heard the previous night. When they had finally left the road, bitter with Headquarters for spurning the lush target they had forged for the Air Commando ('the planes will bomb and destroy the targets you produce') the harassed Japanese at that moment decided to send a force up to rout out and destroy the irritants that had been pestering them. In the darkness they floundered into the rifle company commander who was busy on the track preparing an ambush for any such pursuers. In the noisy action which followed there was a great deal of confusion, as there always seemed to be in our every brush with the enemy, and though the bangs were loud and prolonged, there appeared to have been few casualties suffered on either side. The rifle company dispersed when the action became too much for them and when we met the column that morning there were still thirty men missing but Peter was confident they would rejoin them presently. He was cheerful by nature, never brooded on misfortune and accepted its lessons lightly; he had faith in the men he had trained, and in fact they did rejoin the column two days later, when Peter had moved on about a dozen miles into the hills, illustrating again how well the RV system could work in effective practice.

Stanley joined us that morning to discuss the possibility of building an airstrip to get out the wounded – Sima'pa was much too far away. I told him of a site I had seen near Nalong and he later got them away from there. He had become solicitous about my health ever since that stroke business, and he tried to thrust some rice on me. We spent a pleasant half hour wandering about the village with that tree book and afterwards he helped write them up in my note book. Now that the rains had started I had to be careful with the note book, it was in pencil and the writing could fade to disappearance if the page became mushy so I kept it in K-ration waxed paper most of the time. The diary was written in ink, obsessively every day, and although this ran when wet the book was so small it could be protected by huddling your body over it as you wrote.

Tiny and I left 94 later that morning and continued on our way to rejoin 49 at the rendezvous. It had been raining frequently in the hills since we left the column and you could smell the difference in the air, a moisty fresh scent of growth like that in a greenhouse which has just been watered. We always seemed to have a predominant background scent; in the early days it had been the faintly pepper-tinged dry atmosphere of the indaing then when the taungyas were being fired in April the smell of wood fire tainted all else on the trail, up in the fig-tree forest the prevailing odour was of fecund decay, and now the background was a spring-like scent of rejuvination in the rain-cleared air. Within a few days however the freshness was gone, flooded out by persistent rain, and the background scent had deteriorated into one of dank moisture.

The Brigadier had established his headquarters on a heavily wooded ridge about a mile or so from the Bhamo-Myitkyena road, and had with him not only our column but also 40 column under Monteith, caught up with us at last. When we rejoined them that afternoon we found him with Monteith, very much 'in conference'; he had his big map board out on his knees, spectacles on nose, a new and neater set of red tabs on his shirt, and now and again he would give an occasional sweep of the hand to indicate the road below. He signalled for me to wait till he was free, presently ended his conference, then called me over:

'I'll have your report now, Pat,' he said grandly.

The tone of his voice, and the setting, seemed to call for a ceremonial response. I felt as if I should have stood to attention and responded in officialese:

'Sir! I have to report that I proceeded as instructed with the reconnaissance party to China, leaving Nahpaw Fort coordinate position 4484 at 0730 hours on . . .

However, I squatted down beside him and told him he could have his all-weather strip at Sima'pa if he wished. The space was there, the ground was suitable, but although it was out of my province I did add that it would not be easy to hold, or even to use, if the Japanese decided to intervene. He asked a question or two, then we worked out the signal to be sent back to headquarters about the strip. I think that was the last time we made our ration swop – the K rations had by now become drearily monotonous. I joined David Anderson under his makeshift shelter to discover that we were not allowed to light fires again. It was ridiculous. We were over a mile from the road, a thousand feet up in jungle and with cloud weaving like smoke through the tree tops, and still we were denied fire. Peter Cane would have had roaring blazes everywhere about under the trees – and as a result, higher spirits among the men, also. But the Brigadier could sense only the dangerous light and smoke of fire, not its comforting warmth. The rain was slight but steady and coldly penetrating, I had been looking forward to a hot drink all afternoon on our march and did not intent to forego it, despite the Brigadier's order.

It would have been easy to tell him I had left something back on the track at our last halt, go off a mile or so and light a fire, but instead I decided to utilize the battery-charger. He had already given permission to run it, and now the batteries were well-charged, but that was irrelevant. We piled some branches on top of it then covered these with our blankets; a mess tin filled with water was then jammed between the exhaust and the cylinder, the engine started, and we waited.

It worked. The water did not quite reach boiling point but it was hot enough to give a delicious coffee smell to the drink, and welcome enough to the adjutant and to David Anderson to earn their blessed thanks for the offering.

Towards the end of the afternoon the clouds broke up and lifted clear, and you could then see flecks of the red laterite surface of the road through the trees down below. One curious cloud formation persisted – there was a ridge on the far side of the road and this had a single line of cloud coiled stilly along its rim as the sun went down; it was perfectly straight and smooth, like a white bolster laid carefully along the ridge. The monsoon clouds beyond it to the west were aflame in the sunset, and the base of the vast conflagration was sharply defined by that foam-white line of cloud along the crest of the ridge, straight as the line of the long Pacific breakers seen from the sand of a wide coral beach.

The night promised fine so I shifted the groundsheet clear of the dripping trees and lay down in the open, looking up at the patches of star-strewn sky. It was very still and presently I found myself listening attentively to a brain-fever bird calling from somewhere far away down towards the road, for it seemed the bird was completing the full scale; straining to hear it I discerned another sound, a separate distracting one. It was the revving of an engine, not regular in beat but spasmodic, as though being tested with jerks of the throttle; it was on the fringe of audibility and made me so curious I finally rose and went down the hill to the rifle platoon where David Anderson was on duty. He had not picked it up himself until I made him listen but knew what it was from hearing it a day or two earlier. The Japanese were using a bulldozer on the road. They had moved it in to deal with Peter Cane's demolition, and it was gloomily predicted that the blocked trucks would be able to get away very soon. That very night, it so happened. As we were talking we heard the unmistakeable sound of an engine, a different note to that of the bulldozer, a steady throbbing sound, and then we saw actual lights far down below. The Japanese trucks were moving along the road.

David was mildly distressed. Instead of having a pleasant nostalgic conversation with me about summery days in peacetime he was forced back into war again, into responsibility and action and decision.

'Oh, Lord!' he said fretfully. 'I'll have to go and tell the Brigadier.'

This was not necessary however. Others had heard the sound and started to react. As we were moving back up to headquarters the stillness of the night was rent apart by the shattering uproar of our heavy machine guns from only twenty yards away along the slope, then a moment later the mortars also started sending down their shells. That effectively ended sleep for the night. The Japanese convoy stopped at once, we could see something burning down on the road, but this may have been a decoy for about ten minutes later they put their lights on and started moving once more. The guns and mortars reacted at once and again the convoy stopped. After that we kept firing occasionally, even though the convoy had apparently halted into shelter. It was impossible to sleep; you could perhaps learn to ignore the clatter of the machine guns but the mortars had about them the same tormenting quality as the brain-fever bird's call, they forced you to wait tensely for completion – the difference being that the bird never did give you the final note, whereas the mortar bomb did usually explode a long, long, long time after the thumping sound of its launch. Sleep was fitful, and with the approach of dawn I gave up the vain attempt and went across to join the mortar crew. We had field glasses on the road and kept studying it as the sun rose behind us, searing through the mist and chiselling light into the crevices of the valleys, but we could see no trace of any vehicles on the road itself. The Brigadier, hunting for me, joined us. The convoy had pulled off into the trees beside the road; he pointed out their exact location.

'Could you direct an air attack on there?'

There was still a lot of cloud about, slate-grey slabs of it suspended above the hills, but high enough to give the pilots a clear run beneath and we were well placed to direct them – provided the rain clouds did not again blot out sight of the road, so we prepared a signal. It was headed 'Personal from Brigadier Morris,' and asked for an air strike at 1000 hrs that same morning. We managed to get through to base immediately, but more extraordinary still received an answer about half an hour later to say that a bomber force escorted by fighters would carry out the attack as requested. Peter Cane, a major, with a target about ten times the size of the one we now held, had pleaded urgently for days and received not even a promise of a single aircraft, but a request from the Brigadier for action against a single convoy was granted munificently and at once – it was the last time we were so lucky however, for a few days later Cochrane's Air Commando was taken away from Special Force altogether, and that was the end of our so-called 'artillery'.

Just after we received the signal about the air strike the Japanese started sending mortar shells up into our position. The explosions reverberated across the valley, and you could still hear the last one dying away when the next one blasted over it. They were not very accurate, most of them landing well away to our left, but I saw the top of a tree just below us eject first leaves and twigs then a jet of white smoke when a bomb landed through it. The Brigadier was uneasy and began sending runners scurrying about to discover casualties but he was hugging the impending air strike as vengeful comfort.

'The bombers will soon put a stop to their little game,' he said.

I tried to prepare him for a less drastic outcome, but his confidence would not be shaken by reservations about weather interference or the human failings of pilots. Bombs

209

could miss targets, I told him. He would have none of this; he had seen these boys at work, he said. The Japanese were going to be blasted sky-high.

Unfortunately he was so relishing this prospect that he stayed with me that morning at the observation post from where I was trying to direct the attack, and he was an unmitigated nuisance. The job was complicated anyway because we could not mark the convoy position with mortar fire, we had no smoke bombs. Worse still, a long thin broken shred of cloud drifted across the valley during the attack and this made it fiendishly difficult to direct the pilots, for it was between me and the line of their attack – though they themselves were in the clear. The target was difficult, a heavily wooded gulley at right angles to the line they had to fly, so they had no margin of error to work with. Under perfect conditions, and with the target well marked, they might have had some success, but everything was against them that day. Including ground control. Here is an actual excerpt from my account of the attack written in the notes that afternoon:-

. . . Me on R/T:	'Hello Owen. This is ground. Did you see that mortar explosion? Over.'
Aircraft:	'Calling ground. We saw the smoke. Is that our target? Over.'
Me:	'Negative. Repeat negative. That gives our position. The target is about half a mile south. Do you see that kink in the road? – (Brigadier, interrupting. 'That's not half a mile Pat. Closer to a quarter. Tell him just over a quarter.')
Aircraft:	(confused by two voices) 'Hello ground. Repeat your message. Over.'
	(I repeat the message, giving in to the quibble from the Brigadier – it's not worth arguing about. Aircraft is happy but not the Brigadier. 'You've described the wrong site, Pat. Look, it's this one', pointing stick

	at remote point to the south. 'Tell him it's not –')
Aircraft:	'Hello ground. Turning on to target now. Over.'
Me:	'Okay Owen. I'll tell you when you are opposite us. The target will be a quarter of a mile south from that point. At the kink. They are parked on the western side, to the right of the road, under that thick clump of trees. Got it? Over.'
	(The Brigadier: 'The trees are south of the bend, Pat. On the western side but south of the bend. Tell him. Tell him.'
	Me: 'It's only a guide, for Christ's sake, let's leave him alone.'

The three B25's were in line astern, or very slightly staggered, flying about a thousand feet above the road and so almost level with us on the hill, and I began to talk him into the run-in checkpoint opposite us:

Me:	'Ground to Owen. You are nearly opposite us, coming closer, closer, closer. Now! Straight ahead!
	(The Brigadier cut in again. 'The Japs have got a position further up the hill behind the trucks. Tell them to bomb that too. Just a bit further up the hill.')

Part of this interruption got through to the aircraft, I was slow to shut off the transmitter switch. I really should have called off the run, told the bombers to go around again whilst the Brigadier and I sorted out a Controller between us, and an obstructive cloud shifted to give me a clearer view, but I hesitated about decision and then it was too late. The bombs came down, only vaguely across the gulley, shock waves shivered the trees, the explosions re-echoed through the hills, and a trail of grey smoke began to climb up out of the green ridge. There were cheers about us on the hillside, the

211

Brigadier congratulated me (for what?) as he raised and shook his clenched fists in pleasure. Then the leader gave us his final call:

'Hello ground. We're sending in the pea-shooters now.'

These were the P51 fighters. There were three of them and they came down again and again with cannon blazing, tracer streaming into the smoke about the target area. I did try to help them on to the exact target but the Brigadier kept on intervening. He wanted them to attack an invisible mortar position closer to us on the opposite ridge, to hunt out the bulldozer that was repairing the road further back, to check the bridge at Nalong, and God knows what else. In the end I was snapping at him to keep back from the transmitter, practically pushing him away. But he did not even notice our differences amid the excitement of the attack, and when the planes flew off he actually congratulated me before rushing back up the hill to share his enjoyment with Monteith and the adjutant.

There seemed to me little cause for celebration. There may have been one truck on fire, something was definitely burning down there, and we had given them a bad ten minutes or so, but that was about all. The target, tucked up in that transverse gulley, was not easy to strike, and any tree shelter is hard for fighters to penetrate. I had made strafing attacks myself, and been strafed by both German and Japanese fighters, and knew how easy it is to avoid personal hurt and how unlucky you are to have transport knocked out when it is tucked under trees. So I did not share in the elation of the observers on the hill. But in this I was wrong, as Tiny Langford pointed out a little later when I made a disparaging comment about the raid – I could always be frank with Tiny. He interrupted me with unusual severity:

'Who cares about the number of trucks hit?' he cried.

The raid had been a success even if not a single truck had been damaged, he said. The important result was that it had done a hell of a lot of good to our own men, lifted their morale, and given them a sense of power; this was far more beneficial to our cause at that moment than the destruction of a few trucks. He was right, you had to admit this when you looked at the men about you that afternoon. Smiles and chatter and excitement and bustle – as though the campaign were starting afresh. And the Brigadier's attitude which had seemed to me so juvenile at first was, in fact, just what was required of a commander. It was fortuitous in his case, not contrived, but that made no difference – his excited gratification encouraged the belief we had actually achieved a great victory. For all this, I still had a niggardly reservation: I wished we had inflicted a little more real damage on the enemy, had some physical evidence of this to fortify the psychological success.

When presently there was positive evidence that the convoy still existed despite that thunderous display of destruction, this was not allowed to tarnish the exciting memory of the victory. A tacit understanding was arranged whereby the awkward truth was denied: it was argued that the Japanese convoy must have been replenished by new arrivals who had joined them during the blinding thunderstorm that afternoon, that the main convoy had suffered severely there could be no doubt, the Japanese had then spent the rest of the day huddled in that gulley tending their wounded and salvaging what they could from all the trucks destroyed by the aircraft, and then these replacements arrived. That was how the convoy was able to get moving again. For it did get moving again that same night – so some such explanation had to be concocted if the thrill of our great air success was to be retained.

The behaviour of the Japanese force that night was inexplicable, for when they did start to move the convoy it was with the headlights of all the trucks blazing at full strength, almost as if they wanted to prove that the noise was not a deceit and that their trucks were actually moving on the road. Naturally we opened up with mortars and machine guns.

They stopped, turned off their lights, and we all waited. Then, half an hour later, they put on their lights and tried again, but again we made the obvious response and so once more they stopped. It was not a dark night, the moon was almost full – it was just two months since we had landed – and the cloud was scattered, so they could easily have sent individual trucks up the road without lights, and under a noise cover from the others revving up in the harbour area. But they did nothing to deceive. They just kept trying to move off in brightly-lit unison, advertising their intent with all the fanfare of the start of a great motor race. We kept responding, they kept stopping. This went on all night; light and noise down on the road provoked an explosive reaction from the hillside above. The stupidity of the Japanese commander was bewildering. Dawn found his convoy back in the same harbour gulley where they had been hit by our aircraft the previous day. An appeal for another air-strike went unheeded, however.

Things changed next morning, anyway. The Japanese either extracted some equipment from their trucks or it came out from Bhamo, for from mid-morning they started sending up not only mortar fire but also shells from artillery they had sited somewhere near the road behind the stalled convoy. The shelling of our position went on for over an hour; it was far more accurate than their initial efforts, and we had five men wounded during this prolonged fire. The Brigadier soon decided there was no sense in us staying on the ridge to be shelled indefinitely, so we withdrew into the hills towards the Chinese border to join Peter Cane's column and there decide upon our next sortie against the road.

Our casualties, and those from Peter Cane's fighting, were now sent out by light plane from the strip prepared by Stanley on the site we had discussed. At first the Brigadier had ordered me to do this job, then changed his mind just as we were about to start off; he told me that instead I was to go back to Sima'pa and there construct the all-weather strip we had discussed. It was mid-morning when we were hustled off on this trip, this time without Tiny Langford but otherwise much the same group, and we had climbed up and over two precipitous ridges and were looking for a night harbour when a Kachin scout caught us up with the Brigadier's change of mind. The note, printed letters in pencil, said:

Dear Pat,
 Sorry but there is a change of plan. I want
 you to return and run a SD.
Yrs.
J. R. Morris

By this time anyone in the column could have run a supply drop. The following day when I arrived back about mid-day, in sullen mood, we had walked about twenty-four miles and climbed up and down a total of almost twenty thousand feet according to my furious calculations. All because, as he put it in a typical intransitive evasion: 'there is a change of plan' – not that it was he who had changed his mind, but that some higher authority had intervened. It seemed to me that day, in savage temper after such gratuitous punishment, that it was no wonder the poor adjutant was a physical wreck after two months of such insecurity of decision. He was sent out that afternoon with the wounded from Stanley's airstrip but he died a few days later. Already by this time it was growing easy to die, harder to hold on to life.

15

Someone, somewhere back in the safety of an office in India, thought to economize on the use of cotton and decided to test, at the risk of our hunger, a cheaper type of parachute. It was made out of jute, the same material as the bags of rice, heavy and porous – and totally unfit for the purpose, as we discovered that night in May when they guinea-pigged us. To our dismay most of the dark bundles trailing down after the square loads did not even open at all. They streamed down with frightening speed – fortunately there was a moon-lit sky – the loads hitting the ground with the shattering force of a free drop, bursting explosively open and splattering contents all about the point of impact.

Even when one of these so-called parajutes did open it acted more like a mere directional vane than a retarding force, and the load hit the ground with such speed that the K-ration packs were distorted; it then became difficult to open the little ration tins if at all, the biscuits were crushed, the cigarettes mangled. The murderous hatred which men in the field sometimes develop for staff officers is not always misplaced or prejudiced. A staff officer would be most unlikely to commit himself personally to dependence upon hessian-parachuted supplies for a month unless he were absolutely sure after many tests that the parajutes worked efficiently. We felt, not unreasonably, that we up in the rain-slashed hills of Burma were entitled to that same precious care.

The road action had been on May 6th and for about a

fortnight after this the whole force of three columns pottered about that area with no clear purpose or directive. It was a dithering period, when Force Headquarters had fallen silent and our independent actions seemed arbitrary, hasty, and impossible to justify either on tactical or strategic grounds. All this was a consequence of indecision above, on two levels – that of our own brigade, and that of Force Headquarters. General Lentaigne, as he had now become, lacked the power and prestige that had been invested in Wingate by personal association with Roosevelt and Churchill; Lentaigne was to India Command a mere major-general running a detached force that was quite irrelevant to the titanic battle taking place in the Kohima-Imphal area where over a hundred thousand Japanese had been committed to the destruction of the allied forces in India and the occupation of the country itself. Lentaigne's comparitively small group of Chindits were a distracting irrelevance to Army Headquarters, particularly as we were operating in an area which the notoriously prickly 'Vinegar-Joe' Stilwell considered his bailiwick. The enticing solution, one that got rid of us and might also placate the vitriolic Stilwell, was to hand over the Chindits to him completely and let him give them orders direct rather than keep snapping at high command with his savage criticisms and demands for action. Lentaigne's authority was weakened in this boardroom struggle for survival, and in the meantime the commanders in the field were deprived of directive. All of us from Brigadiers down to my orderly Lilbahadur, had to wait in the anteroom while supreme headquarters crept to the inevitable decision.

We, of all the Chindit groups, probably suffered worst during this period of suspension, because the commander of Morris Force was himself insecure in such an autonomous role. Had the Brigadier been in charge of a normal brigade within a compact regular division, he would have operated with efficiency, for he was a meticulous and proficient administrator of orders; but he was now hundreds of miles away from his next superior officer and radio connections were particularly unreliable during that fortnight. He was forced to initiate his own course of conduct, give effect to an overall plan designed by Wingate many months earlier when conditions were entirely different. With such a wide range of options he was most unhappy. At his best he might have coped reasonably well with this problem, but he was in poor physical condition, so that even when he did get the semblance of a definite order from Force Headquarters he was in no state to make a coherent and effective plan for its execution. He had difficulty in making up his mind and had no confidence in a decision once taken.

'What do you think, eh?' he would ask, telling of his decision about something or other.

He would sit there, looking around at us, groping for reassurance. Or even an outright rejection of the plan, followed by a positive recommendation. Even then his final decisions were rarely secure. He told Peter Cane to keep his column down on the road for a further two days, then when he happened to see a note Peter sent to a platoon commander saying there were masses of Japanese about the area he recalled the whole column – at once, without checking if Peter was just using hyperbole, and not even explaining the reason for the abrupt recall. Then a day later, when Peter had almost arrived back at the hideout in the hills he sent another note to say he could stay down and continue operations if he so wished – I was with Stanley that day and read the note myself. When I saw a stretch of road that seemed to me a good target for an air strike – a cutting around a spur, with a steep drop into the *chaung* – he agreed after much dithering. Once we had sent the signal however he changed his mind in the middle of the night, saying it might jeopardize our harbour base, and we had to spend three hours before managing to get through a message of cancellation.

It was a trying time for the column commanders who had to deal with most of these cancellations and adjustments of orders. Because I was not an Army officer they felt freer to talk to me perhaps – I was part of the battalion but without tribal rank, so breach of loyalty did not arise and when we met on a drop site or somewhere in the hills in passage they felt they could relax and talk. Each of the three commanders suffered in his own way. Peter Cane of 94 was a dashing ebullient leader, with limitless energy, always eager for action, and his major trial was the maddening frustration of having to watch opportunity after opportunity fade away as his commander ignored targets which Peter had laboriously created. Monteith, the commander of the newly arrived 40 column, was a man who liked order and precision in his affairs, he wanted every action to be planned and executed as on a perfect exercise, no attack until an overwhelming force had been assembled and air support perfectly organized, everything well practised and neatly set out in orders, so he was driven to anguished outcry by the Brigadier's impetuous decisions and constant postscripts.

Finally there was Ted Russel who as titular commander of 49 column suffered the worst of all, for with the Brigadier tied to us during the whole campaign poor Russel had no effective command at all. He was treated sometimes as a mere assistant and sometimes as a comforter dispensing reassurance, never as the able commander he was and one who should have been consulted always about the dispositions of his own men. I myself, for example, was supposed to be attached to 49 and therefore technically under Russel's command, but the Brigadier kept me always as part of his headquarters retinue and never thought to include Russel in our deliberations; usually I would tell Russel as a friend when we were to have a supply drop, or where I was going off, with how many men, and why. If the Brigadier had even been consistent in his treatment it might have at least made Russel's life easier, but when a plan was suddenly thrust upon him Russel was never sure if it was meant to be carried out instantly without question or whether it was only a suggestion and would he please reject it at once and produce a sensible alternative. Like the poor adjutant, Russel too suffered physically under the stress of such continuous insecurity and he had to be sent out shortly – he, fortunately, did recover later on in hospital.

I made two trips down to the road in mid-month but all was quiet on both occasions. The second time was when we took down three wounded men and Stanley came back with me on that occasion, for the strip was then being abandoned. We took our time on the trip back that day – Stanley still so concerned about my health he even wanted to carry my pack – and stopped for some time in the morning at a village where a pretty girl in her early teens was laying a posy made of rose-pink begonias on the platform of a nat shrine. She turned and watched us approach up the hill track not at all alarmed. She was wearing a navy-blue lungyi and jacket with a white embroidered cross over each breast. When we paused and called out the usual 'Kaja'e,' she did not just smile but laughed outright, at our accent perhaps, and she accompanied us up into the village repeating the word, savouring it, and glancing with giggles at Stanley and me. Completely at ease – no trace of shyness. A younger girl about ten years old, wearing a scruffy brown smock, came running down to meet her and she mimicked for her our 'Kaja'e' pronounciation; they both broke out into bright laughter, then went running away together presumably to tell all their friends. They left us smiling also.

We heard an extraordinary sound that day. We had stopped for midday break on a ridge looking eastwards to the blue hills over the Chinese border, and afterwards lay there for a languid half hour talking of old times and friends, then just lying there. I heard it first – Stanley was just beginning to start worrying about passing time – but then he too became distracted by the mysterious noise. It was a very faint short-noted squeak, like when a door-hinge flicks over a small rust-spot and it took us a minute or so to trace the unusual source. It came from a moth, bracken-brown with a creamy bar across the wings and about the size of a tortoiseshell butterfly; it was on a tree trunk just behind us and kept making the sound intermittently, at the same time fluttering its wings like a nestling appealing for food. I had never heard of lepidoptera making sounds – except of course that one reported by Wodehouse's golfer who missed a short putt because, so he claimed, he was distracted by the clatter of a passing butterfly in the nearby field.

We also talked that day about our post-Wingate plans, for we were now approaching the end of our jungle-warfare days with the army. Before leaving India we had been told that the whole operation would be terminated definitely at three months – this was not just because it was thought impossible to keep us supplied by air during the monsoon days, but mainly because it was reckoned that three months was the limit of human endurance under such conditions. Wingate himself had declared this to be so, and in accordance with this decree the brigade which had marched in earlier than all the rest of us had now been withdrawn. We had by this time been behind the enemy lines for about ten weeks so had only a fortnight left to complete our sentence.

Planes were still getting through intermittently with supply drops despite the rains but we were still only on half rations and were all losing weight; this was not only a result of the shortage suffered for so long but also because the rations themselves had lost their original appeal – as will any food which you are forced to take for months without variation. The K-rations were designed for assault troops, meant to sustain men for five days in emergency until proper facilities could be provided, never intended to be a sole diet for months at a time. Even one's favoured items had now lost appeal – the swop arrangement between the Brigadier and me ended because it required a tiny effort, and by this time neither of us was sufficiently interested to make that effort.

We were now in wretched physical plight. Though mepacrine can suppress malaria under normal conditions it is not completely effective over a long period – much less so on men in such a debilitated state as we were by mid-May. Even though it may not have broken through completely you can still suffer from bouts of what we in the Pacific used to call 'low fever', when the temperature rises only a degree or so for days at a time and the repressed disease seems to be sapping your vitality like an internally-affixed leech. In such condition, and with the will to live already rickety under stress, you were an easy victim for any other health threat that might arise. Two more officers had to be sent out at about this time, another died, together with seven men in our column alone. It was only the promise of imminent withdrawal that kept many others alive.

The Brigadier had sent out a long report about the fitness of his men – he said nothing about his own physical condition in any message I ever saw – but there had been no response from Headquarters. He asked me to send a signal a few days later, on May 18th, requesting a reply but before we could get it through that afternoon we ourselves heard a dramatic announcement on the radio saying, unequivocally, that Myitkyena had been captured by Stilwell's forces. This brought a shout of excitement from us at the radio and I went hurrying across the hillside to the Brigadier to tell him the news. He wanted to believe it, trembled on the brink of accepting it but it had only been an intercept and there was the possibility, though fantastically remote, it might be a Japanese plant. The Brigadier dare not risk disappointment. Could we raise Force Headquarters for confirmation? We could not – that was what we had been trying to do when we caught that message. But whilst we were actually discussing this a message came through from Monteith of 40 column only a few miles away. It said simply:

MYITKYENA HAS BEEN CAPTURED
BY STILWELL.

They must have been in contact with base. The Brigadier then did joyfully clasp the good news to his bosom and began a fury of planning, starting off with signals to the other two column commanders telling them to join us at once, the object being to discuss how to arrange our withdrawal. The one column commander immediately available, our Ted Russel, was then called over for a prolonged conference on details about our departure. And that rainless evening the fires blazed brightly on the hillside, with us talking and planning and singing – Gurkha voices crooning softly their tender melody, 'The Girl Across the Valley' – yes, the Brigadier allowed even the singing to continue for a little time that joyful night.

To reassure us that the campaign was now definitely over we received a further signal early next morning saying we were to march out of Burma northwards, heading for Fort Hertz where there was a Dakota airstrip whence presumably we would be flown back over the Chin Hills to India. It was a holiday after that. I spent the rest of the morning washing my clothes and body, squatting wrapped in a blanket whilst seeking out the lice in the seams of shirt and trousers, even considered shedding my beard but the mechanics involved – borrowing scissors and razor and soap and mirror – seemed far too laborious to inflict upon oneself for such a trivial purpose.

The Brigadier, revivified by our release, had me with him in his basha shelter that afternoon to examine his maps. We were over two hundred miles south of Fort Hertz, there was no road up there on our side of the Irrawaddy, so the route would be through the hill tracks along the Chinese border, much the same country we had been traversing during the past months. Tiny Langford was included in the discussions, the idea being that we would take a party ahead and prepare drop sites. We all totted up distances on the map like a trio of excited schoolboys planning a holiday, and reckoned it would take us about three easy weeks allowing for pauses to collect supplies. He set me working at once on the selection of possible sites, then went into prolonged conference with Ted Russel, our column commander, to discuss the constitution of the reconnaissance parties that would go with us and various other details of the outward march.

The elation lasted less than twenty-four hours, just time enough to send off a scouting party ahead but not enough to push me away on yet another recalled mission. Our bubble of joy was burst by a signal which indicated that high authority must at last have made the changeover in command, for it was from Stilwell direct to us. It said he was pleased with the contribution we were making to his attack on Myitkyena (*attack*, not capture?), congratulated us on our success in stopping Japanese reinforcements moving north (surely the only time he ever congratulated anyone during his whole wartime command?) and instructed us to stay and continue the good work (stay? what was the point?).

Had Myitkyena been captured or not? You need facts for sensible planning. We sent a signal pleading for confirmation or denial but headquarters would not reply. A repeat, marked PERSONAL FROM BRIGADIER MORRIS, was also ignored. Whatever the truth, however, one thing was cruelly clear from the spate of signals now coming in from Stilwell's headquarters: our ordeal was far from over.

Like the young lady of Riga moreover we soon found ourselves in mortal peril riding the tigerish Stilwell, for scarcely had we decoded that congratulatory message than we received another saying we were to use our maximum effort to block the road and river traffic in the KAZU area. There were two possible explanations for this preposterous signal; the first was that the staff officer had merely made a guess from a map, because the only running water at Kazu was a stream called Nam Tabet which could be a trickle or a torrent according to the amount of rain that had just fallen in the nearby hills; the second possible explanation was that he meant river traffic on the Irrawaddy, but that was about forty miles away at its nearest point to us. The Brigadier made an arbitrary decision that Kazu itself was meant to be the target – that 'river traffic' was a misunderstanding of some kind – and ordered that we should close at once on Kazu twelve miles away down on the plain. This was in mid-afternoon, with rain slashing at us on the clouded hillside.

We loaded the animals and were humping up our own packs, settling into dreary line for the slippery downward march, when he suddenly changed his mind. He decided, in an impulse of valour, to query the order. Everyone unpacked, crawled under shelter of some kind, waited, and then gradually settled for the night. We could not raise base until nearly midnight, and had to wait another couple of hours for a reply to our signal. Then we had not just a simple single answer but three in all, sent out in quick succession, and saying – in order of receipt:

1. All columns should attack Kazu.
2. Do not attack Kazu. Close on Myitkyena with all speed at once.
3. Your instructions are in signal 1.

The Brigadier had to be shaken awake and told the muddled response to our signal. When he heard the first message he immediately told his orderly to fetch Ted Russel and a horse, but then he shouted for him to come back when he started to read the second message. Finally he sat up, torch in hand, reading and re-reading each of the messages, asking for time of receipt and muttering to himself and then, to my relief, stuffed them all into his pack and said he would make a decision in the morning. Nothing to be sent out. So we all had some sleep that night.

What followed as a result of these signals, and his subsequent action, was almost a mutiny. Here, first of all, are my diary entries for the next two days:

Saturday May 20th: Dawns cloudy. Feel today will be ominous, enemy-infested. Now 1100 – have sense of impending action. Later, 1545, O.B. ('Old Boy' was my code for the Brigadier) suddenly decides attack Kazu. Move in 45 minutes! I to wait and pass out Air Support message. Later, march on, arriving in darkness. O.B. has mad plan and Russ gives out the orders in blackness. We sleep?

Sunday May 21st: O.B. gets confounded. Peter turns up after we march down road and told him what a fool he was. So does Russ. Practically a fight. 'Brothel-bred-bastard.' They with two platoons to go ahead and recce area. Peter and O.B. continue argument. We all go down finally – cars and frigidaires and bomb craters. Sleep, intense heat, and flies. Dushman (Gurkhali = 'enemy') bathes in river.

The incidents of those two days and the week that followed were actually far more chaotic than suggested by those laconic diary entries. That Saturday of May 20th started off gloomy and never improved. The clouds drifted cold and damp across the hillside in the grey dawn and from the ridge you could intermittently get a glimpse of the valley to the west with its treetops embedded in cottonwool. The Brigadier talked to Tiny Langford about Kazu – Tiny had done a recce nearby – to Ted Russel about the approach for the attack, and to me about a possible air strike, but then dismissed each of us in turn without making any decision. However he then kept calling one or other of us back from time to time, making notes on a signal pad and then ripping them up, snapping at his orderly, and at one stage calling for a horse to be brought up at once but then sending it back the moment it arrived – not for the first time.

After noting these few sentences in the diary I spent the morning, when temporarily released from the Brigadier, squatting under a rough roof-shelter going over the early material in my note book which the damp had now almost obliterated. A cloud enveloped the hill in the early afternoon and for a couple of hours it either rained down actual drops or the water coagulated on your face and hands and clothing out of the cold sodden air; from the tall trees – like the kanyin, a hundred feet up to the first branch – the drops fell with stinging force on your damp-wrinkled hands, and all around us on the grey hillside the constant melancholy plip-plop sounds of water were thuds of misery to your soul.

The Brigadier erupted finally, as noted in the diary, just before 4 pm, when he decided to attack Kazu at once with all possible speed – no reconnaissance. It was about twelve miles away, we would move at once and be close enough to launch the actual frontal attack early next morning. Without having any idea what targets were there at Kazu, if any at all, where located, or how air support could possibly be directed on them, he ordered me to stay behind with the radio and send through that message for an air strike 'to tie in with the ground assault.'

I thought to argue about the absurdity of such a request but he was in such a frenetic state that I decided to stay quiet and get out of his way. When presently he rushed off with the column I prepared the message for air support but so fouled up the code that there was no possible chance of it ever being deciphered – I had no intention of having us all blown to bits by our own aircraft in an undirected unplanned disorganized air attack. It was a couple of hours before we got our meaningless jumble through to base, then we packed up, loaded the mules, and made the five mile march down the hill in blackness to rejoin the column.

The next morning the Brigadier wanted to continue the march straight on down the road to Kazu. This precipitated that argument with the column commanders, I was involved because he had conceived a lunatic scheme to overcome our lack of information about enemy positions – we would ask the fighter/bombers to make first a reconnaissance run over the tree-covered area and then radio information about the enemy positions down to us. I told him this was an impossible task for pilots as they would see nothing through the trees in that area – and anyway we did not know we would

227

even get any air support (only I knew that). It was crazy to go marching off into an enemy position in the belief that aircraft would come at the last moment and resolve all our planning deficiencies.

Ted Russel supported me strongly. He said we should discover something about enemy positions before advancing into Kazu. Then Peter Cane arrived with his column, and he brought rebellion to a head; he told the Brigadier with blunt force that he would not take his whole column marching down the road, he would send forward only rifle platoons to check what opposition existed and where, the rest of his column would follow up only when the ground had been tested. There was a heated session in the bamboo grove, the Brigadier trying to wave them away to start column march but Peter Cane was adamant that rifle platoons alone should make the move. It was the Brigadier who cracked:

'All right. Do it your way, then,' he said suddenly. He turned away, sat down in the bamboo alcove and started to rummage in his saddle bag, his back positively set against us – Achilles sulking in his tent.

It was shortly afterwards that I heard, from another officer, a suggestion that the Brigadier should be 'accidentally' shot. It may have been a vague hope previously but on this occasion it was put forward in a measured tone as a genuine alternative to be borne in mind should persuasion fail. The phrase noted, 'brothel-bred bastard' was uttered with a quiet venom that left no doubt about the speaker's hostility – and strength of purpose.

We walked straight down the Kazu road because there was no practical alternative, the bamboo on each side was impassably dense and it would have taken days to cut a way through and been noisily apparent the whole time. Ted Russel himself took the lead at the head of the platoon, and there is no doubt in my mind that this was an act of great courage, because he was fully aware of what might be waiting for us – I had just heard him describing the danger, in vivid detail, to

228

support his argument against a column advance. We discovered there had been a Japanese force of about 1500 men in a carefully camouflaged camp just by the rickety bamboo bridge; they had strong defensive positions well concealed in the bamboo, so sited as to make the approach road itself the perfect 'killing ground' and they would have slaughtered us had they still been there that day.

Happily we all lived, the major Japanese force chanced to have withdrawn just the previous day and not a single enemy soldier remained on our southern side of the river. In the camp on the far side however there was still some activity as scouts reported and as I myself saw later when sent up to site an observer post for air control. From about fifty yards downstream that evening Stanley and I, peering through bamboo, saw three Japanese filling water bottles or washing something on the opposite bank; the river level was high, within a foot or so of the decking of the bridge, and this meant there would be no easy alternative to the bridge as our crossing medium. If the dozen or so Japanese seen altogether were part of a large force on the northern bank we recognized it was going to be a bloody battle to force a crossing.

On our way back from the river I told Stanley about the fouled-up signal and he was horrified at first – as expected. He thought I should have 'discussed' it with the Brigadier, or told Russel about it. Suppose the Brigadier found out? It would be a court-martial offence, surely? He became a little easier in mind when I suggested we could ask genuinely for air-support now that we had the river as a positive marker. We could ask for a strike next morning, directed against the northern bank, and to tie in with the time of our attack. He agreed and we sent back the signal to the sergeants with the mule party; it was as the Brigadier originally ordered but now we specified the north bank as the target.

The column attack was planned for late morning, an hour after the time set for the air-strike. We settled down for the night, without fire of course, and carefully silent, amongst the recent bomb craters in a natural clearing amid the bamboo just off the road. It was obvious no bridge had been available in the retreat two years earlier because discarded impedimenta, civilian and military, lay scattered about the area like the detritus after a receding glacier. There was an armoured truck which had been deliberately wrecked with bomb and fire, twisted black metal now with a patina of rust that showed it had died long before the creation of those bomb craters with their edges of freshly-turned earth. There were the stripped remnants of at least four cars, one of which was a Hupmobile sedan like one my father had bought in 1929, the first of its type in Maitland, sent out specially for him from America on a boat whose progress we had followed excitedly across the Pacific. It was fascinating to look about the clearing and see what people had tried to save with their lives when they fled – one of those refrigerators with a big coil on top, the cylinder of a Hoover, a gramophone (most of the big cabinet now gone), a pile of records including thick diamond-disc ones, all broken, two large table fans, and two lawn-mowers from which the handles had been smashed free. We spent the night among this lot, a hot close night with frogs croaking loudly in choral bursts, pestered by a type of biting fly that made a buzzing sound, and mosquitoes so heavy they made a tickling passage over your forehead as they searched for a succulent spot – or perhaps it was just the lice coming out into the less-hot open air to watch them gorge.

The next morning the clouds had lifted, the clearing was dappled and striped with light and shade when Stanley and I made our way quietly to the observation point on the river bank below the second bridge. There was a cool sweet smell from the river, a pleasant relief after that hot and wretched night, the swollen river itself was momentarily covered with a thin pearly mist that was now rising and swirling under the hot rays of the sun as if trying to escape attack; within a minute or so of our arrival it had been whisked away and we could see the dark rippling surface of the rising river as far as the bamboo bridge where a white band of foam now quivered at the base of the decking. We were talking in whispered tones about the bridge, its difficulty as a target, when a single shot rang out from that direction, a shout, then silence. Whether the shot or shout was from a Gurkha or Japanese I never discovered but the next sound, a burst of machine-gun fire, came from a Gurkha section just down the river; there, at the other bridge, a Japanese patrol had tried to cross and the Gurkhas had been forced to open fire, killing eight of the ten men in the party. The shattering echoes of the gunfire reverberated through the bamboo, sustained by other short bursts as we made our way back to column headquarters.

This happened about eight in the morning, and shortly afterwards we heard that we were not going to get any air support; cover had now been blown anyway so the timing was out of our hands. We all waited in position for about an hour but there was still no reaction from the rest of the Japanese over the other side – at this time we did not know their strength over there. The Brigadier then suddenly decided to move himself and his headquarters back into the hills and he set off on horseback with them at once, leaving instructions the attack should not start till an hour later. In the event we crossed the river safely, without any opposition, about midday but I was not confident about the future of the tottery bamboo bridge. The river level was now almost up to the decking, and water was flooding across the top because the branches and dead wood piled up by the strong current created an overflow. The bridge was trembling noticeably under the strain. On the far side we moved cautiously at first, then with growing confidence, into what turned out to be a large Japanese camp, dozens of bamboo huts and at least one truck which we did not touch for fear of booby-traps. The remaining Japanese had fled after the shooting at the bridge, leaving a large amount of equipment and food that included not only plenty of rice for everyone but also several cases of tinned peaches which I found irresistible – regardless of orders and risk of booby-trap I smashed open a tin with my kukrie at once and most of the contents went straight down my throat and the rest about my beard, so that for a long time afterwards my tongue and fingers were tracking down every possible morsel of the deliciously sweet juice. My diary says that Tiny Langford 'took some photographs' but this cannot be true, as we did not have a camera (a pity, that); from about this time onwards there were quite a few diary entries that are now meaningless to me, completely lost to memory which like life itself seems to have started to flicker unsteadily in those final weeks.

The river rose rapidly that day and by mid-afternoon both bridges were gone, leaving all the mules of both columns, loaded with all our equipment and supplies, stranded on the southern bank; they had come up to make the crossing as soon as we had established all was clear but it now seemed they might have to wait on the far side, perhaps for a day or two, until the flood subsided. Whilst Peter Cane was discussing this with David Anderson, and considering whether to try and get a rifle platoon back there just in case there were some isolated Japanese around, there came a burst of firing from the other side, the light chatter of Japanese machine guns and the cracking of rifles. A Japanese force had come up the road; they had obviously contacted our tail, the hundred mules with only fifteen riflemen over there as protection, and now had them trapped against the flood water. Peter Cane looked at the swollen river in dismay.

'What in hell do we do now?' he muttered.

'If it were a problem concerning the medieval popes,' David said, recalling his studies at Cambridge, 'I could give you a definitive answer – but this is a military matter and not my province. You're the military man. It's all yours, old boy.'

Peter hurried off with a group to try to find a crossing

232

further up the river, and meanwhile sporadic fire continued across the far side. I left them to it.

I had to go off with ten men to prepare for a supply drop. It was late afternoon by this time and it began to rain ferociously within a few minutes of our departure. There was no actual track to follow – not until we reached the foothills – but in the sheeting rain we could no longer see the hills and so had to march on compass. In the dry season this would have been easy enough, it was the type of low riverside jungle and thicket through which you could weave a way at two or three miles an hour without much difficulty but the surface had already been softened by the monsoon and the rain that day was changing the whole area into a flooded swamp. It was like clambering along a mangrove foreshore or estuary, at times up to your knees in mud and water, and having to grab at roots and branches to help haul your way onwards. In the remaining two hours of grey daylight we made less than a mile, by my gloomy estimate that night. And all the long night it pelted with rain. We spent it trapped in the swamp, breaking down bushes and branches in a vain attempt to keep ourselves above the water level as it kept on rising inexorably and forcing us to clamber on to higher nests. Leeches tickled over us and there was little we could do except brush at them in the wet blackness. We were cold, shivering cold. It would not have been hard to die that night.

We started off again at first light without waiting to deleech ourselves for by then the water in places was up to our waist and obviously still rising, though fortunately it had stopped raining and we could at least pick out a line of advance through the flooded trees. It must have been about midday when we finally reached solid ground in the foothills, by which time we had probably travelled no more than a couple of miles – and taken only three breaks during the whole morning. By then we were so exhausted that I abandoned normal procedures, dispensed with guards, and after burning off the obvious leeches we slept around a huge fire.

When we awoke we completed the leech hunt, had a meal and a hot drink and in the late afternoon finally roused ourselves to continue the journey. It began to rain again at dusk when we reached the Kachin village which was the planned drop site but we were welcomed in immediately to the chief's house and escaped the worst of the weather. We drank sapa with him and his two sons, speaking a lot but understanding little, and that night we slept blissfully dry in the warm house, collecting a horde of fleas to add to our resident lice. It was a cheap price to pay for dry warmth. Had the cost been life itself it would have still been tempting that night.

All this time the Brigadier had been esconced in a village about six miles away further into the hills, with perhaps a platoon of the column. He was six hours away from his column commanders and the radio was not effective. They were having problems down there with the Japanese and a co-ordinated response might have saved lives, so his remote absence from the scene of action was unfortunate – and not easy to explain charitably, either. By good fortune the immediate defence of the mule group was in good hands. It was a Gurkha havildar, Chakra Bahadur, in command and he established his post on the road with just fifteen men and set about holding up the two hundred Japanese for sufficient time to allow the animal party to escape into the jungle. He achieved this without loss, holding the vastly superior force for over two hours under constant fire, and the transport group managed to get out of the trap and head towards the hills.

The escape was only a temporary one however, the Japanese picked up the trail again later, but this time another group from 94 column came to the rescue by drawing off the pursuers; they exchanged fire briefly, just enough to attract the enemy, then dispersed into the hills leaving the Japanese chasing after shadows. The mule party however still had three desperate days after that in the swampy area about the flooded river which we had so laboriously traversed, at times having to use yakdhans on the flooded ground to give the mules a footing, so many loads were lost. They were then without a single rifleman to protect them and had only the long-range rendezvous as their hope of rejoining the column. Fortunately they were eventually found by a Kachin who delivered them to the rest of the column in the hills. The strain killed our mule officer however – he died the day after he had delivered back his charges safely to the column.

We ourselves had also rejoined the column the previous day, and that same night had a successful supply drop which left us replete with rations the first time for weeks. The Brigadier decided we would all rest up a couple of days to recover strength but then Stilwell sent one of his tetchy signals which, I assume, could only have referred to number two of the three we had received that night before the advance on Kazu. It said:

MOVE IMMEDIATELY AT ONCE TO
MYITKYENA AS ORDERED IN SIGNAL 18 MAY.

This arrived about midday, only a couple of hours after the Brigadier had decided it was essential we had a day or two of complete rest. His reaction to the signal however was so predictable that I told the sergeants to pack up the set before even taking the message to him. Sure enough he ordered the whole column to be ready to move out in thirty minutes' time – and actually got us away ten minutes before that, urging us on from horseback by the side of the track.

16

The Cards which Alice found painting roses in a desperate attempt to ensure the decapitating Queen did not discover their original mistake were not bothered about splashing passers-by in their reckless haste. They were concerned only with survival. Any man trying frantically to retrieve a mistake is a menace, and a lot of allied soldiers were splashed to death when Stilwell had to grab for the paint pots in a cover-up that summer of 1944.

We in Morris Force on the east bank of the Irrawaddy were among the early innocents to suffer in Stilwell's attempt to retrieve his blunder and make good the claim which he had broadcast to the world, without first being certain of its veracity. He had announced, with a fanfare of trumpets, that his troops had captured Myitkyena but when we arrived in the area nearly two weeks later we discovered this was still not true (it was not to be true for another two months, in fact). What actually happened was that Merril's Marauders had made a magnificent fighting march through the inhospitable mountains north west of Myitkyena and then a final surge, at their last gasp as it were, had taken the survivors right on down to the airfield. At once Stilwell had sent out the announcement that the town had been captured – and, incidentally, had given the impression it was not so much the Americans but 'his' Chinese troops that had achieved this victory.

The airfield however is several miles west of the town, an important outpost certainly, but that is all. Its loss did not affect the large Japanese force which anyway had been denied the field for several weeks by American bombers. The Japanese were solidly entrenched in the town, a garrison of nearly four thousand men, with bunkers and pill-boxes and defences that would have presented formidable problems to even the freshest and fittest troops in the whole of the command. And by this time the Marauders, and all the men of the original Wingate force on both sides of the Irrawaddy, were in the worst condition of any troops in South East Asia command.

Once the announcement of the fall of the town had been blared to the world there were requests from war correspondents to visit the scene of the victory. All that could be done immediately was to let them have a look at the airfield, now securely held, spin a story about some isolated Japanese posts in the town yet to be cleared, and hope they did not question further. In the meantime, and as an action of such urgency that there was no care about planning, a sustained assault was ordered on the defences; the surviving Marauders and a couple of Chinese regiments were urged into attack, the Chindits of Calvert's and Masters' brigades and our isolated group on the east bank were all whipped into sacrificial assault against the so-called 'remnants' of the enemy. Journalists and generals and politicians would then be able to see the reality of the proclaimed victory.

The poor Americans in the Marauders Force – Merril himself lasted only a few days after the airstrip capture, then Hunter took over again – had a terrible time of it because Stilwell and his henchmen were right beside them, so they suffered appalling losses. Their treatment by Stilwell's staff was a disgrace not just to the American army but to humanity itself. A typical example of Stilwell's attitude to his troops was innocently disclosed by the civilian Seagrave, one of those medical saints who devote their lives to tending remote tribesmen. He wrote a year or so later that all Stilwell wanted of his medical staff was to get the wounded out of the wards and back into combat as rapidly as possible . . . 'by any means, no matter how unorthodox.'

We on the eastern bank of the Irrawaddy were comparitively lucky. We did not have Stilwell and his second-in-command Boatner actually bayonet-jabbing us into action. We were under their direct command however, they were only three minutes away by plane from our jungle strip, and they asserted their baying presence every fearful day as Stilwell strove to make good his premature claim of victory. When we arrived in the arena two days after receiving his message, having travelled forty miles and crossed two steep slimy-tracked ridges, guided finally by the thudding sound of artillery fire – we received an order to continue straight on with full speed to take over Waingmaw, the village on our bank opposite Myitkyena. We were not to waste time sending reconnaissance parties ahead for there were no Japanese troops in Waingmaw. The Brigadier duly passed on that simple order the same evening: we would march down the road next day to our prescribed destination – only two columns at this time, as Peter Cane's 94 had been delayed by that Japanese attack at Kazu and had yet to catch up with us.

Our harbour on that last evening was on the end of a ridge called Mara Bum that slopes down steeply to the plain from nearly two thousand feet, only about three miles from the Irrawaddy. I went over to the edge early that evening to look at our objective. A single great cumulonimbus covered a major part of the western sky, and draped down from it a grey curtain of rain obscured sight of Myitkyena itself and its throbbing guns; on each side of the cloud mass the western sky was ablaze with fire when the sun went down and this clear clean division of flame-red and white was mirrored in the broad river where it swings due west just below Myitkyena. The lines and patterns of the plain below, the bordered paddy fields and wooded streams and stringy tracks and the river itself began to lose definition in the deepening indigo spread of twilight, as on the hillside about us the crickets started their strident welcome to nightfall. The wind blew cold and damp from the western rain that evening but again we were denied fire by the Brigadier. Over in Myitkyena there was a constant crunch of artillery fire and occasionally you saw faintly the orange flicker of an exploding shell. The thudding of gunfire continued intermittently all through the night, interspersed occasionally with the faint ratcheting of machine-guns.

There is an inane similarity about nearly all the actions we fought in the campaign, we kept blundering into them unprepared then reeling about blinded on impact. That first advance on Waingmaw the following day was typical. The march was led by Monteith's 40 column to which I was temporarily attached, for they were now without an RAF officer. By early afternoon we were well clear of the hills, moving along a cart track towards the river and could hear the guns from close across the river, artillery like the thump on a drum, machine guns like a creaking door. It was a hot still day, a few clouds poised in growth but mostly pale blue sky over the great wide valley, and at one time we saw a flight of three Mitchell B25 bombers dive down on Myitkyena from the west and heard the cr-ump of their bombs.

There were clearings of paddy fields on each side of our track but also some intermittent cover, various ficus including the peepul, screw pines, citrus trees of some kind, one or two pawpaw and several clumps of banana plants. Nearly all cultivated stuff. The best cover however was provided by dense thickets of eupatorium, an introduced aggressor, huge tangled masses of it with the fluffy powder-blue flowers just starting to appear; as we came closer to Waingmaw itself you could see where it had recently been cut back beside the road, as if by a blunt dah, with jagged white stems and splintered stumps jutting out from the green hump of growth. The explanation of this became obvious by its association with slit trenches and defensive positions – the Japanese had been clearing lines of fire. It was a disturbing deduction.

There had been some discussion at the midday halt about the accuracy of Stilwell's reassurance that there were no Japanese at all on our side of the river. The Brigadier had issued instructions that any villager encountered should be taken to him for questioning, but despite all the signs of cultivation about us met no one along the track all morning. There were some of us who felt uneasy about this open march in column line along the track – why should one trust Stilwell? – and when we came to the first deserted machine-gun position this only seemed to confirm the suspicion that the Japanese were still around, for mistrust can utilize the most contrary evidence at times – a man who believes it takes two people to make a quarrel is a man devoid of imagination. However as we trudged on at our steady marching pace and passed three more fortified positions tucked into the side of the road, one built of heavy timber and camouflaged with branches, all of them deserted, doubts began to submerge. Suspicion gave way to curiosity. Why had the Japanese withdrawn? Surely they would want a bridgehead to allow the remnants of the garrison to pull out of Myitkyena finally? They must have known we were on that bank somewhere.

They did. It was about three o'clock on that bright warm afternoon, a few hundred yards short of the village, that they hit us. There was a startling loud clatter of machine-gun fire, joined quickly by another with a flatter tone, a deadly counterpoint, and I actually saw pallid splinters start from a palm trunk just beside us – heard the guns, saw the white flash of tree wounds and dived for cover, all in the same instant. The cover was flimsy, just a couple of spindly palms, but there was a large clump of the eupatorium some fifteen yards or so across the clearing and several of us ran on for this. Two or three mules were with us and they were the only creatures still upright after we reached the shrub – the muleteers were prone like the rest of us, holding the leads close against the ground.

The road, which was on a slightly higher level, was still

visible in patches as I raised my head and looked about, and a group of riflemen crouched on the far side were actually firing towards the village. The way ahead was almost completely empty, just a scattering of mules attached to crouching figures a little further on beside a dense clump of bamboo that had obviously barred their immediate escape from the track. The machine guns continued in sharp bursts, as though the things were gathering breath for each murderous clatter, and you could see bamboo splintering on the road. Then there was a loud explosion from a mortar shell and the nearby leaves shuddered from the blast – or my eyes did. In the midst of all this deadly uproar, when I was loath even to stay as far upright as a crouching position, the Brigadier, who had been well behind us, came striding up the road; he seemed to be utterly indifferent to the enemy fire as he shouted to someone in Gurkhali:

'Where is Colonel Monteith?'

The answer was lost under the explosion of a mortar shell which made everyone duck but when I looked up again the Brigadier was still standing erect; he must have had some sort of answer to his question because he suddenly went striding off into the fields on our right. After a few moments the mortar shells began to land far too close to ignore, the bushes shook and the air shivered at each blast, leaves and twigs were coming down from a tree just behind us, so I decided to go to the platoon commander a little distance ahead to find out what was happening. He was with half a dozen Gurkhas beside a clump of low bamboo, and some of the men were leaning out to fire bursts at a straw hut about fifty yards beyond, on the far side of the paddy field. He encouraged me to have a turn, so I did edge out and gave the hut a burst with the carbine. Mainly to relieve tension. There was no return fire, and no movement from the hut – almost certainly it was empty. A mule bounded and bucked across the open paddy field carrying a pannier on one side only, it had slipped and was practically under the animals's belly, then a mortar shell seemed to explode in the air above the open area and there was a fluttering whizz of flying metal as we flattened ourselves to the ground again.

The sequence of events is difficult to recall. The diary written up that night is not much help in sorting them out:

> '. . . heavy mortar fire . . . one sniper after me personally . . . kutcha-wallah down hole being pulled out by his mule . . . shot one doesn't drop . . . battle chaos.'

Some of this is clear. The mules retreated and for a time I was alone by the spindly palms beside the road, cursing the Brigadier and Stilwell and his staff for landing us in this chaotic action. A Gurkha with a wound in his thigh, blood glistening on the hand clasped over it, was helped back down the track by a friend in search of the doctor. When I returned to the bamboo the four muleteers ('kutcha wallahs') came back in a sudden jangling rush from somewhere and stopped beside me. One of them had a recalcitrant mule that would not stay behind cover but kept dragging the poor wretched driver out of the little bamboo niche where he wanted to crouch; the mule settled back on its haunches and kept trying to jerk him out of his hole, he kept yanking back on the lead to try and get it close in tight with him. Then two men with a Bren gun appeared at the far end of the paddy and opened fire on the little straw hut, which still showed no sign of life whatsoever.

I spent a long time by that bamboo clump that afternoon, growing more angry every moment. What in hell was I doing there? I raged. There was nothing for me to shoot, no aircraft to direct, no signals to send, not even a mule to lead, so why was I there crouching in a field by the Irrawaddy with bullets and mortar shells flying all about? There was no sense in my presence, nor in the presence of a hundred or more mules and all our equipment, no sense in the whole stupid bloody action. Where exactly were the enemy? What were we trying to do just then? And who was doing it? If you lead a party down a hill track where the enemy may be waiting at least you know why you are going to die, logic gives you some support in your trial, but to be killed as you sit witlessly by a clump of bamboo, to lose your life for no discernible purpose, is an obscenity. Had Stilwell appeared I would not have shot him but have smashed his skull with the butt of the carbine. The Brigadier too, perhaps. I wanted to shout above all the clamour of the battle; 'What's happening, for God's sake! Tell me, someone. Tell me.' I went back to the road but could find no sense, down to the big bamboo but a dozen crouching Gurkhas looked at me blankly when questioned, over to a soggy vegetable patch where a mule was nibbling green shoots and not a muleteer in sight, then back to the road to question a medical orderly who could tell me nothing except that he had lost the doctor.

I was still there on the road, still hunting for intelligence, when a mule came hurtling down the track and veered straight into the big bamboo clump through which there was no possible passage. It had a lead but no saddle, it crashed head first into the bamboo just a few yards from me as if it had not even seen the great mass of the obstacle, then pulled back and stood there shivering, white staring eyes, blood pouring from a gaping wound in its neck and another huge one in its belly from which something purplish was obtruding and yellow liquid dripping from it. A mortar shell must have landed almost underneath the poor wretched thing. I gave it a burst from the carbine through the side of the head and it toppled sideways against the bamboo, but some stems had been cut and instead of falling it just slumped over these stumps and stayed like that, draped over them with grotesquely angled legs and bloody head dangling down just short of the ground.

When I moved away from this distressing sight I saw David Anderson, with a jemadar and about a dozen riflemen, coming across from beyond the hut at which everyone had been firing. David stood in the middle of the paddy for a

243

moment, looking about as if unsure where he was heading – or why – and then he saw me and came across to the edge of the road. He gave me the first news of the action. It appeared that the leading group had been held up by a pill-box position, he had been brought up to try and outflank the enemy position but discovered they were spread out wide, so had been nudging along the perimeter of the defences.

He ambled away somewhere, intending to do something or other in due course, and then Monteith suddenly appeared from beyond the hut, running, without his pack. An orderly with him was also packless. He wanted to know if I had seen the Brigadier, or heard from him. He stayed with me by the bamboo, crouching down and scanning the road as he told me what little he knew of the action. He was almost hysterical in complaint about becoming involved in such a casual action without proper reconnaisance or plan, blaming both the Brigadier and Stilwell for the mess.

'We've got to pull back. Make a proper plan. A proper plan,' he kept saying, peering about in the hope of sighting the Brigadier – or a proper plan perhaps.

Finally in a lull in the firing he scurried over to my clump of eupatorium to question a group collected there. He seemed to have discovered something because he pointed away as he spoke to a Gurkha who then started off at once in the direction indicated, running crouched down with his pack thumping up and down as if he had a pygmy-jockey on his back. Monteith followed him presently but then suddenly people began drifting back past us in groups, purposefully, and from them I discovered that orders had been given for a general retreat. By this time there was only desultory shooting, but still quite a few mortar shells – one man on the road nearby was hit in the leg by shrapnel – and I moved back with a group keeping under cover where we could. Finally we all coagulated into a solid mass about half a mile back on the track itself. There we settled ourselves once more into two separate columns, took care of our wounded, then marched away in the direction whence we had come just a few hours earlier.

The sun was setting behind us by this time, and ahead of us the high ridges of Yunnan glowed like a tranquil fire against the dark background of distant rain clouds. All sounds of battle had ceased from both sides of the Irrawaddy, just the creaky jangle of mule harness, soft thudding steps on the muddy ground and lowered voices of defeat as we moved in column along the track. Then suddenly, into this tired dispirited quietness, there began to filter a strange vibrant sound, it grew until the air about us seemed to shiver, we all looked up towards the source and saw a myriad of green parakeets flighting like arrows overhead, a vast continuous stream of them just a little above tree-top height, all heading across the river towards Myitkyena and making that screeching-twittering call that compiled into the massed sound we heard. You wondered if the whole psitticine community of Burma, like all the rest of us, had been ordered by Stilwell to close with all speed on the town to help make up his default. In the days to come we discovered that this mass flight occurred every evening, the birds returning in immense flocks from their feeding grounds in the mountains to spend the night in the same spot somewhere just south of Myitkyena – I never saw them setting off in the mornings. We continued on for about five miles in the opposite direction to their flight, back into the foothills to lick our wounds, bury our dead, and wait to be told what we must do.

Next morning we moved further back to a bivouac tucked well behind the first main ridge on the east of the river. There, about eight miles away from the river we were joined later by Peter Cane's 94 column, and his arrival brought a little sense to the proceedings because the Brigadier had intended to make another dash that same evening at Waingmaw, still without any precise idea of the strength of the garrison and the location of its defences. Peter Cane successfully demanded we delay the assault until patrols had

245

been sent out and discovered something about the enemy lay-out. Stanley and I went on to a site two miles further back and marked out a light plane strip on an abandoned paddy field. We had about a dozen casualties from that Waingmaw attack and a mounting toll of sick and dying, all of whom needed hospital treatment. Seven men had already died since we arrived in the area, the count was to mount steadily thereafter.

When we had finished at the strip we stopped on the way back at a little stream to wash our feet. Stanley was concerned to avoid 'trench foot', he was punctilious about taking all the precautions – he had a list of hygiene and health recommendations copied into his signal book. Since the rains began there had been a sharp and continuous increase in the number suffering from 'trench foot'; the soaked-soft skin of the foot is abraded by embedded mud in the sock, or merely by a tuck in it, and once the weakened flaccid skin begins to go it is almost impossible to stop the wound expanding. The only way to cure it is to keep your feet completely dry, and this for us was almost impossible. In the persistent damp your foot skin became corpse white, clammy, with much the same texture as the belly of a plaice; you could pinch the side of your foot and your fingertips came away feeling a soft clutter from the rubbings of sole-white skin. It was not at all uncommon to see people take off boots and disclose a sock soaked in blood and yet not a leech in sight – I saw one of the Hong Kong volunteers who could scarcely walk, his whole foot was a raw-meat red, he must have been in excruciating pain. Stanley was still clear but I was momentarily depressed to discover that the discomfort felt in the side of my left leg for the last day or two had in fact been caused by the start of that condition; in the pallid damp-wrinkled skin was a bright red patch that flamed in pain when exposed, caused apparently by a tuck in the sock. I would have ignored the damage but Stanley insisted on me bathing and drying my feet carefully before changing socks and starting off again.

He showed far more solicitude for the leg than I did, and on the way back kept fussing at me to wash and dry my socks more carefully. To me it was just another ache. Let the damn thing rot. Not a very sensible reaction, as Stanley told me with some severity.

When we arrived back I discovered that Tiny Langford had prepared a joint shelter for us both – not the first, nor the last, time that he showed such kindness. He had had both our orderlies build not only a double-size shelter but also a dry bed made of strips of bamboo, a sort of shelf on which to sleep clear of the wet earth. We stood about a fire for a while, steaming off some of the moisture before bedding down. That night I was feverish, it was impossible to stop shivering, and every now and then my teeth would chatter uncontrollably. It was a long time to dawn.

The next day we began to send out casualties but the promised drop of ammunition never arrived. Instead we had orders from Boatner to attack the Japanese positions on the river bank without delay, and when the Brigadier replied that we had insufficient ammunition we had back an instruction to prepare a drop site near the point of our attack; the ammunition would then be delivered close to where it was wanted. This was a crackpot plan – suppose it was pelting with rain (not unusual in the monsoon)? I don't know if the Brigadier approved, but he would not let me question it with a signal. He still clung to regulations in insisting we carry out instructions as ordered.

'It doesn't matter if we take the place or not. We've got to put on a show,' is the quote from him in my diary on 1st June.

The attacking force was composed of 94 and 40 columns. We had a meeting just after stand-to that evening – they were El Greco faces around the fire, emaciated, elongated, straggley beards – when we were told the approach this time would not be along the road as before but from the south. The column commanders had by now learned from experience that air support cannot be relied upon to overcome all problems that face infantry in attack but the Brigadier still clung to the old fantasy so both Stanley and I were ordered to attend this operation – he to stand by in the unlikely event we had air support and I to collect the ammunition drop.

The combined force set out just after midnight on 2nd June, still with no precise idea of the location of the enemy forces, but this time we were at least not encumbered with a clumsy trail of mules. We had a local guide. The reason for starting off in darkness was to avoid being caught in the big open area of paddy south of the village in daylight, we wanted to be safely into the trees on the southern outskirts by the first light, so the attack could then be launched from a reasonably secure base. We discovered too late, however, that our guide had never before approached the village by such a circular route even in daylight (why should he?). The result was that we floundered and fumbled about in the black wet night making loud splashing and sucking noises until the grey dawn found us still heaving our way through the mud of the open paddy fields, about a mile short of the trees.

By pure good fortune the Japanese did not see us as we plugged laboriously across this open space, for the rain came down so solidly during the first hour of murky daylight that we were able to reach the shelter of the trees without drawing fire. The enemy opened fire then however, almost at once. Machine guns and mortars. We fanned out but the lack of detailed information about the Japanese positions soon led to confusion; some sections met opposition almost at once when they moved forward, others had a long clear run, so that presently the line became jagged and distorted. Poor visibility in the sheeting rain added to our problems and there was wild firing on both sides – less perhaps from the enemy, as they were in prepared position, with lines of fire and mortar distances all planned.

Stanley had gone off with the column headquarters but the Brigadier kept me with his group. We were about the middle of the line, by a large stone cairn under a peepul tree when the firing started. The Brigadier immediately went off somewhere, then we had a burst of firing close by on the right, close enough to send us edging around the opposite side of the stone cairn – it was about five feet high – and there we sat down in the mud and waited. Resentment grew when mortar explosions began punctuating the rifle and machine-gun fire. A man was hit in the neck, blood streaming down his webbing as he was led away to the doctor's post – leaving his pack behind.

A little later the Brigadier came back, fuming about something or other, and sent off runners in all directions to find out what was happening elsewhere. As he waited his temper grew worse. I think he was feverish that day, you could see a glistening of moisture on his forehead and his right hand, in which he was actually holding his revolver, was tapping and trembling against his thigh. He suddenly seemed to notice me looking at him – I was wondering anxiously if his safety catch was on – and he shouted:

'You should be out there running the supply drop.'

He wanted me to go back out into the open paddy fields which we had just crossed – luckily without being noticed by the enemy. It meant laying out a marker, nothing more. There were perfectly reasonable grounds for argument against the order so there was no need for me to admit that the idea of going back out into that open space, particularly now that the rain had stopped, was not at all attractive: the conclusive argument was that the order was based on an assumption that was ridiculous. A bank of low grey cloud was scudding across us and less than a hundred feet above the paddy fields, there was no possibility whatsoever of an aircraft getting in to drop under such conditions. I explained this to him, as gently as possible because of his immediate state. But he was not to be gentled that day. He was in such unstable mood that any contact at all was dangerous. He cut me short with the usual decisive argument, except this time he shouted it:

249

'That's an order. You get on out there now.'

He flung a quivering arm, the one holding the revolver, in the direction of dismissal. I might have continued pressing reason but with that revolver in hand and that crazy light in his eyes, it seemed safer not to argue. So off I went, returning scowl for scowl.

Stilwell's headquarters had recently suggested a simplified signal for daylight drops in the open, just a plain white plus-sign, the direction being left entirely to the pilot's discretion, so I set this out on the intersection of two paddy-bunds, using parachute panels brought for that purpose. The whine of ricochetting bullets kept demanding attention as I piled mud on the strip ends so as to hold them in position on the bund, for the fields themselves were completely covered with a thin sheet of water. The wind had dropped slightly by this time but although the cloud had now broken up it was still about seven-tenths with some of it carrying rain and so a supply drop remained impossible – even if base ever intended to send one. Therefore once the layout had been complete, I walked back along the bunds and into the trees again.

There was no point in staying out there now the site was prepared. Nor was it attractive. You felt very exposed out there all alone on that flat bare landscape, listening to the crackling of the gunfire and wondering if someone was taking a long-range shot at you personally. The Japanese positions were actually closer to the trees, but the trees offered protection; you could stand close by the big peepul trunk and not be too concerned about the chatter of machine-guns or the occasional fluttering whine of ricochets. Out in the open you were on a stage. You felt that a Japanese machine-gunner, looking about for a positive target, might decide to give a squirt at that lonely figure, just to pick off a bonus victim whilst waiting for another attack to start. So I was glad to get back to the little cairn by the peepul tree, sit down, take off my pack and lean against the protective stones as if merely tired after the walk, and not because of the gunfire and mortar explosions and fluttering metal. I was alone at that time, all the others having gone off somewhere, presumably with the Brigadier.

Monteith then came running back along the track looking for the Brigadier – he always seemed to be running about looking for the Brigadier when action started. There was no chance of getting past the Japanese without heavy artillery, he said. Bombing was no use – the Japanese positions were scattered and in depth. He wanted to pull back his men. Where was the Brigadier?

He was in fact coming back to join us just as Monteith gave this call. Instead of dealing at once with Monteith's battle problem however he came steaming over directly to me and demanded to know why I was not out there waiting for the supply drop as ordered. There was a sharp exchange between us before someone, I think it was Tiny Langford, intervened to support my assertion that the original order had been simply to lay out the signal for a drop and nothing more; Tiny added that he personally had expected to find me back there by then. To this the Brigadier replied that he would therefore make his order perfectly clear:

'You are to stay out there till I recall you. Till I recall you.'

He had put away his revolver but the wild look was still in his eye and it was clear he would have no argument.

So off I went again in glowering silence towards the open space.

The banishment lasted about an hour. At first, after dumping my pack by the white marker, I sat down on the bund and hoped no one would notice the lonely figure marring that classical Chinese picture – the simple wash drawing of flooded rice-fields broken up into squares by the dark bund-lines, puffs of grey clouds overhead. The wind had dropped by now, the clouds had broken up and the whole area was beginning to suffer swathes of bright sunlight – like spotlights on the single moving creature out there in the waste of patterned water. Moreoever, with all the firing going on at the perimeter of the village some of the bullets were actually finishing up in the paddy area. You heard the occasional fluttering whine and the flat water was flicked to life, then a ripple would shiver out from the disturbance where the spent bullet or ricochet must have landed.

In such circumstances, with no distraction and plenty of time to dwell on the subject, you begin to reckon up such figures as the penetrating force of bullets at that extreme range, about angles of elevation and the sizes of targets; having done this you decide you are not just a little tired and want to sit but extremely tired and would prefer to lie down on the muddy ridge of the bund. Once that decision is taken and you lie there listening to the tapping of bullets and occasional slam of mortar from the battle behind your head you discover you are not comfortable using the pack for a pillow as usual, it's a strain on your neck to have your head so high, far better to let your head rest on the mud and have your pack behind it somewhere, merely out of the way but by careful accident between your head and the scene of action. So there you lie, in the mud, staring at the gaps of blue in the broken cloud, now covered in the waterproof sheet but shivering in the clammy cold, running a slight fever probably, and you recite out aloud the ending of the 'Lotus Eaters', with all the passionate longing of those old battle-weary mariners who had had enough of crashing waves and violent action, and wanted only to lie on grassy slopes looking out at the raging seas and sinking ships, remotely serene from it all at last up on their verdant hillside, stretched out beneath the pines.

No aeroplanes came, we ran short of ammunition, we could not advance, and so we all withdrew again about midday. We had five more killed and fifteen wounded, the Japanese probably a few more. You wondered why they had died.

17

Although I kept the diary going right to the end, and also still continued making notes occasionally in the pulpy wodge of the exercise book, there was no longer the same continuity in the record as earlier in the campaign. One reason for this may have been that as the body deteriorated so rapidly in those final weeks, so too the mind wavered, became vague and erratic in its imprints, but the major cause of the patchiness of the record is that the information was no longer so freely available to me. We were now controlled from Boatner's headquarters at Myitkyena, the 22 set was quite adequate for those few miles, but in fact most orders came across by plane, often delivered by hand from the liaison officer. The Brigadier could now maintain personal contact both with his superiors and his column commanders, so I was no longer threaded into the pattern of decision. Both column commanders visited me in an eeyrie where I became established presently and gave me some background information, the Brigadier too opened his heart on one occasion, but it was not until later that I heard many of the explanations.

There was a fresh British division standing by to take over in our area and they could have cleared Myitkyena without difficulty had they been allowed, or the major Chindit force under the inspirational leadership of Calvert could have linked up with the remnants of the Marauders and Chinese to do the job; but Stilwell had already given credit to his troops for the victory, and he refused to allow any other forces attack the place lest they capture it and prove him a liar. But unfortunately his Chinese troops could not take the town, they could make no progress at all against the Japanese, so excuses had to be found. One was us. Neither Stilwell nor Boatner had any conception of the structure of a Chindit column, particularly its lack of artillery; they wanted us to beat out our lives against fortified defences on the east bank that were in fact quite irrelevant to their objective, and when we failed they blamed us for their own incompetence at Myitkyena. They said it was all the fault of Morris Force that they could not overcome the Japanese forces in the town – Boatner actually sent us a signal making that charge – and so our presence several miles away across the river did serve one useful purpose: we provided Stilwell with a scapegoat.

I became an aloof spectator of the action for a time. About a mile upstream of Myitkyena on the opposite bank of the river is a village called Houla where the Japanese were present also in force, but this was thought to be less well protected and so it became our next point of attack. To the east of the village is a large forest reserve covering a series of steep hills, and one of these juts up only a mile from the river bank and the village. It had been reported that this would provide an excellent observation post from which to direct air strikes against the enemy positions, and so the day after that abortive attack across the paddy fields the Brigadier sent me up to the hill with a section of the rifle platoon to examine its possible use for this purpose. It had been reported there was no Japanese presence on the hill but after our recent experiences with faulty Intelligence we moved up there warily that morning, spread out in a line well apart. This time however the reports were accurate, the crown of the hill was empty, though the Japanese had in the recent past occupied a small defence post at the northern end.

'Lookout Point', as it was quickly dubbed, was a perfect site for its planned use. It was an abutment from the main ridge, jutting out on to the plain with a ramp-like approach through a patch of tropical rain forest from the camp site a couple of miles behind it. The crown was almost completely flat, about the size of a football field, with just a scattering of clean-limbed mature trees including two teak, a cassia, and several dipterocarps, and the ground clear except for a few dwarf palms and a large datura in fragrant white dangling-flower – there was a huge bush of it on that Waingmaw road too, I recall. From the western edge there was a clear view across the paddy fields to the Irrawaddy now running in its brown monsoon colours; on its far side about four miles away Myitkyena town was marked by constant puffs of white smoke from shell explosions – the Chinese blazed away with their artillery for weeks, but it was literally as well as metaphorically an aimless performance.

The Brigadier, having had my favourable report on the place, decided I should stay up there, directing any bombers that were sent to help us in the attacks on Houla, so the sergeants and the RAF radio were sent up to join us. We had a section of the rifle platoon as a protective force but the Brigadier withdrew these on the afternoon of the second day when visiting us – and also banned the use of fire, against which I protested in waste of breath. We were not alone for long however, there were regular visitors during the seven days I spent up there – with one break for a sortie to Houla – and the first of them was Peter Cane. It was typical of his adventurous spirit that he should be the one who devised the only practical exercise we ever did attempt from Lookout Point, when he tried to use the post for the original purpose of directing fire on a target.

Unfortunately it was not successful, his radio failed – just after he made first contact with me – we never had another opportunity to try it. David Anderson was with me on the hill that day, it was thought he might try the scheme too if successful, but he was not at all concerned at the failure. 'Oh well, never mind – it's been pleasant up here, away from the Brig.,' he said. David had lasted better physically than many of the rest of us, and with such an equable temperament was not so wrought-up at the strictures from Boatner and the caprices of the Brigadier. Under stress he would drift away mentally to more pleasant pastures.

It was the commander of 40 column, Monteith, who told me most about the problems we were having with General Boatner. His second-in-command had been sent over to Myitkyena to explain just what sort of force we were, what were our capabilities and our limitations, and it seemed Boatner had listened but not heard; the message that had come back with him was that we had to attack again – and again, and again. Monteith wanted the Brigadier to go over and argue it out with Boatner but when I suggested he tell the Brigadier that himself he shook his head and muttered:

'Difficult. Very difficult.'

I don't know if he was describing the Brigadier's character or the question of approaching him. Monteith was in particularly gloomy mood on that second visit. He gave me a detailed account of our losses, of our sick, and the pitiable physical condition of the remainder of us.

'Boatner will kill us all off before he's finished,' he said.

He called to mind a line in one of the poems of John O'Brien about a squatter in the Australian outback who was always prophesying doom . . . '"We'll all be ruined", said Hanrahan, "before the year is out".' His final cheerless news that day was that 18,000 Siamese troops had arrived to reinforce the Japanese in Myitkyena; he seemed to believe it all right, but I had difficulty.

The sergeants and I built a shelter for the three of us on a little mound in the centre of the hill; it was covered with leafy branches upon which we laid a parachute and this protected us somewhat during the incessant showers of rain. It could be gloomy up there on the hill at times. The fallen branches, and even some of the tree trunks, were covered in a sheen of damp furry mould, and amongst the debris on the ground there was a fungus that gave off a faint luminescent glow at night. The whole area was now scattered with pallid flecks of parasol mushrooms which slithered through your fingers and left a slime when you tried to pick one, and the air was so heavy with moisture that every time you touched your beard your hand came away wet. Your clothes were never dry.

In this atmosphere of festering abundance the human body was as susceptible to rampaging nature as anything else, contagion spread, germs multiplied, corruption expanded. The patch of raw abraded skin on my foot grew larger, in my right thigh a leech bite kept suppurating and bursting and would not heal, the attacks of low fever would wake me with violent shivers in the night, and an intestinal infection of some type now had me bowel-tense most of the day. You understand how a man can 'be half in love with easeful death', indeed your heart goes out to him. Release is your only concern, the method not important. Nothing else matters. On the night of June 6th Stanley came up to stay with me on the hilltop and we happened to pick up a news item on the radio dealing with the opening of the second front in Europe that morning. We were only momentarily interested, then left the radio and continued our talk about trench-foot, and rice, and fire, and rumours of our withdrawal and other such important matters – not another word about the momentous event that had occurred far far away in Europe that morning.

Most affectionately remembered visitor to Lookout Point was Wallace, a captain in the American Army. He was actually a member of Boatner's staff and should therefore have been an enemy but within minutes of our first meeting, when hostility had been furiously stoked up for the occasion, he had me in grudging sympathy about their problems the other side of the river. Subsequently, within the next few days, his friendly manner and wondrous kindness in the gift of food, had me so devoted as to consider, at least with him, the possibility that Boatner was not entirely evil – a military automaton perhaps, but not a sadistic Limey-hater. Wallace himself had been sent across the river for two reasons, to urge

257

offensive action on the Brigadier and to report on our capability as a fighting unit. He said he had been unwilling to press the first because in his view we all ought to be sent out; but as no one was going to be relieved or rested until Stilwell's mistake was rectified and the original lie made good, then we had to make the best of the situation.

Wallace never manifested any disloyalty to Boatner, and it was a measure of his personality that he could support his commander and still attract friendship from those of us who met him. The afternoon following his visit Tiny Langford came up from the camp with two tins of that glorious pineapple-and-rice mixture which Wallace had had sent over from Myitkyena specifically for me – I happened to have mentioned to him the glowing memory of my first taste of that ambrosia back at the glider-landing area long ago. It was an act of such thoughtful kindness it almost had me in tears. I don't know if Wallace survived the campaign but he will survive forever with me.

Tiny Langford stayed up there till after sunset that afternoon, talking about the pre-war days in Burma and wondering if life would ever be the same again when war was over. His love for the country was undiminished by our experience, and when we stood on the hill that evening looking out over the plain as he continued with his nostalgic memories you could for a little while imagine pleasant days of peace in such a land. The sun was setting – rapidly now in mid-June, so near the prime vertical – the colours of the landscape fading in the dusk; the bright sunlit translucent greens of the trees on the slope, mirrored squares of paddy fields down below, pale clay-brown of the river and misty blue of the hills to the north were all shading into muted uniformity, except that over near the river a tiny white pagoda still stood out sharply clear against the dark trees along the bank. It was quiet just then, the guns had stopped temporarily, the parrots had all flighted back by now to their haunt below the town, the only sound was a faint scraping-crackle from the radio back behind us. A pair of hornbills sailed across in leisurely flight, they passed every evening about the same time, and after they were gone all was still. No movement to be seen in land or sky, no trace of war in all that peaceful scene. But it was a deceit, of course; the war was still there, had only taken a breather. Before Tiny left a few minutes later the guns were thumping again over in Myitkyena.

The Brigadier ordered me back down to the main camp the night before our second attack on Houla. When I arrived that afternoon in the damp jungley niche between the hills where they were harboured he called me over to join him in the little shelter where he was sitting on the edge of the bamboo-shelf that was his bed. He chatted about Lookout Point and told me of his disappointment that it was not being used to direct bombing raids on the Japanese positions; the Commander over in Myitkyena, he said, had his own 'unusual way' of running things, and we had to accept his decision. He looked tired and dispirited as he chatted about our position and activities. He said that of the original force we were now only slightly better than fifty percent effective, and even without battle casualties he did not think we could survive as a fighting unit till the end of the month. When I asked him if he would himself like to continue with Special Force after this campaign he said at first that he would go where he was ordered; when pressed however he said that if he were offered a choice – 'like you RAF chaps always seem to have' – then he would rather be with a regular division in the field.

'At least you know where you are then,' he said.

You could not help feeling sorry for him at times, for all his infuriating faults. His task was an impossible one. No British commander, and few of any nationality, could hope to satisfy the Stilwell-Boatner combination. A more subtle character might perhaps have sidled away from some of their criticisms, possibly by making claims that bore the same vague relation to fact as the announced capture of Myitkyena or the Wingate signal to Churchill, a little exaggeration about casualties inflicted and objectives gained and damage done would have kept them quieter, but the Brigadier was a blunt uncomplicated man who was totally incapable of such artful evasion. His attitudes had become so solidly rusted into place by years of service life that they were now intrinsic to his being, so he duly obeyed the orders given to him and we all had to bear the consequences.

The action on 10th June was just as chaotic as the previous unprepared ones. Peter Cane's platoons captured the first objective in the village just before dawn, but then were held down by concentrated fire from set positions as they waited for us in the main body to arrive at dawn. But we were late. We had difficulty finding our way in the dark, I was with a rifle platoon that lost the column completely at one stage and only found them again with the help of a local Indian who came whispering out of the darkness to guide us on our way. The result of this paddy-floundering was that we were far too late reaching our positions; by the time we came marching along the road at about eight o'clock a large number of Japanese had been sent down from the village to the north to reinforce the Houla troops there and they outflanked us coming up the road.

The first contact we in our group had with them was a sudden burst of fire from the open ground to our right. It took us completely by surprise because we knew others had marched down this wide track just before us and met no opposition at all. The track was rather like a forest fire-break, wide as a main road but covered in grass and with a bamboo wattle fence about four feet high running along the sides. Fortunately there was a break on the side opposite the crackling guns and we all stumbled and clattered across the fallen panel into a small field where some low-growing crop like melons or pumpkins was in yellow flower. At the far end of the field was a little clump of trees, dark citrus I remember, and we halted there, rifles cocked, facing the road and waiting for the enemy to appear. But they didn't. The firing stopped and then presently we all began to drift back towards the road again where a dead Gurkha was lying in the wattle fence, but before we were assembled in line the ragged column started off at a smart pace and I found myself with two mules and their drivers hurrying along in a jangling run to catch up the fleeing group ahead.

Firing broke out again on our right, this time from a grove of trees and again we had to swerve off into cover – a ditch that was shielded by some prickly shrub pruned as a hedge. One of our group was hit in the shoulder and was sent back with a friend. It was apparent by this time that the whole column snake was presenting a broadside target to Japanese groups coming down from the village to the north, so we abandoned the road altogether and made an attempt to continue on course more or less parallel to it. This was a mess. The whole column broke up into straggley groups, and it was difficult to grasp where we were actually heading, and to decide whether other groups about us were enemy or friends. Some mortar shells began to land in the field where we found ourselves and another man was hit, so instead of continuing straight on into these bursts we swung away to cross a small flooded field of paddy and on to another grass track where I found myself eventually waiting by a clump of closely grouped oleander bushes with four riflemen from another column. We all stood there, peering about the pink-flowering bush with guns at the ready but not the faintest idea where any targets were nor indeed what they might be. A mule without saddle or lead, possibly not one of ours, bolted down the track past us in a mad flight for freedom in the hills. But we had to wait.

What a stupid senseless nonsense it all was! It was about ten o'clock by this time, a sticky humid morning, and the sweat was already dripping from my eyebrows and tickling down my beard. Again I began to fume about being stuck in such a place at such a time – a trained and experienced pilot who had cost the RAF thousands of pounds and man-hours to get to that state, and there I was without any possible use or justification peering through the oleander bushes along a narrow shady track in northern Burma with the sound of gunfire all about and the occasional crack of mortar explosion behind us. The scent of the oleander . . . a memory of Australian boyhood suddenly struck me, of playing cricket on the side lawn at our home in Maitland, my brother Frank hitting the ball into the shrubs against the fence, me rummaging after it furiously while he was making a run, and our mother on the veranda cried out:

'Mind my oleanders, Terry! My oleanders!'

Far away and long ago . . . and how the scent of the dawn-pink flowers brought it all back!

But in the immediate present a runner came from the Brigadier ordering me to join him, so I followed along the track a short distance then off the side through some shrub and past a little straw hut with a pumpkin plant sprawled over its roof to find the Brigadier on the far side talking to a platoon commander from 40 column. I learned that one of the platoon commanders from 94 column had been killed, together with three of his men, in the opening burst from the outflanking Japanese, that we had still not made contact with Peter Cane's group in the village, and that there was an enemy group with a machine gun somewhere near two tall palms about a hundred yards or so ahead as pointed out by the Brigadier. Would it be possible for an aircraft to bomb those palms, but not along the line of the track because we had men the far side? Of course it wouldn't! It was impossible to identify to any aircraft those particular palms, we had no idea what other palms were scattered about this area. To my surprise he accepted this abrupt rejection without question. I felt he himself had never really thought air support would help but had just been reaching back in this moment of trial for that dream from our training days – when he had decided air strikes could solve all problems of opposition.

Back on the grass track I found the platoon squatting

against a stretch of that bamboo fencing with one or two men peering over it at a narrow flooded field with a water buffalo tethered at the far end on a raised muddy patch; it was nudging through a pile of straw, quite indifferent to all the shattering noises of our presence. As I was looking at the animal there was a long burst of automatic fire from further back along the track which sent us all to the ground, and turning to face the sound of danger. Were we cut off? A section was sent back to investigate. Whilst we waited a messenger arrived to tell us Peter Cane's group were now in contact with the head of the column but were perilously low on ammunition, so we sent him off in the direction of the Brigadier's party to pass on his message. Then the group that had gone to investigate the firing from our rear came back with one man to say that a party of Japanese were in fact astride the track in some force.

We sent on this message also to the headquarters group and in reply were told to move up to join them – I think it was the reserve platoon I was with. We moved happily enough, for a mortar shell had just landed in the field beside us and shrapnel had actually penetrated one man's pack, without harming him. The runner led us across a small muddy patch of ground to a tangle of shrub by a little stream which was in spate; but the Brigadier had meanwhile moved headquarters, he was now on the far side apparently but there seemed to be no crossing place, and the stream when tested proved to be at least shoulder high and therefore impassable. Whilst trying to discover his crossing place we saw a dozen men in line come across the clearing beyond the flooded streamlet and for a few seconds there was frantic argument as to whether we should fire or not, but fortunately for them our platoon commander decided against it – they turned out to be a group from 40 column who had been cut off. They called out the news that Monteith and another officer had been killed, a Japanese encircling party having caught them on the track. Whilst the jemadar was yelling across to us a flock of ducks, domesticated ones, came paddling down the muddy stream between us in line astern, quacking away happily in the midst of our shouts and the mortar explosions and the starts of machine-gun fire.

We finally discovered a makeshift bridge but by this time ammunition was low everywhere and it was evident we could make no further progress against the entrenched Japanese. Nor could we stay in that vulnerable and disorganized position for any length of time. The Brigadier ordered a withdrawal, with the relieved approval of Wallace who had been impressed by the column effort, and who duly reported this impression to Boatner – to no mellowing however, as we discovered.

Stanley was sitting against the bamboo wattle-fence along the road, waiting for me on our return. He had been with a group caught by one of the Japanese parties and had finished up firing at the attackers from a pig pen shared with a pregnant sow. He had later passed by Monteith's body at the side of the road; it appeared that when he fell after being hit his pack had kept his body upright in a kneeling position and the Japanese officer had taken a swipe with a sword that almost completely decapitated him. When we took the count subsequently we discovered there had been ten others killed and rather more than twenty wounded, almost all of whom had to be sent out the following day.

You expect casualties in war, of course, but this again was an unnecessary waste of life because advice was not heeded. We had been rushed into action against carefully prepared positions and achieved nothing, when an experienced campaigner like Peter Cane had been insisting that reconnaissance was essential before any further attacks on that particular target. We might actually have achieved the objective had his counsel been accepted, certainly would not have suffered as many casualties in the process. Had that been the first time Boatner had killed off some of us in blind obedience to Stilwell's orders you might have found an excuse for his conduct; but it wasn't the first time – and more damning still, it was not the last. So it can be assessed, literally and quite impartially, as a stupid bloody mistake by Boatner.

The whole command structure of Morris Force had to be altered after that last action because now Peter Cane was the only surviving column commander out of the original three. The decision was that the remains of 49 and 94, now reduced to less than the strength of a single column would be amalgamated under Peter Cane himself; 40 column, which was still at about three-quarter strength, was to come under Monteith's second-in-command. That same day, whilst reorganizing the depleted force, evacuating casualties, and moving the bivouac back about a mile closer to the airstrip, another message came over from Boatner urging continuous effort against the eastern bank of the river. As there was no specific order contained in the message, just a General bitching, the Brigadier nervously noted the contents but took no convulsive action.

This was sensible, but his decision to send me up to Lookout Point again made no sense at all. There were no actions projected that day, indeed it was planned we would take two days off to rest and reorganize and move camp, so there was no purpose to be served by having me sitting up on that hill three miles away. There never had been, with no aircraft to control. The Brigadier however grew impatient with argument at this stage, he just waved a hand at me and finished the interview with his customary closure. It was an order, Pat – but no longer as decisively as it once was, just a fretful dismissal. It seems I continued the argument however and was shouting at him until David Anderson and Stanley managed to persuade me away – but like so much that happened towards the end I remember nothing of this rowdy insubordination. All I know is that the Brigadier had his way and I did go back up the hill – alone, as Lilbahadur had gone down with fever a few days earlier.

It rained heavily all that afternoon and a mere three miles

trek up the muddy track to the hilltop was as physically exhausting as any march on the whole campaign. The path dipped down into a narrow valley about halfway up the hill, a sombre spot of dank rain forest and stagnant air. The squelchy debris on the forest floor was littered with toad-stools and strangely shaped fungi, spotted as if in some dreadful contagion, and there were parasitic growths crawling up the tree trunks and creating shadowy niches in which lurked weird epiphytes. A dead tree had crashed across the path weeks earlier and we had always had to haul ourselves up over the trunk by a branch stub that jutted out at knee level, but on that day the rotten branch collapsed when it took my weight. I crashed down against the exposed rupture with my face almost touching a fat white beetle larva big as a thumb and writhing in sluggish aversion from this sudden exposure to dreadful daylight.

It was a slight relief to emerge into the grey clarity of the open hill, out into the direct pouring of the rain, but by then I was physically exhausted. I remember dropping the horrific pack and leaning against a tree to regain breath and sight before finally stumbling across the plateau to join the sergeants huddling under the parachute. By then I had decided I had had enough fire deprivation. There could be no danger of compromising their situation now that they had moved camp, so we built up a blazing fire just outside the shelter – the K rations were still welcome, for the waxed paper could make a fire flare up even in pelting rain. And that night, at least, I slept a little.

The next few days we spent up on the hill, nothing to do, no reason for our presence. We had visitors with whom I seemed to have discussed at length, boring length apparently, the futility of our situation up there and they promised to carry the arguments to the Brigadier but he was still unwell, his judgment wayward, and this secondhand pressure had no effect. I had developed raw patches on both feet by then, was in actual pain from dysentery and one night was shivering so violently with fever that I brought down one of the supports of our shelter. The fever did abate somewhat during the day, I don't know why, so the days were bearable, but most nights were misery. We continued with our illegal fire when food or comfort needed it, and by now I had ceased to concern myself with the possibility that it might attract attention from the enemy. Or the Brigadier.

The last afternoon up on the hill I do remember, because we had a rare visitor. I had gone over to the northern edge of the hilltop to look again at an ironwood tree – it had leaf-buds like the tiny flame-red lights of a decorated Christmas tree. I stood there for a minute or so, quite still, looking at it, then heard a rustling noise from away to the side. I turned just in time to see down below a figure splash through some leaves and out of sight. The immediate reaction to this was a sharp return to war consciousness – and an awareness that the carbine was back in the shelter. But then there was a similar sound from much closer and this time I saw the figure. We both saw. A gibbon. We looked at one another for an instant, less than twenty yards apart, about the same level, he in a tree down the slope and me on the ground of the hilltop. The frost-white eyebrows on black face accentuated its surprise. Then he turned, hurled himself down through the branches with a cough of alarm and showing white tail-patch of his behind till he finally disappeared in a crash of leaves. I waited quietly for a long time but neither saw nor heard them again that evening – but at dawn next day I did hear them halloo-ing in joyful chorus from the hills behind us to the north.

When we came down that next day we heard that Lentaigne had paid a visit to our airstrip and instructed that a basha hospital be built by the strip to deal with those sick and wounded who did not need to be evacuated. What message he gave to the Brigadier I don't know, or cannot remember, but the mere establishment of a makeshift hospital suggested we were certainly not going to be relieved as promptly as had been hoped. There had been another attack on Houla during this time, more casualties suffered, and these together with the regular loss of twenty sick a day suggested that the end would soon arrive one way or another – either we would be withdrawn or all finish as casualties.

The Brigadier was reasonably fit the first day and Stanley and I had a long discussion with him, quite evenly tempered at times, about the RAF group's continued presence with the force. By now we were in constant contact with Myitkyena headquarters by air so had no need for radio communication, we were getting all supplies by aircraft landing at the strip so there were no drops for us to arrange, and our operations were no longer suited to air-support so we were not needed for any of our original purposes. Why hang on to us? we asked. Most of the other RAF officers of Special Force were out by this time, Stanley and I were losing the chance of grasping the best opportunities available in squadron work. We would get the leftovers. And all for no purpose. We suggested that he let at least one of us go – we would toss for it, I said (Stanley was determined that I should go out first).

The Brigadier however was as unwilling as any other commander to reduce the strength of his force, particularly by giving up a specialist unit – this is to downgrade one's command, so naturally is resisted. He said he did not know when we would be relieved, it might be weeks (God help us!) but until he knew for certain that operations were finished he felt he had to retain us both.

'Why?' I asked. 'You still haven't said what use we are to you now.'

He waved away further discussion, not imperiously as of old but by turning his head, flapping a hand by his ear to cut off sound. Stanley hauled me away, again.

That attack on Houla was the last attempted there. Attention was then directed on a village about a mile to the north, and over the next few weeks we made a series of assaults against that area, most on a limited scale. The last major attack attempted by the force was on June 19th; neither Stanley nor I was involved in this, we waited in camp with the rest of the non-combatants and sick – Stanley himself was still reasonably fit but my foot had now worsened, I was still feverish most nights, still suffering from the dysentery and not too sure most of the time where I was – or even who I was. There were plenty of others worse than me, and some of them had actually marched off in that last attack.

It cost us twenty casualties. We were now down to about 250 riflemen, less than a quarter of our original strength, and had no realistic chance of dislodging from well-fortified positions a force that surpassed us in number, were far fitter physically, and had plenty of ammunition and supplies within their perimeter. But still Boatner kept shouting for attacks, and this despite the report from Wallace that for all our willingness to obey we were no longer physically capable of attaining his objectives. As the remains of Merril's force were in as bad, if not worse condition than us and Boatner was still driving them into battle over at Myitkyena it is not surprising that he paid no attention to Wallace's report and recommendations. In the end the last of the Merril force practically mutinied, its commander (Hunter) went back bitter to the States, the men were all withdrawn and the whole thing hushed up – Stilwell himself was sacked from command shortly afterwards.

At this time, towards the end of June, the basha hospital was having difficulty coping with the wounded and sick, even though we were sending out the more seriously ill every day. The doctor filed a report stating that our force was 100% unfit, and the Brigadier thought it necessary to plan for a mass fly-out of survivors just in case headquarters responded sensibly to this information. He sent me up to the strip to prepare some sort of report about this – I can't recall the details, my diary just says 'Report on poss. fly-out.' Anyway, off I went, accompanied by Lilbahadur who had now re-covered from his fever. It was only about a mile from the jungle camp to the strip, and along a flat muddy path, but I was so weak or light-headed that day that I fastened two parachute trace-lines to my pack and dragged the terrible thing behind me like a sleigh through the slippery mud – I think the ground sheet was under it, but can't be sure.

I remember a discussion with an American Captain in charge of the strip but of the report drafted later that afternoon I can recollect practically nothing at all except that it was written in a corner of the basha hospital, sitting on my pack with the rain pelting down outside. I must have been running a temperature at the time, the Doctor discovered this and kept me there in the hospital in a feverish condition that night. He did send back my report to the Brigadier and with it – as I discovered weeks later – a note from himself saying he intended to send me out by the next aircraft that landed.

The first I knew of this was next morning when a sheet of paper arrived with various goodwill messages scribbled on it from column friends – from Stanley, from Tiny Langford and David Anderson and others, and above all (literally) from the Brigadier. I remember sitting under the basha shelter in the roaring rain, reading again and again the faint pencilled farewells, but I can't recall actually receiving the letter nor the discussion I must have had with the doctor about my evacuation. During this time, and right up to that last day, I had kept the diary going but many of the incidents recorded in it towards the end made no imprint on memory whatsoever. A haze hangs over that period in retrospect, and yet the final entry of the diary – written, I imagine, back in hospital in India that night – seems lucidly matter-of-fact:

Thursday 22nd June: Aircraft arrives about 1000. Put out signal OK but quibbles before drops down. We take 22. Say goodbye Lilbahadur and give carbine. Up front for take-off as Wing Commander. Says strip too short but fault slow start. High over Chins, tossed about in cloud. Land Sylhet and truck to hospital. Indian driver skids in hospital gate, hits culvert, cut cheek blood-soaked beard. Walk dripping into hospital. It's finished.

I remember little of this . . . just shaking hands with Lilhabadur in the slipstream by the open door of the aircraft and going through into the cockpit, saying I was a Wing Commander and claiming a cushioned seat for my protruding bones. No memory of the flight itself, nor the incidents on arrival, now remain. I suppose that final sentence epitomized all that mattered that day . . . It was ended.

*   *   *

P.S. And that was how Morris Force campaign ended also – not with a bang but a whimper. The others stayed on in rapidly diminishing numbers for another fortnight, as disease and death took their toll, and then were relieved by a regular army division; at that final count we had just over one hundred men left out of the 1350 of us who had marched out from Chowringee less than four months previously. I myself spent six weeks in hospital – I had lost 70 pounds, and the malaria had complications – before being sent on convalescent leave, which I spent with David Anderson up in the hills by the lake at Naini Tal as we had promised ourselves.

Stanley and I left the Army then. He had avoided hospital and so got to air headquarters long before me, and there accepted an offer to join a Liberator bomber squadron. He had wanted Mosquito photographic reconnaissance but they told him there was no vacancy and, being Stanely, he accepted this instead of kicking up a fuss. He said they would keep a place for me but I was finished with bombers for ever after Nalong. This narrowed severely the scope for operational work – a staff job had no interest at all. But the promise made by the Air Marshal that he would ensure we got the work we wanted afterwards turned out to be reliable in my case – particularly when I quoted it, suitably improved, to Personnel – for they finally produced the offer of a flight command with a Special Duty squadron then being reformed. Its role was to service the illicit organizations and guerilla units operating behind the lines throughout South East Asia, to parachute them in, supply them on operations, to land and pluck them out when necessary. The job could have been designed specifically for the post-Wingate me; I was to complete two tours of operations with the squadron right through to the end of the war.

Stanley had already started with his Liberator bombers by the time I received the Dakotas for our new flight. He phoned me one night to say how fascinated he was by the type of work our squadron was doing, and when I told him we had a Liberator flight to which I could certainly get him and his complete crew transferred if he wished, he was keen to examine the possibility. I arranged to fly over and pick him up with his crew a few days later so that he could have a closer look at our squadron set-up and talk to the commanding officer. The night after this conversation he and his crew went missing, presumed killed in action, on some stupid trivial bombing raid over Indo-China. The war was never the same for me after Stanley died.